Feminism, Labour and Digital Media

There is a contradiction at the heart of digital media. We use commercial platforms to express our identity, to build community and to engage politically. At the same time, our status updates, tweets, videos, photographs and music files are free content for these sites. We are also generating an almost endless supply of user data that can be mined, re-purposed and sold to advertisers. As users of the commercial web, we are socially and creatively engaged, but also labourers, exploited by the companies that provide our communication platforms. How do we reconcile these contradictions?

Feminism, Labour and Digital Media argues for using the work of Marxist feminist theorists about the role of domestic work in capitalism to explore these competing dynamics of consumer labour. It uses the concept of the Digital Housewife to outline the relationship between the work we do online and the unpaid sphere of social reproduction. It demonstrates how feminist perspectives expand our critique of consumer labour in digital media. In doing so, the Digital Housewife returns feminist inquiry from the margins and places it at the heart of critical digital media analysis.

Kylie Jarrett is Lecturer in the Department of Media Studies at the National University of Ireland Maynooth. With Ken Hillis and Michael Petit, she is co-author of *Google and the Culture of Search* and has researched a range of commercial web platforms such as eBay, YouTube and Facebook.

This publication was supported by a grant from the National University of Ireland.

Routledge Studies in New Media and Cyberculture

Feminism, Labour and Digital Media

The Digital Housewife

Kylie Jarrett

Routledge
Taylor & Francis Group

LONDON AND NEW YORK

First published 2016 by Routledge

2 Park Square, Milton Park, Abingdon, Oxfordshire OX14 4RN
711 Third Avenue, New York, NY 10017

Routledge is an imprint of the Taylor & Francis Group, an informa business

First issued in paperback 2017

Library of Congress Cataloging-in-Publication Data

Names: Jarrett, Kylie.
Title: Feminism, labour and digital media: the digital housewife / by Kylie Jarrett.
Description: 1 Edition. | New York: Routledge, 2016. | Series: Routledge studies in new media and cyberculture; 33 | Includes bibliographical references and index.
Identifiers: LCCN 2015027343
Subjects: LCSH: Information society—Social aspects. | Alienation (Social psychology) | Feminism. | Social media.
Classification: LCC HM851.J377 2016 | DDC 303.48/33—dc23
LC record available at http://lccn.loc.gov/2015027343

ISBN: 978-1-138-85579-3 (hbk)
ISBN: 978-1-138-57566-0 (pbk)

Typeset in Sabon
by codeMantra

For Janet.
I should have listened when you told me my mother was my best friend.

Contents

Acknowledgements

The argument in this book emerged over a decade and across two countries, so I am sure I am missing important people who have contributed to its making. You have my apologies. I do know that I must thank my family, friends and work colleagues in Australia who were there for the genesis of this project. Special thanks go to my father Eric, my sister Tracey and my non-biological sister, Lyn Adams, for continuing to provide me with a home whenever I return to Adelaide, and my friends Kirsten Wahlstrom, Tammy Franks and Sergei Stabile for making it feel like I never left. My new family in Dublin, Maynooth and at the Department of Media Studies at Maynooth University – Caroline Ang, Amanda Bent, Chris Brunsdon, Anne Byrne, Laura Canning, Martin Charlton, Íde Corley, Denis Condon, Aphra Kerr, Sophia Maalsen, Jeneen Naji, Cian O'Callaghan, Tracy O'Flaherty, Catherine O'Leary, Eoin O'Mahony, Helen O'Neill, Stephen O'Neill, Caroline O'Sullivan, Maria Pramaggiore, Stephanie Rains, Moynagh Sullivan and Gavan Titley – have also provided me with support, intellectual stimulation and just enough of the craic to keep going. I must also give Sheamus Sweeney special recognition for allowing me to strip-mine our friendship for the purposes of my research. My transnational family at the Association of Internet Researchers – Alison Harvey, Ken Hillis, Sal Humphreys, Ben Light, Sharif Mowlabocus, Susanna Paasonen, Michael Petit, Tamara Shepherd and Julia Velkova, to name a few – have also been invaluable in the framing and reframing of this argument over the years. I am always learning so much from you all. This book wouldn't exist, though, without the GBBC – Mary Gilmartin, Sinéad Kennedy and Anne O'Brien. Their wisdom, kindness, support and insightful reviewing not only added to the quality of my argument, but these amazing women helped me find my voice. I had lost the sense of myself as a researcher. They helped me build that confidence again. I owe them pints.

Introduction

From the Mechanical Turk to the Digital Housewife

In the late eighteenth century, inventor Wolfgang von Kempelen unveiled a wonder of the age – the Mechanical Turk. This automated clockwork chess player dressed in "traditional Turkish robes" toured extensively, beating many opponents until it was destroyed in 1854. The theatricality of its exhibition drew upon the exoticism of "the Other," invoking in its orientalism the world of nature and mysticism (Aytes 2013), but also the scientific imagination of the day that conceived the human as a reified subject inhabiting a machine-like body (Sussman 1999). Through this process of enchantment and rationality, and the ensuing suspension of disbelief, the machine was ascribed intelligence and agency. As is well known today though, the Mechanical Turk was an illusion, if not a hoax. Despite the elaborate construction of cogs and gears revealed behind the doors of the cabinet, hidden behind that was a living chess master who used magnetic systems to move pieces around the chessboard from under the table.

The Mechanical Turk serves as a useful metaphor for understanding today's greatest technological wonder – the Internet (Aytes 2013; Dyer-Witheford and de Peuter 2009; Gehl 2011; Ross 2013; Scholz 2009). While ostensibly cold machinery of great technological sophistication, the commercial Internet and the web in particular are also animated by living beings and their often playful labours. Amazon.com has adopted the name of the Mechanical Turk for its crowdsourcing labour market in which users fulfil tasks requested by other users in exchange for micropayments. Suitable tasks are those requiring human intelligence, such as trawling databases or searching live satellite feeds for particular information, and those tasks such as coding that benefit from a critical mass to distribute workloads and to multiply forms of expertise. Mechanical Turk users who designate themselves as workers are paid for their contributions although, given the reliance on the crowd, these payments are often only a few cents. The name of the eighteenth-century automaton was borrowed because in both instances, "the performance of the workers who animate the interface is obscured by the spectacle of the machine" (Aytes 2013, 81).

Bringing the metaphor of the Mechanical Turk to bear upon the Internet allows us to peek behind the seamless and engaging interfaces of popular digital media platforms such as Facebook, YouTube, Pinterest or Twitter to identify the very human energies that are integral to their functioning. Just as the original Mechanical Turk was merely an empty shell without its human operator, so too the various websites of the commercial web do not function without the uploading of content, social interactions and affective engagements of their users. The Mechanical Turk reveals that behind even the most sophisticated technological marvel lie the material energies of living human beings.

Enter the Digital Housewife

The Mechanical Turk, both the eighteenth century machine and the contemporary labour market, is a useful mechanism for understanding the commercial web because it reveals that below the interfaces of digital media is the ceaseless productivity of a multitude of users. However, what the concept describes is the work of a labourer – the chess master – who is directly and knowingly employed by the exhibitor. It does not, therefore, accurately describe the work of consumers whose willing acts of information-sharing or whose phatic gestures of solidarity are experienced not as work, but as pleasure. The Mechanical Turk, while usefully pointing to the importance of human actors and interactions in digital media, maps that labour onto that of the paid industrial workforce and, in doing so, fails to capture the nuances of the kinds of work associated with digital media. I contend that there are better parallels to be seen between consumer labour and the unpaid, quasi-voluntary work of the private, domestic sphere. Consequently, rather than drawing on the metaphor of the Mechanical Turk, the figure that will animate this book is "the housewife."

Domestic labour can consist of menial physical work, but it also has a set of immaterial qualities, summarised by Leopoldina Fortunati as "affect, care, love, education, socialization, communication, information, entertainment, organization, planning, coordination, logistics" (2007, 144). Even the repetitive, physical, menial chores of housework are often driven by, or serve as expressions of, the immaterial values of care work. This work also produces immaterial products such as health, dispositions or esteem. These products and activities map closely onto the types of unpaid labour associated with digital media industries. The work involved in, for instance, the management of community forums, uploading new data to the Wikipedia commons, commenting on a friend's Facebook status or coordinating a guild run in a massively multiplayer online game (MMOG) has the same qualities Fortunati associates with the immaterial aspects of the domestic sphere. As Christian Fuchs (2008, 186) puts it, the "labor that characterizes Web 2.0 systems is labor that is oriented on the production of affects, fantasy (cognitive labor) and social relations (communicative, cooperative labor) – it is like all labour material because it is activity that changes the state of real world systems. The difference to manual labor is that it doesn't primarily change the physical condition of things, but the emotional and communicative aspects of human relations." The correspondence between the socially significant aspects of housework and these depictions of user activity suggests that work in the domestic sphere is a valuable model for thinking about the nature of consumer labour on the commercial web. It suggests the figure of a digital media user involved in creative acts of social reproduction; it suggests the Digital Housewife.

As I will expand throughout this book though, it is specifically the way domestic work has been understood within the work of Marxist, socialist or materialist feminists (henceforth Marxist feminist) that illuminates the complexity of this labour. As pointed out by Mariarosa Dalla Costa and Selma James (1975), Leopoldina Fortunati (1995) and Silvia Federici (2004; 2012) among others, domestic work provides for the reproduction and renewal of the labouring body and, importantly, the labouring subject. It is unpaid or severely under-compensated work that is, nevertheless, integral to the maintenance of capitalism. Furthermore, it generates surplus-value by reducing the costs of reproduction. From this perspective, domestic work *is* productive labour. However, the activities of a domestic labourer are rarely experienced in the same way as organised, industrialised work. Domestic work is often individually and socially enriching, and remains replete with use-values, despite its role in capitalism. There is therefore a contradiction at the heart of domestic labour in that its social functions are outside, and often antagonistic to, capitalist modes of accumulation, even while they remain necessary to that system.

This dialectical relationship is also at the heart of consumer labour in digital media. There are a variety of studies pointing to the economic value of the unpaid contributions of consumers (see particularly Fuchs 2009; 2014b). However, as John Banks and Sal Humphreys (2008) point out, analysis of the practices of users can rarely be reduced to their function as inputs into the fiscal calculations of capitalism and certainly not without diminishing their complexity and social function. Both are important to the mental and emotional health of individuals and to group cohesion at a family, community, class or societal level. Domestic labour and the work of consumers online thus manifest similarities in their relationship to capital.

This correspondence leads to the argument at the centre of this book that the forms of immaterial and affective labour that are exploited in the economic circuits of the commercial web can be usefully interrogated using frameworks already identified as relevant to understanding domestic labour's role in capitalism. Knowing more about the mechanisms by which domestic labour enters into exploitative economic circuits, but still retains so much of its social potency, can tell us much about the contradictory dynamics of exploitation and agency associated with digital media capitalism. The figure of the Digital Housewife will, therefore, be used to place consumer labour in relation to this dialectic and to demonstrate the greater insights that can be gained from conceptualising digital media users' activities as a form of social reproduction. Most importantly, the Digital Housewife is a product of Marxist feminist theorisation of domestic work, and the figure will also place that critique at the heart of its analysis.

Troubling the Digital Housewife

The term, the Digital Housewife, describes the actor that emerges from the structures and practices of the ostensibly voluntary work of consumers as they express themselves, their opinions and generate social solidarity with others in commercial digital media while, at the same time, adding economic value to those sites. The use of the term "housewife" may seem problematic – I could have readily used the non-gender specific term "domestic worker" for instance – but it is used here quite consciously. The figure of "the housewife" has a complex role in the political, economic and social history of women. Using it here is intended to foreground the importance to this project of feminist thought about this history. It also highlights the importance of gender within the social and theoretical history of labour and in particular the kinds of labour associated with the sphere of social reproduction. However false the attribution of certain kinds of activity to biological sex may be, it is from this attribution that domestic work draws its valence and what allows it to be mobilised within the oppressive machinery of patriarchal capitalism. To use the gendered term is to acknowledge this context.

I also use the term "housewife" for the key metaphor rather than "domestic work" as this analysis draws primarily on theories about the unpaid, quasi-voluntary labour of the domestic sphere rather than the paid sphere of domestic and care work. This is not because the sphere of paid domestic labour is not important nor a growing, highly gendered sector marked by severe conditions of exploitation (International Labour Organisation 2013). It is because the figure of the Digital Housewife draws on insights that have been generated about unpaid domestic labour, typically undertaken in a family context. This is also a vital, but often unmeasured, area of work. OECD statistics (Miranda 2011) on unpaid work, including domestic work and volunteering, claim that on average between one-third and one-half of all valuable economic activity in the OECD area is unpaid. Although there are national differences, and differences related to the developmental status of nations, women still spend more time on unpaid work than men – on average, 2 hours and 28 minutes more per day. This remains the case even in nations where women are well represented in the paid workforce. Despite its economic importance and the light these figures shine on continuing inequities in household labour division, such work is rarely used in calculations of economic activity, including GDP. The term, Digital Housewife, thus focuses attention on the kinds of labour that are too often elided from economic history.

More pointedly, my use of the gendered form also draws attention to the fact that, despite an emphasis on feminised activity such as affect and care in conceptualisations of immaterial labour and in user activity on the web, there has been little engagement with feminist interrogations of unpaid domestic work in this literature. In the current "return to Marx" (Fuchs 2014b) associated with interrogations of digital media economics, the insights from feminist thinkers have rarely been integrated. As I will argue further in Chapter 2, this omission is surprising as a key framework for interrogating consumer labour draws on the concepts of affective, cognitive or immaterial labour that are integral qualities of domestic work. These are also precisely the kinds of labour involved in the economically significant social networks of digital media, constituted as they are by the generation of (dis)-affective intensities and/or the sharing of intangible information and symbols.

I acknowledge, though, that it is difficult to draw on this history of the gendered division of labour without re-inscribing its binary logic. The term Digital Housewife may imply that the work of social reproduction is exclusively done by women, naturalising its categorisation as essentially feminine activity. This is clearly not the case, as Kathi Weeks summarises: "Women and men are indeed still often engaged in different laboring practices, but these differences cannot be mapped onto a binary gender schema secured by recourse to a model of separate spheres" (2007, 238–239).

Moreover, to use understandings about labour that draw on domestic work may also imply that it is only in these spheres that gender is a structuring principle and where feminist critique need apply. As such, the term may register as a "flashback to moments where women could only legitimately be considered if cast in the language of either domestic labour or reproduction" (McRobbie 2010, 65). These critiques are valid. However, it is equally important to mobilise the contributions of a range of feminist scholars, mostly women, whose understandings of the specificity of domestic work, regardless of who performs it, are a useful analytical tool. This book is therefore not *about* domestic work in its various forms, nor about unpaid and paid work done by women. Rather it is about bringing feminist theorisation and activism about that unpaid reproductive work out of the domestic sphere, applying its insights to contemporary digital media. It is about bringing that which feminism has taught us about domestic work to the centre of debates about immaterial labour.

Finally, the term the Digital Housewife is not used here with the assumption that domestic labour directly correlates with the activities involved in being a user of digital media. It certainly would be absurd to suggest that there was an exact resemblance in terms of form, materiality, intensity, personal investment or the social consequence of the two forms of labour. The Digital Housewife as s/he is used in this book is primarily a rhetorical device. S/he is used to draw attention to the long history of capital's incorporation of immaterial labour, as well as to the already existing feminist paradigms we have for understanding this practice. S/he is also specifically a *Digital* Housewife whose arena of activity is the commercial web. While I maintain that the ways of conceptualising immaterial labour's relationship to capital that Marxist feminist thinking opens up have wide relevance and applicability, a point I will expand in the conclusion, this book is predominantly about digital media. Its main function is to describe a model for thinking about consumer labour that will be of utility to digital media scholars. To that end, we must first place the Digital Housewife in her/his technical, economic and theoretical context. This field is marked by the wide distribution of interactive and participatory commercial media and a growing acceptance of Autonomist Marxist arguments that value-generating labour can be attributed to the inalienable products and dispositions of the working subject. The Digital Housewife is also a figure that specifically emerges from feminist thinking so that setting must also be articulated. The following sections will offer sketches of these contexts, locating some key concepts that will be drawn upon throughout the book.

"Web 2.0" and the Productive Consumer

The Digital Housewife emerges out of two apparently competing dynamics of the World Wide Web – the emergence of participatory media, and its attendant participatory culture, and the intensification and extensification of commercialised content. These trends are captured in the concept of "Web 2.0." This is not a term I typically use (hence the scare quotes) because it implies a historical break between different dominant iterations of web forms (Allen 2012; Fuchs 2014a; Scholz 2008). Nevertheless, its definition captures some of the dynamics that have positioned consumer labour centrally in the digital economy.

"Web 2.0" emerges within the context of the post-Fordist drift from a dominant focus on demand-side innovation occasioned by the oil crisis and "stagflation" problems of the 1970s (Harvey 1990; Jessop 1997; MacDonald 1991; Thrift 2005). During the latter part of the twentieth century, with the economic mobility emerging from class struggle and post-World War II Keynesian economics, consumption was increasingly viewed as an economic and social driver (Cross 1993; Miles, Steven et al. 2002). This is not to suggest that during this period there was not transformation in production, particularly as informed by technological change such as computerisation. The export of manufacturing to the global South, and the continued exploitation of primary resources and cheap, un-unionised labour in the same regions, is evidence enough of a continued drive for economies in the costs of production. However, it is to emphasise that this occurred in conjunction with the expansion and management of demand through advertising, branding and marketing, as well as through technological change that enabled small-batch production. The ensuing aestheticisation and personalisation of consumer goods emphasised economies of scope rather than scale.

It is difficult to designate cause and effect, but these changes in production and economic focus correlate with the domination of material culture by commodity consumption. Anthropology tells us that material goods play important roles for identity and community making in all societies. Throughout the twentieth century though, goods that perform these roles in the global North have increasingly been mass-produced and disposable products, purchased in the commercial marketplace. The appropriation of consumer goods has become a key plank of identity construction, supplementing or supplanting class as a primary source of self-making. This was a key finding of various studies into youth subcultures that emerged from the "Birmingham School" of Cultural Studies in which the debased, mass-produced goods of consumer culture were shown as integral to emerging constructions of subjectivity and community (for example, Hebdige 1979; Humphery 1998; Thornton 1995).

The emergence of consumer culture, and its centrality to socioeconomics, is an important point to recognise in the context of this book, for consumption is routinely cast as frivolous, unimportant, base and a feminine activity. It belongs in the domestic sphere, where it is often seen as a wasteful "using up" of resources, particularly when compared to the productive activity of the workplace. However, Celia Lury (1996) reminds us that consumption is creative and involves active acts of appropriation that often generate new meanings and, in effect, cultural products. A key example that Lury (1996, 121–143) offers is the transformation of shop-bought goods (raw materials) by a housewife as she produces edible food for her family, or as she transforms herself and her body into appropriate models of femininity. Lury's argument makes the links between consumer labour and domestic work clear, even though this has rarely informed critiques in relation to digital media and "Web 2.0." Nevertheless, the concept of the productive consumer is a logical extension of the growing emphasis on consumption as a valuable social and economic phenomenon connected to creative expression. Moreover, the commercialisation of the Internet, and the growing significance of it as a cultural mediator, has meant the integration of consumer culture "ever more firmly into everyday routines of anticipation, purchase and display" (Murdock 2014, 130).

The term "Web 2.0" was popularised in 2005 by Tim O'Reilly from technology publishing house O'Reilly Media and used to describe a supposed shift in the nature of web content from relatively static monologic home pages for individuals or companies, to dynamic, dialogic spaces shaped by participatory architectures demanding engagement by consumers. It described a continually updated web, delivering "rich user experiences" by allowing for remixing, sharing and updating by the diverse user base of any website. It was centred on Internet users framed as individualised and creative consumers. "Web 2.0" was conceived by O'Reilly, and others as diverse as business analysts Don Tapscott and Anthony D. Williams (2006) and IT Law academic Yochai Benkler (2006), not only as an opportunity for businesses to increase brand loyalty and build new relationships with customers, but also as having transformative social potential. In allowing users to interact with and to inform the outputs of commercial enterprises in an ongoing, dynamic process, "Web 2.0" broke the choke-hold on information flows that create imbalances in markets, as well as allowing for participation in generating broadly distributed cultural texts that would otherwise be controlled by media corporations. "Web 2.0" was described both as a new paradigm of economics and as implicated in the emergence of a wide-spread participatory culture.

The concept of participatory culture is often associated with Henry Jenkins (2006a; 2006b), whose influential work in the 1990s on the creative practices of TV fans brought attention to the dynamic participation of audiences in the meaning-making associated with media. While it had long been recognised that audiences were active in producing their own meanings, Jenkins' (1992) work underscored that this activity often manifested materially in the form of texts that were, effectively, a co-production between fans and producers. Rather than being mere avid consumers, fans were highly productive. What he went on to document in *Convergence Culture* (2006b) is a similar process of co-production in which the types of media associated with "Web 2.0" further activate audience participation in meaning-making. Importantly such participation is not a marginal activity of a dedicated group of media fans, but is the general background of the contemporary web. Like the housewife described by Lury, digital media users are engaged in everyday acts of meaningful creative work. Participatory culture and "Web 2.0" exemplify and make visible the creativity of consumption.

The Commercial Web and the Labouring Consumer

A key aspect of the "Web 2.0" phenomenon was the framing of this participatory culture and media co-creation as a site of value-generation for the industry. This process was described as harnessing the collective intelligence of users. As O'Reilly summarises: "*Network effects from user contributions are the key to market dominance in the Web 2.0 era*" (2005, n.p.; emphasis in original). The term "network effects" here refers to the economic benefits associated with using the massed contributions of users as content, to solve problems (in the way of Amazon's Mechanical Turk), or to promote products through word of mouth. Key examples O'Reilly offers are eBay in which the company serves merely as an enabler of exchanges between users, and the user-generated encyclopedia Wikipedia. O'Reilly articulates this production to the goals of commercial enterprises, arguing for the economic value that can be gleaned either directly or indirectly from authorising users to create content and to meaningfully interact with your site.

It is this aspect of the "Web 2.0" phenomenon that is most closely associated with another key term for understanding today's commercial web – social media. This term may be considered a redundancy as all media requires the construction of shared meanings and therefore is social. It is most commonly used, though, to describe those sites and practices that are about the construction of sociality and, thus, of collective intelligence. As summarised by Fuchs in his critical introduction to social media, the term is associated with the following concepts: "collective action, communication, communities, connecting/networking, co-operation/collaboration, the creative making of user-generated content, playing, sharing" (2014a, 37). The term social media can be used to describe sites and practices associated with the construction of the "general intellect" or commons; a space of meaningful social symbols, their construction and mutually beneficial distribution. The term "Web 2.0," particularly as defined by O'Reilly, captures such sites but also includes corporate webpages in which some user-generated content such as comments, reviews or ratings is allowed, but which do not involve a meaningful exchange between users. It is a broader term than social media which tends to be linked more extensively with sites such as blogging platforms, social networking sites, or image-sharing facilities whose content is primarily that provided by users.

Whatever the preferred definition, the figure of the Digital Housewife, whose cognitive and affective efforts in building and sustaining interpersonal relationships online, in communicating and coordinating activity with others, in producing and sharing content, is at the heart of the collective intelligence of digital media's commercial properties. This worker provides content in the relatively material form of videos, game play, status updates, tweets or podcasts, but s/he also adds that affective stickiness (Ahmed 2004a; 2004b) which makes engagement with these sites meaningful. This latter contribution is valuable for it is the affective investment of users that produce "lock-in" to particular sites. To make a site meaningful and to subsequently generate a critical mass of users makes continued engagement with that site desirable and increases the emotional costs of choosing another site. A single consumer engaged in this work may not contribute enough content, nor generate enough stickiness, to sustain an entire website or ensure its continued dominance of the market. En masse, however, these users become invaluable to the economics of the industry.

Another quality that O'Reilly attributes to "Web 2.0" is that it is driven by the value of user data over that of hardware or even software. The harnessing of collective intelligence does not, therefore, refer only to capitalising on the provision of free content. Collective intelligence can also be harnessed as clickstream data, user-preference information and search terms that are of value to marketing companies. As will be discussed in more detail in Chapter 3, the economics of the web are predominantly based in advertising (see McStay 2010). They rely on the generation of what, in 1977, Dallas Smythe (2014) famously called the "audience-commodity." Smythe argued that the key product of broadcast media was not programmes, but audiences, or more precisely information about the audience that could be sold to advertisers. In "Web 2.0," the abstraction of user data is intensified and made almost instantaneous as each interaction can be measured and collected in the back-end databases of any commercial media site. From the

1990s, this ability to extract more and more accurate data about users, and to do so in real-time, was recognised as the benefit of digital media to corporations (Forbes 1999; Hoffman et al. 1995; Hoffman and Novak 1996; McStay 2010; Strauss and Frost 1999; Stroud 1999 for instance).

The labouring consumer and his/her valuable material and immaterial contributions thus serve double duty in the economics of the industry. S/he is unpaid and freely contributes content that provides these sites with their appeal to other users, while also generating readily repackaged data about consumer trends, tastes and desires. Moreover, s/he also produces shared meanings and builds social solidarity in those same interactions. There is, as the title of Benkler's (2006) book says, both cultural and economic wealth in the networks of collective intelligence generated by users. The Digital Housewife, as emblematic of the actively productive consumer whose activities are both culturally and economically valuable, becomes conceivable in this context.

Immaterial Labour and Exploitation in Digital Media

This dynamic, which attaches value to consumer activity, is also that which links "Web 2.0" to the growing critique in the field of Internet political economy research that draws extensively on ideas from Marxist theorists of the *Autonomia* or Autonomist Marxist movement (for example, Berardi 2009; Hardt and Negri 2000; 2005; 2009; Lazzarato 1996; Marazzi 2011; Negri 1989; Virno 2004). The discussion of this theoretical paradigm will be expanded in the first two chapters, but for now it is most important to note its emphasis on the expanding incorporation of various life processes such as cognition and affect into the economic calculations of capital. This argument has become central to understanding the labour of consumers in "Web 2.0." The application of this paradigm to digital media is typically traced to the work of Tiziana Terranova (2000) and her explication of the dimensions of unpaid labour inherent to many digital media industry business models. While never making the connection to domestic work, she importantly identified the role of voluntary, unpaid contributions by industry workers but also Internet users within the economy of the digital media sector. For Terranova, digital media environments – both production and consumption contexts – function with the same dynamics as contemporary capitalism in which value can be traced to the affective energies of workers and consumers. Because these attributes are developed, maintained and exercised outside of formally defined labour contexts, Terranova argues that work increasingly occurs in time for which the labourer is not compensated.

Since Terranova's nuanced analysis and its expansion by a range of theorists (for example, Andrejevic 2002; Arvidsson and Sandvik 2007; Banks 2002; Fuchs 2008; 2009; 2014b; Potts et al. 2008; Zwick et al. 2008), it has become possible to see how digital media consumers are integral to capitalist valorisation in various digital media industries, but as part of a broader trend in socioeconomics. It is through this paradigm that we have been able to conceptualise consumer activity as labour. Moreover, we can see it as *exploited* labour. Like housewives, consumers receive little or no direct financial compensation for their contributions to the revenue-generating mechanisms of digital media sites so that all of their labour produces surplus-value for the website provider. Using Marx's definition, such labour is therefore exploited and alienated. This is the social relation at the heart of "Web 2.0" and the digital economy as theorised by Terranova and Autonomist Marxism.

This exploitation of user activity is not absolute, however. For Michael Hardt and Antonio Negri (2000; 2005; 2009), the excessive energies associated with cooperative production, such as that associated with social media's collective intelligence, manifest as the power of what they call "multitude" to overturn and reshape the production process. This is the dialectical tension that Hardt and Negri argue typifies contemporary cognitive capitalism and it is also evident in the dynamics of "Web 2.0," social media and participatory culture. This tension is recognised in the definitions of "Web 2.0" offered by O'Reilly (2005). He celebrates a context where users are exploited for their immaterial labour while simultaneously describing how these media sites serve as hubs for the expression of agency and potentially transformative politics. Because of its resistance to effective and totalising means of capture, immaterial labour and the labour of digital media consumers manifest the excess of multitude and thus serve as potential sites of agency.

A central contention of this book is that the same tension Hardt and Negri associate with cooperative production also animates unpaid domestic labour as it has been understood by a variety of feminist scholars. Exploited in and vital to capitalist circuits, domestic work is often simultaneously socially meaningful and resistant to capture, particularly in its immaterial forms. Thus, not only do the immaterial aspects of domestic labour bear resemblance to the kinds of value-producing contributions associated with digital media consumers, unpaid domestic work also articulates the tension between agency and exploitation that animates the politics of digital media.

To place the figure of the Digital Housewife at the heart of our analytical models as proposed in this book is thus a means for understanding more than the economy of social media. The Digital Housewife is a useful figure for understanding the types of labour relations that arguably dominate in the high-technology, service and finance sectors of the global North. This is why it is essential to bring thinking about domestic labour back to the centre of critical analysis in order to know digital media and contemporary capitalism more generally. The key theorists who have addressed this arena are, of course, feminists and typically feminist women, so the following section will set the figure of the Digital Housewife within the particular dynamics of feminist theorisation, activism and politics.

Feminist Contexts

Mapping any discipline or research field in a short introduction is fraught with difficulty, reductionism and necessarily exclusions and it would be impossible to offer an exhaustive account of feminist thought in this section of an introductory chapter. Consequently, the typology I present here describes only a small slice of feminist thinking, almost exclusively focusing on those theoretical paradigms that are directly drawn upon in my argument. Consequently, there are almost as many exceptions as there are adherents to the typology I present and many more theoretical paradigms that go unrecorded. Nonetheless, this sketch provides a conceptual background to key ideas that inform this study, but also locates the Digital Housewife in feminist traditions, explaining more of the relevance of this thinking to the political economy of digital media.

Many of the sources about domestic work drawn upon in this analysis can be defined, albeit loosely, as Marxist, socialist or materialist in origin. In particular, they draw on the "wages for housework" movement associated with 1970s feminism, particularly those theorists who emerged from within, or beside, the field of Italian Autonomist Marxism. Marxist feminism, as Zillah Eisenstein (1979) insists, is defined, not by a commitment to challenging patriarchy, but by a commitment to challenging capitalist patriarchy, a term she uses to refer to the "mutually reinforcing dialectical relationship between capitalist class structure and hierarchical sexual structuring" (1979, 5).

This framework emerged as a distinct strand of Marxist thinking in the 1970s as growing feminist, queer and race consciousness highlighted the problems of collapsing all power relations and social dimensions into class. The usual suspects of reflexive modernisation and post-Fordist socioeconomics challenged the primacy of labour and class location in the actualisation of identity and in the politics of struggle. Social and economic mobility in the global North; the "victory" of the "artistic critique" in labour struggle which lead to a greater emphasis on creativity and aesthetics in the workplace (Boltanski and Chiapello 2005; du Gay 1996); the rise in service and tertiary industries in the global North as manufacturing industries were exported to cheaper labour markets in the global South (Wölfl 2005); the growing economic and social valence of consumption activity and correspondent consumption-based identity options; and, more recently, neoliberal governance structures that entail "an assault on the resources and agencies which have defended working class interests" (McRobbie 2010, 63) have all worked to decentre class in identity construction. Moreover critiques centred on race, gender and sexuality – so-called identity politics – forcefully suggest that power dynamics are not singular, but a series of intersecting articulations that create specific contingent relations of dominance. The nexus of these conceptual shifts has led to an emphatic focus on the specificity of the experiences of capitalism and work for subordinated social groups such as women. Documenting the particular qualities of women's labouring has consequently become an important feature of contemporary feminist Sociology and Cultural Studies.

The nexus of Marxism and feminism has historically been problematic though, partly because of the neglect of a clearly articulated gender dimension in Marx's writing (Arruzza 2013; Barrett 1980; Hartmann 1979b). It is also partly due to the primacy given formal production in orthodox Marxist economics and the subsequent limited conceptualisation of the feminised realms of consumption and domestic work. The tensions also emerge in the typically hostile view of the female workforce taken by trade unions when women's under-compensation was used to undercut male wages (Wright 2002, 134; Hartmann 1979a). But perhaps most importantly, the tension is caused by the deferment in most Left politics of women's equality until after the conquest of class domination (Cuninghame 2008; Zaretsky 1976). The privileging of white, male, industrial labour in Left politics typically means the selection of only "certain sectors of the working class as revolutionary subjects" (Federici 2012, 28). For feminists who are also socialists or Marxists, paradigms that recognise these other actors and dimensions of social reality are an important political avenue.

Nevertheless, Marxist feminism argues that Marxism provides useful tools for understanding the specific contours of women's oppression. As Eisenstein notes, "there is nothing about the dialectical and historical method that limits it to understanding class relations" (1979, 7; Brown 2013). She goes on to say, though, that the particular importance of Marxist feminism is that the "relations between the private (personal) and public (political) become a major focus, having particular consequences for the relations defining sexuality, heterosexuality, and homosexuality" (1979, 5–6). The paradigm emphasises ideology, culture and meaning-making, extending the traditional Marxist dialectic to realms of consciousness and lived experience. Eisenstein (1979, 5) says: "This new way of viewing things – that society's ideas and people's consciousness are part of the objective lived experience and that they operate out of the relations of class, sex, and race – is a product of the feminist assault on the inadequacies of the left, both in theory and practice."

This refocusing of Marxist methodology in the 1970s directed attention to the sphere of social reproduction as much as to the economic and labour relations of the capitalist mode of production. Consequently, it validated the focus on domestic work as an important, integrated component of capitalist society. In the late 1960s, Margaret Benston (1997) noted the material production of use-values in the unpaid labour of the domestic sphere, characterising the family as a production unit, albeit for products outside of fiscal, market economics. This position was subsequently challenged by Mariarosa Dalla Costa (Dalla Costa and James 1975) and various other feminists cited in this book. While agreeing with Benston that domestic work is a form of material production, these scholar/activists instead place that work firmly in the circuits of capitalist economic exchange. Explained more thoroughly in Chapters 2 and 3, Dalla Costa's argument identifies the role played by the housewife in the production of surplus-value because she is producing the essential and special commodity that is at the heart of capitalism: labour-power. Despite Benston and Dalla Costa's differences, through both their arguments it became possible to see both the structural location of domestic work in the economy and the role of the gendered division of labour in the oppression of women.

Nancy Fraser (2013, 215–216) neatly summarises the insights of this feminist second-wave. She describes how these theorists and activists identified the androcentrism that forms the basis of the gendered division of labour, further arguing how this generated a systematic devaluation of activities associated with women in both paid and unpaid contexts. She adds that in applying their analysis to the capitalist system, these feminists "uncovered the deep structural connections between women's responsibility for the lion's share of unpaid caregiving, their subordination in marriage and personal life, the gender segmentation of labor markets, men's domination of the political system, and the androcentrism of welfare provision, industrial policy, and development schemes" (2013, 215). In particular, she points to the exposure of the family wage as a key site for the misrepresentation of women, the misrecognition of their labour and for the maldistribution of resources. The result, she says, was a "critique that integrated economy, culture, and politics in a systematic account of women's subordination in state-organized capitalism" (2013, 216).

Incorporating Radical Feminism

Feminism is, however, a diverse field; it is better understood as feminisms in the plural. Indeed, some of the controversy about the relationship between domestic work and the generation of surplus emerges from more radical feminist positions that refuse to discuss affective and care work in the masculinised terms of economics. This approach contends that it is important for this work to be understood and valorised using concepts that come from women's experience and, accordingly, logics of care and sociality. These more radical positions tend to emphasise patriarchy and struggle between the sexes as the source of women's oppression rather than locating it within capitalist dynamics as does Marxist feminism. Nevertheless, these paradigms intersect in that they both emphasise the ideological dimensions of reality and the concept of gendered subordination within their understandings of capitalism. Lise Vogel (2013) describes the incorporation of radical approaches into Marxist feminism during the 1970s that brought the concepts of patriarchy and biological reproduction (as the paradigmatic female experience) into consideration, allowing for interrogation of the mutually constitutive relationships between patriarchy and capitalism. Significantly, the articulation of these concepts into Marxism allows for the existence of female oppression under patriarchy prior to and beyond the capitalist system, with important consequences for revolutionary politics. While the argument about the Digital Housewife primarily draws on Marxist feminist thinking, some of these radical arguments are picked up on in Chapter 3 to assert the specificity and inalienability of immaterial labour such as that done by housewives and digital media consumers.

Thus, while Marxist feminism's recognition of the vital economic function played by domestic work has remained controversial within the spheres of both Marxism and feminism, it has nevertheless re-shaped understandings of both labour and economics. By de-naturalising the gendered division of labour – by arguing that care for others, cleaning, cooking and, importantly, sexual availability were not an organic birth-right of those born to the female sex but instead a product of and productive of capitalist dynamics – these feminists articulated an agenda that re-constituted the terrain of struggle. It became possible to see that women are not only integral to capital because they serve as the industrial reserve but also because they produce labour-power. It was also possible to demonstrate how women's relationship to capitalism is shaped through the gendering of labour and cultural practices. Feminist theorists enabled the conceptualisation of capitalism specifically as a patriarchal system (Adkins 1995; Eisenstein 1979; Hartmann 1979a; 1979b; Pateman 1988), drawing connections between gender oppression, and resistance, and the capitalist mode of production. It was through identifying the important economic contribution of unpaid work to the generation of surplus that it became possible to articulate demands that domestic activity be waged as a means to challenge the economic dependence structurally imposed on women by the gendered division of labour. This insight also allowed the refusal of domestic work to serve as a political tool. The rejection of the inevitability of domestic work is a lasting legacy of this approach in feminist theorisation, activism and, most importantly, in the lived experience of women.

Emerging from this paradigm was also an expanded definition of labour. This expansion is deeply entwined with the work of Autonomist Marxists. Indeed, Patrick Cuninghame (2008; n.p.) declares the women's movement "one of the foremost practitioners of autonomy." Often acknowledged, but rarely developed (a point I will return to in Chapter 2) is the importance of feminist theorisation and activism in the emergence of *Autonomia* out of the broader workerist movement. In his history of Italian Autonomist Marxism, Steve Wright (2002) describes how a failure to address areas of concern to women, such as childcare, education, violence or reproductive rights, and the ongoing hostility towards labouring women in trade unions, led Italian feminists to develop their own political organisations. *Lotta Feminista* (Feminist Struggle), the group from which the wages for housework movement emerged, criticised the privileging of male workers in Left politics, aligning the attack on women and racialised others with the oppression of one class by another (Wright 2002, 134).

These feminists drew on and then transformed the lessons of workerism, the Civil Rights movements and anti-War activism, re-describing the capitalist circuit as they did so (Federici 2012, 6–7). Along with the student groups associated with Italian labour activism during this period, these feminists expanded the range of activities, locations and actors that could legitimately be involved in class struggle to include those outside directly contracted wage relations. In recognising the social value of unpaid, (quasi)-voluntary work, Italian feminist activists and scholars thus contributed significantly to the re-composition of class that is the legacy of Autonomist Marxism. Their articulation of the economic importance of labour associated with affect, ideation, socialisation and care is also what connects domestic work to the labour of digital media consumers, giving rise to the concept of the Digital Housewife.

In the closing years of the twentieth century, however, the critical force of such materialist feminist politics was challenged by the emergence of a "post-feminist sensibility." Although interpreted in various ways (see Gill and Scharff 2013 for a short summary), a critical view of this paradigm describes it as a mode of engagement with feminism in which women claim power and agency, but in a form that is stripped of its critical, transformative force. Post-feminism is marked by more or less active repudiation of feminist activism, either predicated on an assumption that its work is finished or in rejection of its core principles. It is also marked by nostalgic retreats to normative gender roles and activities, often in the form of highly feminised and/or sexualised gender performance or hyper-domesticity, as well as an emphasis on individual choice over collective action. A feminist identity and politics are adopted as yet another individual consumer decision taken within a market, disarticulating feminism from systemic critiques of gender politics, as well as those of capitalism, race, sexuality and ability (Budgeon 2001; Faludi 1992; McRobbie 2009; 2010; Negra 2009; Tasker and Negra 2007). Post-feminism has also been associated with a retreat to individualised responses to labour struggles and also with the entrepreneurial, flexible, agential subjectivity that is demanded within neoliberal consumer capitalism (Adkins and Jokinen 2008; Adkins and Lury 1999; Gill and Scharff 2013).

This sensibility can be located in the changes in feminist theoretical frameworks and activism since the 1980s that Nancy Fraser (2013) documents. She describes a shift from the politics of redistributing power and wealth associated with 1970s socialist feminism to politics centred on the recognition of difference. Fraser describes the decline of the political project of this latter form of feminism in the neoliberal, consumption-driven politics of post-Fordism. As the welfare state came under ideological assault and lost its legitimacy, feminist groups lost their agency for redistributing power. "No longer able to assume a social-democratic baseline for radicalization, they gravitated to newer grammars of political claims-making, more attuned to the 'post-socialist' zeitgeist" (Fraser 2013, 4). Feminist projects, she says, became oriented toward the politics of identity instead of critiquing the gendered systems of capitalism. The transformation of culture rather than capitalism became central to the feminist imaginary. As she notes, this new struggle continued the expansion of the political agenda beyond waged labour and class struggle, but also "dovetailed all too neatly with a rising neoliberalism that wanted nothing more than to repress all memory of social egalitarianism" (2013, 5). In effect, the critical function of feminism was swallowed up by the very focus on identity and the cultural dimensions of socioeconomics that was the important contribution of radical feminist thinking to Marxism.

As I write this, however, we seem to be emerging out of that post-feminist moment. The global financial crisis of 2007 and the ensuing imposition of austerity politics on various nations in the global North has brought attention in this region back to issues of political economy and social justice. Alongside the return to Marxist thinking already described, I would suggest there has also been a resurgence of feminist activism and theorisation. This may be due to backlash politics mediated through the Internet becoming more visible, the inequitable burden of austerity measures placed upon women (Cronin 2012; McVeigh 2013) and/or the continuing retrenchment of gains made in women's rights across the global North (for example, Kennedy 2015), all of which underscore the need for continued feminist struggle.

In relation to theories about labour, the turn to feminist critiques may also reflect the "feminisation" of work under neoliberal capital as, on one hand, women take up a greater share of paid work, and on the other, as all kinds of work become increasingly precarious, under-compensated and reliant on "soft" skills such as communication, affect and cognition (Adkins 2001; Mies et al. 1988; Veijola and Jokinen 2008). Over recent years, various female and male celebrities have also actively declared themselves feminist in public forums, increasing the valence of the term, if not a clear politics. Across a variety of cultural arenas it has become increasingly difficult to avoid feminist critiques, although, as I will argue in Chapter 2, this has not been a feature of discussions of immaterial labour within Autonomist Marxism, nor in critique of consumer labour in digital media. This book contributes to the reclamation of this feminist ground.

To summarise then, the Digital Housewife emerges as a logical synecdoche of the labouring consumer because of the reliance on users' creative and productive engagement in the business models of "Web 2.0" and the framing of this activity as a form of exploited labour using Autonomous Marxist insights. S/he manifests the kinds of immaterial and material practices that are integral to the digital media economy and has the same complex relationship to capital accumulation that feminist theorisation has attributed to the unpaid domestic worker. Furthermore, the contributions of both digital media consumers and housewives are exploited, but they are not only this. The history of feminist thinking documented above suggests a continuing need to incorporate analysis of the subjective dimensions of labour and consumption alongside the economic concerns of socialist or materialist feminism (Budgeon 2013; Federici 2012; Fraser 2013).

In its various forms, feminism's long engagement with criticising domestic work means it offers useful tools for interrogating labour that is both exploited and socially meaningful and, therefore, for unpacking both its economic and cultural significance. Using this paradigm, the work of consumers can be understood in relation to its role across the whole mode of accumulation. Using feminist frameworks thus promises to add clarity and nuance to our understanding of consumer labour in digital media. It seems timely and appropriate then, if not overdue, to bring radical, but mostly Marxist, feminist theories of domestic work to bear upon consumer labour in digital media. This is what this book will do. It will firstly make a comprehensive case for using these materialist feminist perspectives to understand digital media. It will then articulate a particular model for understanding the incorporation of unpaid domestic work into capital, before going on to apply this model to a particular example of consumer labour. Through the figure of the Digital Housewife, this book will place feminist thinking at the centre of both digital media and contemporary conceptualisations of labour.

* * *

The long history of domestic work and other unwaged labour in capitalism asserted by the Digital Housewife corrects a tendency to view the incorporation of subjectivity into capital as a novel set of circumstances, a common feature of many Autonomist Marxist conceptualisations. S/he brings the specificities of that work and, importantly, the theorisation of that labour once more into view. Articulating this history is the goal of the first two chapters. Chapter 1 documents the key concepts of Autonomist Marxism that have been incorporated, perhaps celebrated, in contemporary theorisations of digital media. This chapter thoroughly describes the concepts of immaterial labour, the social factory and multitude, going on to identify how these have been mobilised in the interrogation of consumer labour. Chapter 2, however, draws in feminist theories of domestic work, as well as some ideas from cultural Marxism, to critique these concepts and their application in this field. Recent uses of the concept of the social factory are particularly scrutinised for their elision of the long history of domestic labour's role in capitalism, apparently lost within the "shock of the new" attributed to the symbolically and affectively laden work of post-industrial capitalism. That immaterial labour, and the saturation of private life with the dictates of capitalism, is not new challenges preconceptions about the nature of cognitive capitalism and allows for an interrogation of this work using pre-existing models for understanding culturally and affectively rich activity.

This critical perspective subsequently enables a re-consideration of the economics of digital media and in particular the long-running and unresolved debates about whether this work is productive or unproductive and, relatedly, whether such work is alienating or a generator of social agency. Chapter 3 explores these unproductive dichotomies that dominate theorisations of consumer labour, applying a diverse range of feminist frameworks to challenge and support arguments on all sides of these disputes. Specifically, it uses insights from Marxist feminist critiques of domestic work to establish the productivity of this form of labour, and then draws upon more radical feminist economic theories to underscore how such work is also simultaneously outside of economics. In doing so, this chapter articulates the need for an analytical approach that embraces hybridity, such as that advocated in Donna Haraway's (1991) post-humanist "cyborg theory," in order to encapsulate the complex nature of such labour.

This hybridity is further explored in Chapter 4 which initially provides a critique of another binary that animates studies of digital media economics and labour – that between gift and monetary economies. This is a particularly important consideration when we recognise the importance of sociality and affective exchanges to digital media industries and the long association of the Internet with non-commercial gifting practices. These interactions are more readily associated with moral economies than monetary exchanges and so understanding their incorporation into capital requires some specific analytical tools. It becomes an important critical question as well, for gift economies are often posited as a "solution" to the inequities and exploitation of capitalism. In this chapter, the work of John Frow (1997), Arjun Appadurai (1986), Igor Kopytoff (1986) and Viviana Zelizer (2005; 2011) are drawn upon to challenge the binary between gift-giving and commodified exchanges, and then to propose an approach exploring the "biographies" of labour and its products as they move in and out of commodity relations.

This approach leads back to domestic work and on to the particular model for understanding consumer labour advocated in this book: that described by Leopoldina Fortunati (1995) in *The Arcane of Reproduction*. This model, which proposes a multiphasic incorporation of domestic work into capital, allows for moments that produce use-value and moments that produce exchange-value but, importantly, also asserts that all these moments are part of capitalist circuits. This model establishes that gift exchanges are not necessarily outside of capitalism or exploitative regimes, contradicting the neat alignment of gift economies with progressive outcomes. The persistence within capitalism of use-values and moral economies that this model allows also flags the importance of incorporating cultural critique into the understanding of media economics.

The implications of this model are explored in Chapter 5. Throughout the book, illustrative examples of key concepts are separated out from the main body of the text, allowing expansion of their explanatory power and, if desired, the capacity for the reader to skip these sections and avoid digression from the core theoretical argument. The final chapter, though, differs from this format as it is constituted by a single example. Here, the model of consumer labour's incorporation into capital that has been developed throughout the previous chapters is applied to one particular instance of digital media consumer labour: a banal Facebook exchange between me and a friend that, in the course of writing this book, has become affectionately known as The Ballad of Kylie and Sheamus. The analysis of this exchange indicates the complexity of the value such labour generates in the digital media economy, including the ways the use-values generated in this exchange also do "work" within the capitalist mode of production. It explores how the affective intensities generated in such interactions work to produce consumer lock-in and brand value, but also serve as disciplining techniques that drive desire for the kinds of digitally mediated experiences that can be exploited by capital.

The interrogation of The Ballad of Kylie and Sheamus incorporates both the productive and reproductive functions of consumer labour. In doing so, this chapter testifies that the blending of theoretical frameworks; of culture and economics; of affect and labour; of exploitation and agency; of Marxism and feminism that is proposed in this book is not a category error but is, in fact, necessary for a full understanding of the messy complexity of the exchanges we are involved in whenever we use commercial digital media. The broader implications of this framework for understanding paid labour contexts and for political activism are considered in a short conclusion. This is where the salience of the Digital Housewife and the feminist thinking that animates this figure are taken beyond the confines of digital media's consumer labour.

The complex inter-relationship between economics, culture, society and individual embodied identities that this conclusion advocates has been a central concern of my research for many years. Indeed, this book can be read as the synthesis of the various investigations of the commercial web that I have undertaken since my undergraduate studies. The core argument has been developed within a variety of journal articles, book chapters and conference papers (see Jarrett 2003; 2006; 2008; 2009; 2014a; 2014b; 2014c; 2015a; 2015b). These publications document the working through of the concept that is essential to combine social, cultural and economic analyses, and particularly feminist perspectives, in the critical study of digital media economics. Throughout the writing of this book, this idea has become articulated in different ways than in preceding versions with valuable new connections being made between the various concepts. Nevertheless, all these publications stem from a long series of niggling frustrations about the persistent mobilisation of unproductive binary frameworks in the debates about user activity. Tackling these binaries is a driving force behind this book.

The argument described here is also motivated by a generalised anger at the elision of feminist thinkers and domestic work from debates about media economics and labouring practices, a particularly pernicious outcome when set against the regression of women's rights that has followed the conservatism of post-feminism. The loss of feminist perspectives in this field, especially those that speak to the gendering at the very heart of capitalism, is profoundly disturbing and detrimental to social justice. Consequently, the other goal of this book is to place these important and useful frameworks at the centre of contemporary analysis. I trust that in the following pages, I do justice to the arguments of the many (predominantly) women whose work I cite and whose insights have contributed to its argument. Most importantly, I hope this book and the concept of the Digital Housewife encourage further recognition of these women's valuable contributions to debates about work, and to the interrogation of the intersections between power, economics, labour, gender, race and sexuality.

References

Adkins, Lisa. 1995. *Gendered Work: Sexuality, Family and the Labour Market.* Buckingham: Open University Press.

———. 2001. "Cultural Feminization: 'Money, Sex and Power' for Women." *Signs* 26 (3): 669–695.

Adkins, Lisa and Eeva Jokinen. 2008. "Introduction: Gender, Living and Labour in the Fourth Shift." *NORA – Nordic Journal of Feminist and Gender Research* 16 (3): 138–148.

Adkins, Lisa and Celia Lury. 1999. "The Labour of Identity: Performing Identities, Performing Economies." *Economy and Society* 28 (4): 598–614.

Ahmed, Sara. 2004a. "Affective Economies." *Social Text* 22 (2): 117–139.

———. 2004b. *The Cultural Politics of Emotion.* New York: Routledge.

Allen, Matthew. 2012. "What Was Web 2.0? Versions and the Politics of Internet History." *New Media and Society* 15 (2): 260–275.

Andrejevic, Mark. 2002. "The Work of Being Watched: Interactive Media and the Exploitation of Self-disclosure." *Critical Studies in Mass Communication* 19 (2): 230–248.

Appadurai, Arjun. 1986. "Introduction: Commodities and the Politics of Value." In *The Social Life of Things: Commodities in Cultural Perspective*, edited by Arjun Appadurai, 3–63. Cambridge: Cambridge University Press.

Arruzza, Cinzia. 2013. *Dangerous Liaisons: The Marriages and Divorces of Marxism and Feminism.* Wales: Merlin Press.

Arvidsson, Adam and Kjetil Sandvik. 2007. "Gameplay as Design: Uses of Computer Players' Immaterial Labour." *Northern Lights* 5 (1): 89–104.

Aytes, Ayhan. 2013. "Return of the Crowds: Mechanical Turk and Neoliberal States of Exception." In *Digital Labor: The Internet as Playground and Factory*, edited by Trebor Scholz, 79–97. New York: Routledge.

Banks, John. 2002. "Games as Co-creators: Enlisting the Virtual Audience – a Report from the Net Face." In *Mobilising the Audience*, edited by Mark Balnaves, Tom O'Regan and Jason S. Sternberg, 188–212. St Lucia, Queensland: University of Queensland Press.

Banks, John and Sal Humphreys. 2008. "The Labor of User Co-creators: Emergent Social Network Markets." *Convergence* 14 (4): 401–418.

Barrett, Michéle. 1980. *Women's Oppression Today: Problems in Marxist Feminist Analysis.* London: Verso.

Benkler, Yochai. 2006. *The Wealth of Networks: How Social Production Transforms Markets and Freedom.* New Haven: Yale University Press.

Benston, Margaret. 1997. "The Political Economy of Women's Liberation." In *Materialist Feminism: A Reader in Class, Difference, and Women's Lives*, edited by Rosemary Hennessy and Chrys Ingraham, 17–23. New York: Routledge. Originally published 1969.

Berardi, Franco "Bifo." 2009. *The Soul at Work: From Alienation to Autonomy*. Translated by Francesca Cadel and Giuseppina Mecchia. LA: Semiotext(e).

Boltanski, Luc and Eve Chiapello. 2005. *The New Spirit of Capitalism*. Translated by Gregory Elliott. London: Verso.

Brown, Heather A. 2013. *Marx on Gender and the Family: A Critical Study*. Chicago: Haymarket Books.

Budgeon, Shelley. 2001. "Emergent Feminist(?) Identities: Young Women and the Practice of Micropolitics." *European Journal of Women's Studies* 8 (1): 7–28.

Cronin, Deirdre. 2012. "Women and Austerity." *Irish Marxist Review* 1 (1). http://www.irishmarxistreview.net/index.php/imr/article/view/6.

Cross, Gary. 1993. "Time, Money, and Labor History's Encounter with Consumer Culture." *International Labor and Working-Class History* 43: 2–17.

Cuninghame, Patrick. 2008. "Italian Feminism, Workerism, and Autonomy in the 1970s: The Struggle Against Unpaid Reproductive Labour and Violence." *Amnis: Revue de Civilization Contemporaine Europes/Amériques* 8. http://amnis.revues.org/575.

Dalla Costa, Mariarosa and Selma James. 1975. *The Power of Women and the Subversion of the Community*. 3rd edition. London: Falling Wall Press.

Du Gay, Paul. 1996. *Consumption and Identity at Work*. London: Sage.

Dyer-Witheford, Nick and Greig de Peuter. 2009. *Games of Empire: Global Capitalism and Video Games*. Minneapolis: University of Minnesota Press.

Eisenstein, Zillah R. 1979. "Developing a Theory of Capitalist Patriarchy and Socialist Feminism." In *Capitalist Patriarchy and the Case for Socialist Feminism*, edited by Zillah R. Eisenstein, 5–40. New York: Monthly Review Press.

Faludi, Susan. 1992. *Backlash: The Undeclared War Against Women*. London: Vintage.

Federici, Silvia. 2004. *Caliban and the Witch: Women, the Body and Primitive Accumulation*. New York: Autonomedia.

———. 2012. *Revolution at Point Zero: Housework, Reproduction and Feminist Struggle*. Oakland, California: PM Press.

Forbes, Walter. 1999. "A Store As Big as the World." In *The Future of the Electronic Marketplace*, edited by Derek Leebaert, 63–89. Cambridge, Massachusetts: MIT Press.

Fortunati, Leopoldina. 1995. *The Arcane of Reproduction: Housework, Prostitution, Labour and Capital*. Translated by Hilary Creek. New York: Autonomedia.

———. 2007. "Immaterial Labor and its Machinization." *ephemera* 7 (1): 139–157.

Fraser, Nancy. 2013. *Fortunes of Feminism: From State-managed Capitalism to Neoliberal Crisis*. London: Verso.

Frow, John. 1997. *Time and Commodity Culture: Essays in Cultural Theory and Postmodernity*. Oxford: Clarendon Press.

Fuchs, Christian. 2008. *Internet and Society: Social Theory in the Information Age*. London: Routledge.

———. 2009. "Information and Communication Technologies and Society: A Contribution to the Critique of the Political Economy of the Internet." *European Journal of Communication* 24 (1): 69–87.

———. 2014a. *Social Media: A Critical Introduction*. London: Sage.

———. 2014b. *Digital Labour and Karl Marx*. Oxon: Routledge.

Gehl, Robert W. 2011. "The Archive and the Processor: The Internal Logic of Web 2.0." *New Media & Society* 13 (8): 1,228–1,244.

Gill, Rosalind and Christina Scharff. 2013. "Introduction." In *New Femininities: Postfeminism, Neoliberalism and Subjectivity*, edited by Rosalind Gill and Christina Scharff, 1–17. Basingstoke, Hampshire: Palgrave MacMillan.

Gregg, Melissa. 2011. *Work's Intimacy*. Cambridge: Polity Press.

Haraway, Donna J. 1991. *Simians, Cyborgs, and Women: The Reinvention of Nature*. London: Free Association Books.

Hardt, Michael and Antonio Negri. 2000. *Empire*. Cambridge, Massachusetts: Harvard University Press.

———. 2005. *Multitude*. London: Penguin.

———. 2009. *Commonwealth*. Cambridge, Massachusetts: Harvard University Press.

Hartmann, Heidi. 1979a. "Capitalism, Patriarchy and Job Segregation by Sex." In *Capitalist Patriarchy and the Case for Socialist Feminism*, edited by Zillah. R. Eisenstein, 206–247. New York: Monthly Review Press.

———. 1979b. "The Unhappy Marriage of Marxism and Feminism: Towards a More Progressive Union." *Capital & Class* 3 (2): 1–33.

Harvey, David. 1990. *The Condition of Postmodernity*. Massachusetts: Blackwell.

Hebdige, Dick. 1979. *Subculture: The Meaning of Style*. London: Methuen.

Hoffman, Donna L. and Thomas P. Novak. 1996. "Marketing in Hypermedia Computer-Mediated Environments: Conceptual Foundations." *Journal of Marketing* 60 (3): 50–68.

Hoffman, Donna L., Thomas P. Novak and Patrali Chatterjee. 1995. "Commercial Scenarios for the Web: Opportunities and Challenges." *Journal of Computer Mediated Communication* 1 (3). doi:10.1111/j.1083-6101.1995.tb00165.x.

Humphery, Kim. 1998. *Shelf Life: Supermarkets and the Changing Cultures of Consumption*. Melbourne: Cambridge University Press.

International Labour Organisation. 2013. *Domestic Workers Across the World: Global and Regional Statistics and the Extent of Legal Protection*. Geneva: International Labour Office. http://www.ilo.org/global/publications/books/WCMS_200962/lang-en/index.htm.

Jarrett, Kylie. 2003. "Labour of Love: An Archaeology of Affect as Power in e-Commerce." *Journal of Sociology* 39: 335–351.

———. 2006. "The Perfect Community: Disciplining the eBay User." In *Everyday eBay: Culture, Consumption and Collecting Online*, edited by Ken Hillis, Michael Petit and Nathan Epley, 107–122. New York: Routledge.

———. 2008. "Interactivity is Evil! A Critical Investigation of Web 2.0." *First Monday* 13 (3). doi:http://dx.doi.org/10.5210/fm.v13i3.2140.

———. 2009. "Through an Interface, Darkly: Consumer Agency on the Commercial Web." In *The Computer Culture Reader*, edited by Joseph R. Chaney, Judd Ethan Ruggill and Ken S. McAllister, 159–175. Newcastle: Cambridge Scholars Publishing.

———. 2014a. "The Relevance of 'Women's Work': Social Reproduction and Immaterial Labour in Digital Media." *Television and New Media* 15 (1): 4–29.

———. 2014b. "A Database of Intention?" In *Society of the Query Reader: Reflections on Web Search*, edited by René König and Miriam Rasch, 16–29. Amsterdam: Institution of Network Cultures.

———. 2014c. "The Alternative to Post-Hegemony: Reproduction and Austerity's Social Factory." *Culture Unbound* 6: Article 8. doi:10.3384/cu.2000.1525.146137.

———. 2015a. "'Let's Express our Friendship by Sending Each Other Funny Links Instead of Actually Talking': Gifts, Commodities and Social Reproduction in Facebook." In *Networked Affect*, edited by Ken Hillis, Susanna Paasonen and Michael Petit, 203–219. Cambridge, Massachusetts: MIT Press.

———. 2015b. "Devaluing Binaries: Marxist Feminism and the Value of Consumer Labour." In *Reconsidering Value and Labour in the Digital Age*, edited by Eran Fisher and Christian Fuchs, 207–223. Basingstoke, Hampshire: Palgrave MacMillan.

Jenkins, Henry. 1992. *Textual Poachers: Television Fans and Participatory Culture*. New York: Routledge.

———. 2006a. *Fans, Bloggers, and Gamers: Exploring Participatory Culture*. New York: New York University Press.

———. 2006b. *Convergence Culture: Where Old and New Media Collide*. New York: New York University Press.

Jessop, Bob. 1997. "Post-Fordism and the State." In *Post-Fordism: A Reader*, edited by Ash Amin, 251–279. Oxford: Blackwell.

Kennedy, Sinéad. 2015. "Abortion in an Era of Neoliberal Choice." *Socialist Review* 400, March. http://socialistreview.org.uk/400/abortion-era-neoliberal-choice.

Kopytoff, Igor. 1986. "The Cultural Biography of Things: Commoditization as Process." In *The Social Life of Things: Commodities in Cultural Perspective*, edited by Arjun Appadurai, 64–91. Cambridge: Cambridge University Press.

Lazzarato, Maurizio. 1996. "Immaterial Labor." In *Radical Thought in Italy: A Potential Politics*, edited by Paolo Virno and Michael Hardt, 132–146. Minneapolis: University of Minnesota Press.

Lury, Celia. 1996. *Consumer Culture*. Cambridge: Polity Press.

MacDonald, Martha. 1991. "Post-Fordism and the Flexibility Debate." *Studies in Political Economy* 36: 177–201.

Marazzi, Christian. 2011. *Capital and Affects: The Politics of the Language Economy*. Translated by Giuseppina Mecchia. LA: Semiotext(e). Originally published 1994.

McRobbie, Angela. 2009. *The Aftermath of Feminism: Gender, Culture and Social Change*. London: Sage.

———. 2010. "Reflections on Feminism, Immaterial Labour and the Post-Fordist Regime." *New Formations* 70: 60–76.

McStay, Andrew. 2010. *Digital Advertising*. Basingstoke, Hampshire: Palgrave MacMillan.

McVeigh, Tracey. 2013. "Spending Cuts Hit Women Worst, says Report." *The Guardian*, September 21. http://www.theguardian.com/society/2013/sep/21/spending-cuts-women-report.

Mies, Maria, Veronika Bennholdt-Thomsen and Claudia Von Werlhof. 1988. *Women: The Last Colony*. London: Zed Books.

Miles, Steven, Alison Anderson and Kevin Meethan, eds. 2002. *The Changing Consumer: Markets and Meanings*. London: Routledge.

Miranda, Veerle. 2011. *Cooking, Caring and Volunteering: Unpaid Work Around the World*. OECD Social, Employment and Migration Working Papers No. 116. Paris: OECD. http://www.oecd.org/els/workingpapers.

Murdock, Graham. 2014. "Producing Consumerism: Commodities, Ideologies, Practices." In *Critique, Social Media and the Information Society*, edited by Christian Fuchs and Marisol Sandoval, 125–143. New York: Routledge.

Negra, Diane. 2009. *What a Girl Wants? Fantasizing the Reclamation of Self in Postfeminism*. Oxon: Routledge.

Negri, Antonio. 1989. *The Politics of Subversion: A Manifesto for the Twenty-first Century*. Translated by James Newell. Cambridge: Polity Press.

O'Reilly, Tim. 2005. "What is Web 2.0: Design Patterns and Business Models for the Next Generation of Software." *O'Reilly Media*, September 30. http://oreilly.com/web2/archive/what-is-web-20.html.

Pateman, Carole. 1988. *The Sexual Contract*. Cambridge: Polity Press.

Potts, Jason, John Hartley, John Banks, Jean Burgess, Rachel Cobcroft, Stuart Cunningham and Lucy Montgomery. 2008. "Consumer Co-creation and Situated Creativity." *Industry and Innovation* 15 (5): 459–74.

Ross, Andrew. 2013 "In Search of the Lost Paycheck." In *Digital Labor: The Internet as Playground and Factory*, edited by Trebor Scholz, 13–32. New York: Routledge.

Scholz, Trebor. 2008. "Market Ideology and the Myths of Web 2.0." *First Monday* 13 (3). doi:http://dx.doi.org/10.5210/fm.v13i3.2138.

———. 2009. "On MTurk, Some Examples of Exploitation." *Collectivate.net*, June 11. http://collectivate.net/journalisms/2009/6/11/on-mturk-some-examples-of-exploitation.html.

Smythe, Dallas W. 2014. "Communications: Blindspot of Western Marxism." In *The Audience Commodity in a Digital Age: Revisiting a Critical Theory of Commercial Media*, edited by Lee McGuigan and Vincent Manzerolle, 29–53. New York: Peter Lang. Originally published 1977.

Strauss, Judy and Raymond Frost. 1999. *Marketing on the Internet: Principles of Online Marketing*. New Jersey: Prentice Hall.

Stroud, Dick. 1999. *Internet Strategies: A Corporate Guide to Exploiting the Internet*. Basingstoke, Hampshire: MacMillan Press.

Sussman, Mark. 1999. "Performing the Intelligent Machine: Deception and Enchantment in the Life of the Automation Chess Player." *TDR* 43 (3): 81–96.

Tapscott, Don and Anthony D. Williams. 2006. *Wikinomics and its Discontents*. New York: Penguin.

Tasker, Yvonne and Diane Negra. 2007. "Introduction: Feminist Politics and Post-feminism." In *Interrogating Post-feminism: Gender and the Politics of Popular Culture*, edited by Yvonne Tasker and Diane Negra, 1–25. Durham: Duke University Press.

Terranova, Tiziana. 2000. "Free Labor: Producing Culture for the Digital Economy." *Social Text* 18 (2): 33–58.

Thornton, Sarah. 1995. *Club Cultures: Music, Media and Subcultural Capital*. Cambridge: Polity Press.

Thrift, Nigel. 2005. *Knowing Capitalism*. London: Sage.

Veijola, Soile and Eeva Jokinen. 2008. "Towards a Hostessing Society? Mobile Arrangements of Gender and Labour." *NORA – Nordic Journal of Feminist and Gender Research* 16 (3): 166–181.

Virno, Paolo. 2004. *A Grammar of the Multitude*. Los Angeles: Semiotext(e).

Vogel, Lise. 2013. *Marxism and the Oppression of Women: Toward a Unitary Theory*. Chicago: Haymarket Books. Originally published 1983.

Weeks, Kathi. 2007. "Life Within and Against Work: Affective Labor, Feminist Critique, and Post-Fordist Politics." *ephemera* 7 (1): 233–249.

Wölfl, Anita. 2005. *The Service Economy in OECD Countries: OECD/Centre d'Études Prospectives et d'Informations Internationales (CEPII)*. OECD Science, Technology and Industry Working Papers 2005/03. Paris: OECD Publishing. doi:http://dx.doi.org/10.1787/212257000720.

Wright, Steve. 2002. *Storming Heaven: Class Composition and Struggle in Italian Autonomist Marxism*. London: Pluto Press.

Zaretsky, Eli. 1976. *Capitalism, the Family, and Personal Life*. London: Pluto Press.

Zelizer, Viviana A. 2005. *The Purchase of Intimacy*. New Jersey: Princeton University Press.

———. 2011. *Economic Lives: How Culture Shapes the Economy*. New Jersey: Princeton University Press.

Zwick, Detlev, Samuel K. Bonsu and Aron Darmody. 2008. "Putting Consumers to Work: 'Co-creation' and New Marketing Govern-mentality." *Journal of Consumer Culture* 8 (2): 163–196.

1   Sexts from Marxists and Other Stories from Digital Media's Social Factory

Karl Marx has a rich second life on the web. The opening up of production and distribution tools associated with networked, digital communication systems has enabled dissemination of diverse Marxist, socialist and communist political perspectives in websites, blogs and online magazines or journals. From individual sites for political organisations to archives of Marxist literature (*Marxists Internet Archive*) to online versions of newspapers and journals such as *Socialist Worker*, it has never been easier to distribute information about Marxist politics and ideologies or to organise and engage others in political discussion. The Internet has also enabled more flippant engagements with Marxist thinking, ranging from Facebook pages where one can literally "like" Karl Marx himself, socialism or, indeed, capitalism, to Tumblrs such as *Sexts from Marxists* (in which quotes from Marxists are reconceived as tools for seduction), *Marxist Cats* (in which quotes from Marxist thinkers are superimposed over images of cats) or *Marxwear* (in which images of Karl Marx's head are grafted onto fashion photographs), to the *Socialist Meme Caucus* Facebook community where users can share their comic interpretations of Marxian political perspectives. Digital media offers fertile ground for the expression and distribution of Marxist theory and praxis.

Digital technologies have been associated in practical and conceptual ways with resurgence in Marxist frameworks for political activism. In 1996, Manuel Castells linked the network structures of the Internet to the particular form of distributed political activity of the Mexican leftist political group, the Zapatistas. From the so-called anti-globalisation protests of the 1990s, through to the recent visibility of the Occupy movements and the "Arab Spring," networked communication systems have been linked to transformative political change and credited (perhaps erroneously) with the capacity for radicalising individuals and collectives. While not all of the politics driving these protest movements could be described as formally Marxist, socialist or communist, there has nevertheless been a tendency to associate the network structures of the Internet with alternative modes of political organisation and control. The same idea has been applied to media institutions. Open source systems, peer-to-peer networks and open publishing models such as indymedia or Wikipedia arguably "advance principles of

open access, free distribution, cooperative production, and common ownership of goods" that offer "alternative production models that undermine
corporate power and suggest social spaces in which goods are jointly produced and freely distributed" (Fuchs 2008, 164).

There has also been a related reinvigoration of research into the political
economy of media, but particularly of digital media. This is, in part, due
to the rapid development of commercialised property on the web making
the economic infrastructure highly visible. With companies such as Google
reaching a US$400 billion market capitalisation in 2014 (Farzad 2014) and
Facebook having one of the most valuable initial public offerings (IPO) in
the technology sector with a peak valuation of US$107 billion (Pepitone
2012), the economic significance of digital media is obvious. It is not surprising then that there has been a renewed emphasis on critically exploring
the political economy of these sites.

This emphasis intersects with the increased influence of the Autonomist Marxist movement, but particularly the work of Michael Hardt and
Antonio Negri, in interpreting recent economic and political trends. From
their depiction of the shift from a process of capitalist imperialism to a
state of Empire to their identification of the politics of multitude, Hardt
and Negri (2000; 2005; 2009) are pivotal figures in understanding the fabric of contemporary society. The Western consumer society they depict is
marked by the saturation of market imperatives throughout all facets of
life; sociality is industrialised and industry is socialised. They have also
provided the key framework for understanding how immaterial, cognitive
and affective labour have become central to capitalism. This in turn has
rendered these theorists and their interpretation of Marxist political economy vital for understanding digital media. Hardt and Negri, and various
other theorists associated with the *Autonomia* movement, have provided
the dominant framework being used to interpret the economic relationship
between creative consumer activity and digital media economics. The figure
of the Digital Housewife emerges partly because of the tools they provide
for articulating unpaid and creative work undertaken in digital consumer
contexts as labour. Their insights have also linked that labour to broader
socioeconomic tendencies, providing for complex critical interrogations of
such activity.

This chapter documents this intersection of Autonomist Marxism and
digital media. It explores three key concepts – the centrality of immaterial
labour, multitude and the social factory – and it then places the labouring consumer within those contexts. This consumer, though, is not yet the
Digital Housewife. As I will go on to argue in the following chapter, feminist perspectives and insights relating to domestic work are neglected in
this analysis. Nevertheless, to understand the Digital Housewife requires
outlining the dominant theoretical concepts being applied to consumer
labour, which means we must begin by understanding Autonomist Marxist
thought.

Autonomia and Immaterial Labour

The *Autonomia Operaia* movement originates in 1960s labour protests by Italian students, academics, feminists, unemployed youth and factory workers. The original conceptual framework of the movement was of a non-hierarchical, non-unified organisational structure, focussed on struggle to re-define work rather than for better conditions and wages (see Wright 2002 and Lotringer and Marazzi 2007 for a rich engagement with the group's history). It emerged out of the wider *operaismo* (workerism) branch of the Italian Left that analysed the nature of working-class life and struggle, but was more specifically focussed on the relative autonomy of workers from the dictates of capital and their ensuing capacity to effect change. It also emphasised the relative autonomy of these workers from the politics of the Communist Party and the trade unions (Cleaver 1979). Various wings of the Italian Left became radicalised from the mid-1970s with breakaway groups – in particular the *Brigate Rosse* or Red Brigades – engaging in direct action. The intensification of state suppression of Leftist opposition, but particularly of *Autonomia*, ultimately led to the arrest and incarceration of trade unionists and key members of the movement, including Antonio Negri.

More recently, *Autonomia* has regained influence, with key theorists such as Franco "Bifo" Berardi, Paolo Virno and Maurizio Lazzarato continuing to develop the Autonomist framework. However, this paradigm is most commonly associated with the work of Hardt and Negri and in particular the ideas developed across the three volumes of *Empire* (2000), *Multitude* (2005) and *Commonwealth* (2009). The name of the movement comes from the argument in the "fragment on machines" in Marx's *Grundrisse* (1973) that describes the relative autonomy given to worker's intellectual energies – the general intellect – through automation of labour processes. This idea is explored further below, but it is important from the outset to note that this interpretation of labour's qualities has become increasingly influential as digital technologies, driven by the vital energies of creative, social labourers, have been integrated into post-Fordist capitalism. It has also emerged as a model for thinking about, and activating, the range of plural, disaggregated political movements such as Occupy or the anti-Austerity protests in Europe (Douzinas 2010; 2013; Thorburn 2012; Venn 2007) that have characterised political resistance since the 1990s.

In particular, the emphasis on the role of immaterial labour in capitalism articulated by Autonomist Marxists has been singled out for its explanatory power and used to re-conceptualise labour relations within digital media industries, providing explanation of the work of direct employees and consumers alike. *Autonomia* theorists argue for the centrality of knowledge, social relations and communication – the troika of affective immaterial products – within contemporary capitalism. In *Empire*, Hardt and Negri (2000) describe a new global economy where digital systems and technical innovation are at the core of the developed world's economic growth.

Akin to long-rehearsed arguments about the rise of post-Fordism (Amin 1997; Bell 1973; Castells 1996; Harvey 1990), Hardt and Negri point to the decentring of extractive and manufacturing industries and their associated industrialised, physical labour in favour of industries associated with symbol manipulation. Evidence of this trend is supplied in the growth of the service sector. Accurate statistics of the growth of such work are difficult to find, primarily due to problems of definition as well as uneven distribution at a global level. Nevertheless, in 2005 the OECD estimated over 70 per cent of total value-adding in that region was from areas defined as "services" and that the sector was responsible for the same percentage of total employment (Wölfl 2005).

Consequently, labour that generates non-material products – code, data, ideas, interpersonal relations, knowledge – has become an increasing source of value and central to market economics. Hardt and Negri (2005, 208–209) typify not only the products but also this kind of labour as "immaterial," distinguishing two different kinds of work under the umbrella term. The first is that involving intellectual, cognitive or communication skills, while the second is affective work that involves interpersonal relations and emotion. They suggest that most contemporary work involves both kinds of labour. Digital media industries such as those associated with social media, but also those in the broader software and digital entertainment sectors, are exemplary of this trend in which production predominantly consists of symbol manipulation and the articulation of creative and intellectual energies (Lazzarato 1996). These are the inputs that generate the products of this sector and, as the rise of social media indicates, often continue to inform products as they further engage cognitive and affective energies in their consumption cycles.

More importantly though, Hardt and Negri suggest that while most workers today may not actually be involved in producing immaterial goods – globally, agricultural and manufacturing work remain central to employment – immaterial labour has become "hegemonic in qualitative terms" (2005, 109). The valorisation of this mode of accumulation has "imposed a tendency," meaning that "today labor and society have to informationalize, become intelligent, become communicative, become affective" (2005, 109). There has been an increasing reliance on social relationships and communicative capabilities within factory walls. Cognition and affect generate value abstractly in the calculations of "human capital" that have become integral to the share price of most commercial companies. Furthermore, non-material processes have taken on renewed importance on the industrial factory floor as so-called "soft" skills, particularly those associated with communication, intellectual achievement and interpersonal skills, become vital to computerised industries. This restructuring of the capitalist mode of accumulation, the Autonomist Marxists argue, has lead to a fundamental restructuring of labour, emphasising immaterial activity such as cognition, affect and communication over physical activity (Virno 2004), even in industrial contexts.

As Berardi summarises: "Cognitive activity has always been at the basis of human production, including production of a more mechanical variety. There is no human labor process that does not imply the exercise of intelligence. But now cognitive capacity is becoming the essential productive resource. In the sphere of industrial labor, the mind was put to work as a repetitive automatism, as the physiological support of muscular movement. Today the mind is at work as innovation, as language and as a communicative relation" (2007, 76). In this context, labour-power (as potential energy) is no longer only associated with the force of the living body but with subjectivity, cognition and affect (Virno 2004). It has become immaterial. Because of its ability to capture the kinds of labour associated with consumer-driven, symbolic industries such as commercial digital media, the concept of immaterial labour has become a crucial prism through which to explore the labour of consumers and for understanding the Digital Housewife.

The Social Factory

Autonomist Marxists go on to argue that this re-organisation of labour around immateriality extends the influence of the capitalist mode of accumulation, especially its practices of expropriation and alienation. In immaterial capitalism, life processes often considered outside of capitalist logics, and necessarily so to maintain their validity, become re-organised so that they reflect the logics of industrialised capital. Most simply this occurs in the extension of the working day for those who do intellectual labour where "an idea or image comes to you not only in the office but also in the shower or in your dreams" (Hardt and Negri 2005, 111–112). Evidence of this industrialisation of sociality also comes in the form of the "presence bleed" generated by mobile communications technologies that blur boundaries between work and intimate personal life (Gregg 2011). It can also be found in the logic of "workfare" programmes, lifelong training initiatives and in the expanding phenomenon of unpaid corporate internships (Ross 2013). In these instances, often pleasurable and (quasi)-voluntary social activity manifests the alienating, expropriating and commodifying logics of industrial capitalism (Negri 1989).

What Autonomist Marxists refer to is also about the direct involvement of practices historically considered to be outside the market into the economic calculations of capital. As Christian Marazzi says (2011, 94), cooperative social relationships, interpersonal communication, affective intensities both inside and outside the workplace all become "the fixed capital whose combination with live labor makes that live labor productive." In consumer capitalism, personal, social and leisure activities can be mined as data, captured in economic calculation as brand value, or be factored into share prices in the form of a corporation's "human capital" (Gorz 2010, 11). To contribute to this value, workers are encouraged/required to incorporate economic logics into their identities and to make the production and performance of that identity a core aspect of work (Gorz 2010; Ilouz 2007; Rose 1999). Virno (1996a, 14) suggests that the "permanent mutability of life enters the productive process by way of 'job description'" in which the flexibility, opportunism and willingness to absorb contexts of precariousness that are required of a contemporary productive workforce are integrated into the socialisation of all subjects.

Incorporation of such labour into capital in both traditional leisure and paid work contexts blurs the boundary between the social being and industrialisation processes. As Nick Dyer-Witheford summarises, the "world of the socialized worker is thus one where capital suffuses the entire form of life" (1999, 81). This intermeshing of sociality and the dictates of capital is mobilised in Autonomist Marxist thinking as "the social factory." This concept, attributed to Mario Tronti, explains a context in which there is little distinction between those activities normally associated with leisure (and, I would pointedly add, the domestic sphere) and those that occur in the contexts of industrialised labour. It is, Tronti (1973, 105) says, the "arrival point of a long historical process" in which "all social production has become capitalist production" and so forms the basis for a truly capitalist society.

The General Intellect

In this context, the most valuable labour-power is no longer that instantiated in the labouring body, but is instead that emerging amongst and within the social subjects of capitalism. Successful software, for instance, is not only the product of a single actor pressing the keys on a computer keyboard, but the amalgamation of a range of tacit or explicit knowledges instantiated in various forms, communicated between individuals and bearing the traces of previous iterations and understandings. In *Grundrisse*, Marx (1973, 693) describes how automation changes labour into "a conscious organ, scattered among the individual living workers at numerous points of the mechanical system." What he articulates is understood in the work of Autonomist Marxists as the "general intellect," the collectively shared cognitive and affective inter-relationships of workers that serve as the commons, but from which value is also increasingly being extracted.

As prefaced in the introduction, there are two competing effects of the absorption of the general intellect into capital's social factory. On one hand, its increasing valorisation marks a process of intensified expropriation and alienation that constitutes a totalising system of subjection to capital. Marx describes the subsumption of workers' consciousnesses as they are objectified both in machinery and the output of those machines. He conceptualises this human-machine assemblage as "an automaton, a moving power that moves itself ... consisting of numerous mechanical and intellectual organs, so that the workers themselves are cast merely as its conscious linkages" (1973, 692). It renders labour an abstraction, regulated by the machinery, acting upon the worker rather than being animated by the worker's skill and agency. To put this another way, through systems of automation, an individual's immaterial labour is expropriated from the commons and then is alienated from her or him, returning to confront this individual in the form of machines over which he or she has little control.

Marx says: "In machinery, objectified labor materially confronts living labor as a ruling power and as an active subsumption of the latter under itself, not only by appropriating it, but in the real production process itself" (1976, 693–694). He goes on to say: "The accumulation of knowledge and of skill, of the general productive forces of the social brain, is thus absorbed into capital, as opposed to labor, and hence appears as an attribute of capital" (1976, 694). This effect is described in Shosana Zuboff's (1988) interrogation of the introduction of computerisation in the print industry (see *The General Intellect in the Automated Workplace* below) where not only were workers' knowledges objectified in machines, these machines were also used as systems of surveillance in relation to their work. This materialisation of general intellect that Zuboff's empiricism identifies constitutes the "real subsumption" of life into capital described by Marx (1976, 1,034–1,038). This goes beyond the absorption of fundamentally unaltered labour and life processes to capitalist accumulation (formal subsumption) to a context where these same processes are reformed so that they actively support that mode of production. In doing so, life processes and the general intellect are considered to become directly productive and the social factory comes into being. The social factory is thus associated with an extensification of the expropriating and alienating effects of capitalist accumulation and with a system of control that permeates the entire social fabric, even to the core of individual subjectivity (Lash 2007).

Multitude

On the other hand, automation and the absorption of the general intellect reduces the labour-time required to generate surplus and also the effort and concentration required by the worker. This creates a contradiction as it effectively sets free "the artistic, scientific etc. development of the individuals" (Marx 1973, 706). The machine takes on the physical and/or intellectually challenging aspects of the job allowing the creative energies of the worker to be engaged beyond the needs of capital. Consequently, there is an antagonistic dialectic at the heart of the social factory. The development of the machine "indicates to what degree general social knowledge has become a *direct force of production*" (1973, 706; emphasis in original) suggesting the subsumption of workers' whole subjectivity into capital. However, the capacity of this general intellect to transform material processes and practices indicates its agency and its relative autonomy from capitalist production. Thus, even though it is incorporated into capital, the general intellect nevertheless remains a form of social capital (Tronti 1973). It is described by

Negri as "potentia" (1991; Lash 2007), as active, potent, emergent energy that is creative, inventive, excessive and always potentially in resistance.

Virno demands that the concept of the general intellect be expanded beyond the knowledge instantiated in fixed capital, to include all "the intellectual activity of mass culture" (1996a, 21) such as "all those forms of knowledge which structure social communications and which impel the activity of mass intellectual labor" (1996b, 270). To generate value from the general intellect is thus to generate value from socially embedded, cooperative work. But this type of activity is difficult to measure, challenging the possibility of calculating exchange-value. It also has a meaningful social core, and so contains within it the potential to disrupt the alienating logics of capital. Hardt and Negri attribute a degree of autonomy to social production that generates powerful tensions in the processes of capital. "The autonomy of the biopolitical labor process and the immeasurable, overflowing nature of the value produced are two key elements of the current contradiction of capitalist command. To capture surplus value, capital must alienate the productive singularities, seize control of productive cooperation, neutralize the immaterial, exceeding character of the value, and expropriate the common that is produced – all of which pose obstacles to and undermine the production process itself" (2009, 270; Lazzarato 1996).

Virno argues for the "indivisibility" of the general intellect for "an important part of knowledge cannot be deposited in machines, but rather … it must come into being as the direct interaction of the labor force" (1996b, 270). This is the autonomy that nominates the movement. It is the freeing up of the general intellect that results "from the free-flow of information in technological societies and the possible re-use of social knowledge for a re-invention of a more communal life" (Lotringer 2007, vi). The Autonomist Marxist movement thus emphasises the active agency of workers, focusing on moments of struggle and independence from the exploitative conditions of work organised by capital. This is the labour context of the Digital Housewife.

The General Intellect in the Informated Workplace

Marx's "fragment on machines" describes how the introduction of increasingly complex machinery – objectified labour – into the workplace often has contradictory effects. It provides more mechanisms for control over the worker's body and knowledge, but at the same time it potentially frees that worker from the intensity and degradations of that labour. This premise was empirically tested in Shoshana Zuboff's (1988) important study of technological innovation: *In the Age of the Smart Machine*. She describes the incorporation of computerised information technologies into manufacturing and white-collar industries, noting differing outcomes particularly in relation to the agency of workers. These machines, she says, are not only automating processes, but "informating" them. Rather than merely replacing the human body with a mechanised version, as was the logic of early industrialisation, IT systems also generate background information about activity, rendering previously opaque processes, events and objects "visible, knowable and shareable" (1988, 9).

For industrial workers, whose agency, power and status was often tied to their embodiment of skill and knowledge, adaptation to these systems transferred industrial knowledge from something that was "sentient, embedded, and experience-based to knowing that was explicit and thus subject to rational analysis and perpetual formulation" (1988, 56). It amounted to deskilling and disenfranchisement. It also entailed a secondary transfer of knowledge about the production process from labour to the management tier. Consequently, not only the abstraction of knowledge but also the surveillance of activity in informated systems became a source of antagonism in the workplace. Consequently, Zuboff's study documents the scepticism, hostility and more or less active forms of resistance generated during the automation of industrial systems in the various sectors she explores.

She also notes, however, a contradictory tendency. For some workers on the factory floor of the pulp mills she studied, the re-organisation of their work around cognition and symbol manipulation was experienced as empowering. Zuboff identifies a distinction between the trajectories of labour associated with blue-collar and white-collar work. In manual labour, the body is used for the transformation of materials and the use of equipment (acting-on) while white-collar work is associated with interpersonal communication and coordination of others (acting-with). For Zuboff's pulp mill workers, increasing involvement in and reward for acting-with behaviour, hitherto associated with management and executive roles, became a source of agency and limited class mobility. In effect, her empirical work documents both the greater subsumption of work into the machinery of capitalism as embodied knowledges of the pulp-mill become codified and abstracted, but also the (potential) freeing of the general intellect as it became increasingly vital to the production process. These positive effects were not evenly distributed but, nevertheless, are a striking feature of her study.

Zuboff's study, though, does more than confirm Marx's point about machines. Avoiding technological determinism, she also identifies the complexity of the incorporation of machinery into already complicated social systems riven by hierarchies and power dynamics. For middle management, whose monopoly of knowledge and information had been a key source of status and power, the increasing automation of activity threatened the distinctiveness of their labour. Consequently, the automation of lower-level white-collar activity such as clerical work became viewed as a threat to managerial status and authority. In response, rather than freeing up workers for innovative, self-directed activity, the rollout of computer systems into the office spaces she studied were often accompanied by a routinisation and simplification of work that reduced reliance on existing know-how. She documents the re-organisation of office layout to reduce social exchange, a feature associated with the managerial function. Rather than increasing the intellectual

(Continued)

> engagement and autonomy of these workers, the introduction of computer
> technology at the level of office-work encountered a social system that limited
> its radical potential for individual employees and for society as a whole.
>   Ironically, the existence of processes to regulate and contain the general
> intellect supports ideas about its relative autonomy and its challenge to organ-
> ised capitalism. If it did not manifest agency, it would not be policed. How-
> ever, Zuboff's study also provides a sobering framework for thinking about
> the actual autonomy of labour in contemporary capital. While at the abstract
> level, immaterial, cognitive and communicative work escapes confinement, it
> nevertheless emerges in well-established social-cultural-economic systems in
> which bodies and subjectivities are constantly regulated and controlled. This
> is the same system into which Hardt and Negri's multitude emerges and so
> Zuboff's study serves as a useful cautionary tale for assumptions about its
> capacity to effect social change.

It is this emphasis on "the capacity of living labor to wrest control away
from capital," (Dyer-Witheford 1999, 66) and in doing so to recompose class
relations, that provides the optimistic perspective Hardt and Negri articulate
in their concept of multitude. They describe multitude as distinct from other
collectivities of individuals such as the people, the masses or the working
class. These labels, they say, reduce diversity and generate a unity and singular identity that is false. In keeping with the rhizomatic, non-hierarchical
organisational framework of *Autonomia*, the concept of multitude instead
describes a multiplicity. It is "composed of innumerable internal differences
that can never be reduced to a unity or a single identity – different cultures,
races, ethnicities, genders, and sexual orientations; different forms of labor;
different ways of living; different views of the world; and different desires.
The multitude is a multiplicity of these singular differences" (Hardt and
Negri 2005, xiv). It is also distinct from the concept of the working class in
that it is a more inclusive concept, capturing those who work in ways not
traditionally recognised as labour, and also those whose work does not correlate with the extractive, manufacturing sectors most commonly associated
with working-class labour. This includes those involved in the generation of
symbolic and immaterial products, like digital media workers or housewives.
   The multitude, they say, is about producing a common interest within
diversity and acting collectively upon that ground. Collective action, generated not through sovereign control but through a radical democracy of
interests that emerge out of an increasingly autonomous intellectual commons, enables radical political change, but importantly political change that
emerges from within capitalist labour relations.

> When the flesh of multitude is imprisoned and transformed into the
> body of global capital, it finds itself both within and against the pro-
> cesses of capitalist globalization. The biopolitical production of the

multitude, however, tends to mobilize what it shares in common and what it produces in common against the imperial power of global capital. In time, developing its productive figure based on the common, the multitude can move through Empire and come out the other side, to express itself autonomously and rule itself.

(Hardt and Negri 2005, 101)

It is in multitude that the autonomy of labour freed by technological change can express and actualise its transformative agency.

Immaterial Labour, the Social Factory and Digital Media

Ideas drawn from the work of Hardt and Negri as well as other *Autonomia* theorists have been particularly influential in understanding the digital economy. The connection is, perhaps, obvious. The primacy they accord to industries associated with symbol manipulation and knowledge generation seem to map closely onto the types of work involved in creating the technical infrastructure of the vast array of websites, apps and data systems we use daily, as well as the varied content we encounter there. When the work primarily involves using symbolic language to generate lines of code, and when the products generated are, in reality, nothing more than ephemeral 0s and 1s, immateriality seems an apposite, if not literal, designation of the digital labour context. The distribution of productive and distributive agency amongst users enabled by the Internet also seems to physically manifest an autonomous, general intellect in the form of the participatory web, giving particular salience to the concept of multitude in relation to digital media. However, the connection between Autonomist thinking is much deeper than this superficial connection to the immateriality of digital products and the much vaunted agency of users.

As documented in Nick Dyer-Witheford's (1999) *Cyber-Marx: Cycles and Circuits of Struggle in High-Technology Capitalism*, Autonomist Marxist ideas have been particularly useful for understanding the circuits of capital in digital media. He first documents the social and economic changes associated with Bell's post-industrial society (1973) and its intersection with expanding computerisation as a means for economic revival, shaped particularly by the success of the technologically advanced Japanese economy in the 1960s and '70s. Dyer-Witheford goes on to map the various responses to the "information revolution" by different strands of Marxist thinking, but focusing particularly on the Autonomist Marxists. He identifies the two opposing themes of this approach: technology as an instrument of capitalist oppression and as a tool for class struggle. As alluded to in the subtitle of Dyer-Witheford's book, this integrates technology closely into the circuits of capitalism but also to resistance.

His work then goes on to document sites of struggle and exploitation within a range of labouring practices associated with high-tech industries.

He explores the introduction of robotised systems into factories, the labour of service staff such as cleaners, gardeners and cafeteria staff in Silicon Valley, in the work of academics and, importantly for our purposes, in "cyberspace." Despite the commercial development of the Internet and the web being driven by the need to generate efficiencies and greater capital returns, Dyer-Witheford nevertheless recognises the contradictions between the exploitative regime of the social factory and the agency of multitude. He describes the "proliferation of autonomous activity" (1999, 122) associated with the web, but the simultaneous drive to constrain the agency that is set in motion. Presaging the emergence of digitally mediated participatory culture, but locating it within organised labour rather than consumption, he says:

> To create and operate computer systems, commerce has had to summon up whole new strata of labor power, ranging from computer scientists and software engineers, through programmers and technicians, to computer-literate line and office workers, and ultimately to whole populations relegated to tedious, mundane jobs yet required to be sufficiently computer literate to function in a system of on-line services and electronic goods. As this virtual proletariat emerges, there also appears a tension between the potential interest and abundance it sees in its technological environment, and the actual banality of cybernetic control and commodification (1999, 123; Huws 2003).

Consequently, there is an ongoing tension in capitalism's enabling of activity through digital technologies.

This same tension is documented in what is perhaps the pivotal text for thinking about labour in digital media: Tiziana Terranova's (2000) article "Free Labor: Producing Culture for the Digital Economy." Drawing directly on Autonomist Marxist theories, she documents the particular regimes of control and exploitation associated with digital media industries. She describes the increasing backlash against popular media constructions of the glamour of the sector, identifying instead the important role played by uncompensated labour, often performed outside of formal working hours. Examples of this exploited work include the devolution of responsibility for skill development to unpaid time, but also the incorporation of sociality in the form of networking events important for maintaining employability and/or a client-base. This links her argument directly to the concept of the social factory and to the economic structures of the broader society. She correlates the particular dynamics of labour within the digital media sector with the "contemporary trends toward increased flexibility of the workforce, continuous reskilling, freelance work, and the diffusion of practices such as 'supplementing' (bringing supplementary work home from the conventional office)" (2000, 34).

The problems of under-compensation in this sector have been subsequently developed by various researchers who have interrogated the particular problems of work-life balance, the intensive and extensive working hours and the exploitation of unpaid internships throughout this economy and in various other kinds of computer-mediated or creative work. Andrew Ross (2009; 2013), for instance, recounts the "race to the bottom" in relation to employee remuneration in web companies such as *The Huffington Post* and the Mechanical Turk where contributors either provide content gratis or are paid merely piecemeal rates. These "wages" pale in comparison with the significant profits of the "employer," indicating a directly exploitative relationship. Like Terranova, Ross places this form of digital labour in the context of broader socioeconomic trends, including the increasing use of unpaid internships and the rise of workfare social programs. The computer games industry also provides important examples of, as Dyer-Witheford and Greig De Peuter (2009) put it, the politics of empire. The example of crunch-time, when employees work well beyond paid hours in order to meet deadlines, has been a particularly notable example of the significant under-compensation of the industry. In a *Live Journal* blog post in 2004, EA Spouse, the wife of an Electronic Arts employee, famously described the demand for her partner to work thirteen-hour days, seven days a week in order to meet deadlines, claiming that this time "just goes away," causing untold personal stress and family dysfunction.

Consumers as Content Producers

What is more important for this analysis though, is how Terranova's mobilisation of the concept of immaterial labour is useful for understanding the exploitation of the Digital Housewives of the commercial web. Her framework has been elemental in reconceptualising their activity as value-generating labour, and also placing it within the economic and ideological functions of the wider economy. She describes the digital economy as involving specific forms of institutionalised production such as web design but that it also includes "forms of labor we do not immediately recognize as such: chat, real-life stories, mailing lists, amateur newsletters, and so on. These types of cultural and technical labor are not produced by capitalism in any direct, cause-and-effect fashion; that is, they have not developed simply as an answer to the economic needs of capital. However, they have developed in relation to the expansion of the cultural industries and are part of a process of economic experimentation with the creation of monetary value out of knowledge/culture/affect" (2000, 38). Informed by Lazzarato's (1996, 133) inclusion into capital of labour that produces the cultural content of a commodity such as those "involved in defining and fixing cultural and artistic standards, fashions, tastes, consumer norms, and more strategically public opinion," Terranova's argument identifies the contribution made by consumers in populating otherwise empty websites with meaningful content such as videos, memes or photographs, as well as social interaction.

Calling on the general public to provide media content is not a novel practice. Bridget Griffen-Foley (2004) offers a useful history of audience content creation in various media ranging from newspapers' letters-to-the-editor features, to real-life stories in magazines to talkback radio. Nevertheless, Terranova's argument makes it possible to understand that the labour involved in creating user-generated content such as the play experience of an online multiplayer game, an amusing YouTube video, a tweet about a television program, or a comment on an online newspaper's forum is part of a de-centred production process that is central to the value-creating mechanisms typical of contemporary capitalism. The example of volunteer AOL community moderators, who later sued for back wages, exemplifies this logic (see *AOL and Organised Volunteer Labour* below). In these communities, volunteers generated content and managed the flow of threads. They also policed the compliance of posts with community rules, as well as offering a vital induction service for new users. These moderators were compensated in a limited sense – moderator's time spent online generated a corresponding rate of free access to this pay-by-the-hour service – but this was a much cheaper means of generating content than paying in-house writers to develop and sustain meaningful relationships with its millions of members. For AOL, users' undercompensated labour was the cornerstone of its business model.

Chris Werry (1999) documents the increasing importance placed upon building community throughout the early history of the Internet's commercialisation. Community began to be recognised throughout the 1990s as a means of attracting audiences and producing the site "stickiness" that maintains users' attention and increases the emotional costs of shifting sites, thus producing both brand-value and ongoing user traffic (Armstrong and Hagel 1996; Kelly 1998; Shapiro and Varian 1999; Tapscott 1998). Community shifted from being an additional feature of commercial sites to an audience for micro-targeted advertising through to the core business of many commercial providers. In this context, consumers' interactions with digital media sites and with other users via those sites are thus a source of economic value. This indicates that the digital economy is fundamentally driven by consumer labour and, consequently, operates with a very blurry distinction between production and leisure activity.

AOL and Organised Volunteer Labour

In January 2000, the world's premier Internet service provider and web portal, America Online (AOL), announced it would merge with media conglomerate Time Warner, buying the older firm for US$160 billion in stock (figures vary but this is a low estimate of the final cost). It was announced that the new company, AOL-Time Warner, would be 55 per cent owned by AOL and 45 per cent by Time Warner and have a market valuation of US$350 billion with annual revenue of over US$30 billion (Johnson 2000). With over 30 million members worldwide at its peak, the merger with AOL promised Time Warner a significant inroad into the growing web economy, as well as access to a large advertising market and a site from which to generate synergistic value for the array of offline media products collected under their umbrella. For AOL, the deal enabled access to Time Warner's more than 13 million cable subscribers (Johnson 2000). At the time, this was the largest merger in corporate history. The initiative soon faltered though, scuttled by poor timing in relation to the dot.com crash that occurred before the finalisation of the deal in early 2001. The same period also marked the decline of the consumer portal model for which AOL was known. The expected synergies between the company's properties also never emerged. Recently, Time Warner chairman Jeff Bewkes described the merger as "the biggest mistake in corporate history" (Barnett and Andrews 2010).

The abject failure and hubris of this mega-merger was not the only controversy associated with AOL and it is not the one of most interest to us here. AOL was also involved in a long-running dispute over its exploitation of volunteer community moderators, involving a labour strike and a class-action lawsuit. Documented by Hector Postigo (2003; 2009), the emergence of a labour consciousness by AOL volunteers offers a salutary example of the slippage between paid and unpaid work in online environments and the particular role played by unwaged consumer labour in the digital economy. AOL's revenues came from subscription to their dial-up Internet service which also granted access to the range of bulletin board systems, chat rooms and communities of interest (Postigo 2003). In these spaces, users could aggregate and congregate, engaging in discussion and information-sharing with like-minded others. AOL saw themselves as offering access to community for their users, facilitating communication between people rather than merely operating as an Internet service provider (Postigo 2003, 209). Notably, these community spaces were predominately moderated by volunteers whose duties included hosting chat rooms, monitoring electronic bulletin boards, managing other volunteers, helping other members, guiding new members and enforcing the Terms of Service.

Community was core but it was also highly lucrative, not least because it was primarily managed by unpaid volunteer labour. In a pay-per-hour service, time spent online was money in AOL's pocket. Attracting and keeping people engaged was therefore core business so the communities that constituted AOL were really a co-production of users and the company (Postigo 2009). In 2001, *Forbes* magazine estimated that since going public in 1992, AOL had saved US$973 million by using unwaged voluntary labour (Raymond 2001). Describing its "cyber-sweatshop" in *Wired* magazine, Lisa Margonelli (1999, n.p.) calculated that "one-fourth of all user hours were spent in chat – and those hours generated tons of money. Put a popular remote staffer in a chat room with 22 other people for an hour and – boom! – that was nearly 70 bucks in AOL's pocket. All that chat added up; according to some estimates, by 1996 the service's non-sex chat was pulling in at least $7 million a month with the help of 33,000 volunteers. Chat was far cheaper to produce than content – and far more lucrative."

In the early period, volunteers were compensated with greater access privileges and credits toward Internet access. This reward of access time was one key reason for logging long hours in community moderation practices but, as Postigo documents, there were also less rational reasons for users to contribute

(Continued)

time and energy to the AOL communities. For many, their contributions were based in belief in the hacker ethos of the early Internet, for others it was the sense of community they encountered that drove their continued involvement. Postigo describes the references to kinship in the discourse of volunteers based in mentoring relationships. He says: "This sense of 'family' was not only created as a marketing tactic by AOL but existed and was propagated among some volunteers in the early days" (2003, 209).

This changed in 1995 when AOL altered its pricing plan, moving from an hourly rate to a flat monthly rate. The incentive for volunteer involvement based on the banking of access hours became irrelevant but, more importantly, the plan also involved moving volunteers to accounts that reduced their privileged access and their relative equity with in-house staff. Over 450 disgruntled volunteers discussed their concerns with an AOL representative in an online chat where the possibility of a strike was proposed. A letter to this effect was later sent to other volunteers, leading to the "firing" of a number of senior volunteers. These firings met existing tensions as volunteers were already concerned about their ability to manage the growing number of members and AOL's increasing attempts to regulate their labour, which included the setting of minimum shift requirements, formalising training and reducing their autonomy in managing aspects of the portal.

As these changes became entrenched, "various community leaders began to see their volunteerism in a different light... To them, AOL was no longer a family affair but an exploitative relationship, no longer fun but drudgery" (Postigo 2003, 216). There was also a pre-existing lawsuit from volunteer Errol Trobee who was seeking compensation for the hours he had banked before being let go by the company. What ensued from this re-framing of volunteer labour in 1999 was a class-action lawsuit by a group of ex-volunteers that contended they were employees of the company and that AOL was in breach of Fair Labor Standards for failing to provide a minimum wage. After years of legal limbo, AOL finally settled the case in 2009, reportedly for US$15 million (Kirchner 2011; Grove et al. 2001).

The case of the AOL volunteers marks an important shift in understandings of consumer labour that continues to resonate. As Postigo says, in their struggle for wage justice and more importantly validation as workers, AOL volunteers were forcing the reconceptualisation of affective activity such as community building as "no longer altruistic or an act of familial responsibility, but rather as a commercial service" (2003, 221). This re-framing has recently featured in criticisms by *Huffington Post* unpaid bloggers who wondered whether they should receive compensation out of the US$315 million paid by AOL for its acquisition (Kirchner 2011). It also underpins the resentment of contributors to the crowdfunding of virtual reality company Oculus who saw their affective investment in supporting "creators" through Kickstarter turn instead into "bait for venture capitalists" (VCs) and huge profits for those VCs when the company was sold to Facebook for US$2 billion (Johnson 2014). The case of the AOL volunteers takes the otherwise academic question of immaterial labour, its economic value and its capacity to generate antagonism in the capitalist process and grounds it in the materiality of lived experience.

The Interactive Audience-Commodity

This re-framing of consumer activity as productive, value-generating labour incorporated into corporate designs has also enabled a closer interrogation of the economics of digital media industries and in particular of the commercial web. In the early 1990s, the Internet was characterised by a general rejection of authority and control associated with the libertarian "Californian ideology" of the Internet's key developers (Barbrook and Cameron 1996; Barbrook 1998; Himanen 2001). While there was not structural or legal impediment to commercialisation after 1991 when the US National Science Foundation changed its regulations, there nevertheless was a prevailing cultural pressure that enforced "an unofficial ban on commercial activity on the internet" (Halavais 2009, 71; Streeter 2011). It was only with the popularisation of the World Wide Web in 1993–1994 that the economic potential of the Internet became widely recognised, and the discourse around the technology began to shift towards the concept of audiences using the web to access information (Kenney 2003, 38; Roscoe 1999).

In her exploration of the economics of the search industry, Elizabeth Van Couvering (2008) provides a useful history of the overlapping periods of the web's commercial development. The first period, approximately 1994–1997, is associated with technical entrepreneurship in which many start-ups that began in non-commercial settings such as universities sought venture capital funding to develop their products. These newly commercialised technology companies used product licensing and/or pop-up and banner advertising to generate revenue. The dominance of portals marks the next phase of the web industry. Commercial websites became aggregations where various kinds of commercial transactions were available under a single-brand umbrella, thus allowing for the generation of a mass audience. Typically an arm of, or in alliance with, existing media corporations, portals such as MSN, AOL and Excite@Home became proprietary walled gardens on the web (Van Couvering 2008, 186) funded by the commercial transactions they facilitated, corporate synergies and advertising.

Both of these periods were associated with the high-technology investment boom based primarily on projected revenues from technically and economically untested technologies. This bubble collapsed in 2000 with the NASDAQ technology index losing forty per cent of its value in six months. The period that followed this crash was marked by the withdrawal of established media and telecommunications companies as primary providers of web content, paving the way for new, independent entities such as Google and Facebook to emerge as destinations in their own right. More than a decade after the crash, the advertising market has been reinvigorated, particularly with the advent of pay-per-click metrics developed most effectively by Google, and it continues to provide the key revenue source for commercial websites.

A key thread running through this history is the provision of free access to sites, as opposed to subscription services, that has led inexorably to a sector dominated by advertising-based revenue models. The particularity of this economy, and what it means for understanding the integration of consumer activity into capital, has been explored in great detail by Christian Fuchs (2008; 2009; 2014a; 2014b). The greater complexity of his arguments, and how they relate to processes of alienation, will be dealt with in more detail in subsequent chapters. For now though, it is important to outline the basic principles of this economy in order to understand how it may relate to the social factory. The basic tenets of the contemporary Marxist critique of consumer labour can be traced to Dallas W. Smythe's (2014) argument that the key product of broadcast media was not programming. Rather, he said, it was the collation of information about audiences that could be sold to advertisers. He describes this product of media companies as the audience-commodity, a reduced representation of actual viewing activity (Ang 1991) that can be sold in the marketplace in the form of ratings data and taste-identifying information. Watching television or listening to radio – being an audience of advertising-driven media – can thus be understood as value-generating labour (Green 2001; Jhally and Livant 1986; Shimpach 2005).

As Fuchs explores in detail, the audience-commodity is also the key product of advertising-driven digital media (see also Andrejevic 2002; Caraway 2011; Cohen 2008; Manzerolle 2010; Marshall 1997; Napoli 2010; Petersen 2008; Zwick et al. 2008). However, the ability to capture audience behaviour and to monetise it is greatly enhanced in interactive digital contexts where mechanisms for capturing user data saturate the complex. In the 1970s when Smythe was writing, the key method for measuring audiences was market research and audience diaries that captured viewing habits after the event. Digital media, however, enables the capture of every action in real-time, from status updates on Facebook that indicate taste preferences, to search information that indicates particular interests, re-tweets that indicate political alignment right through to the ability to capture patterns of consumption such as time spent on particular sites, geographic location of IP addresses and "click-throughs" (instances where links are followed from a primary site). It is even possible to capture individual keystrokes. In the hyper-activated surveillance machinery of digital media, each invitation to interact with a commercial site on the web is an invitation to add data that potentially increase a company's profits. The systems of digital media also generate finely grained consumer information rather than homogenous mass categorisations, ensuring the continuous production of new, finely calibrated market segments (Zwick and Denegri-Knott 2009). Consumers are thus not only a source of value because the job of content creation is outsourced to them, as Terranova identifies. It is also because their activity generates advertising revenue, and so is perhaps the primary source of profit in the sector.

However, it is important to reiterate that, for all its ability to generate value, the work of the digital media consumer involved in providing unpaid content and user data does not occur within the spatial, temporal or even conceptual frame of the factory. As Fuchs says: "Social media and the mobile Internet make the audience commodity ubiquitous, and the factory is not limited to our living room and your wage workplace – the factory and workplace surveillance are also in all in-between spaces" (2014a, 118). This is work that is, in fact, leisure or play. It is also this work that generates the general intellect, both in terms of the cooperative creation of knowledge as evidenced in Wikipedia but also in the creation of community and meaning-ful social relationships mediated by commercial websites. I, for one, have a few important friendships whose origins are entirely in Facebook. As I will return to in later chapters, real, meaningful sociality, and the kind of soci-ality that constitutes multitude, are also produced in the economic systems of digital media. Nevertheless, these activities are happening in a context saturated by mechanisms for exploiting the unpaid labour of consumers. Digital media industries thus do not only exemplify the social factory as understood by Autonomist Marxists because the types of labour they draw on is cognitive, affective and immaterial and that this is exploited by being uncompensated. When it comes to consumer labour, it exemplifies the social factory because it leaves no space that is not available to the logics of capi-talist expropriation and alienation.

Sexting from the Digital Sweatshop

Terranova (2000, 51) suggests that today it is "technically impossible to sep-arate neatly the digital economy of the Net from the larger network of late capitalism" because it is "part of larger mechanisms of capitalist extraction of value which are fundamental to late capitalism as a whole." Similarly, it is impossible to separate out the desiring, meaningful affective activities of users – their potential manifestation as multitude – from the exploitative frameworks of digital media. It is in this light that we must also view the various manifestations of Marx described in the opening paragraph of this chapter.

On one hand, there are the overtly ideological, informative activist sites manifesting a direct ideological challenge to mainstream capitalist thought. On the other, there are the variety of sites which, while political, couch their message in humour that sometimes detracts from or undermines their par-ticular perspective. Furthermore, despite their diversity, each of these sites and the activities of the individuals whose labour generates their content are at once inside and outside of capitalist logics. These sites are the material expressions of the ideological and affective excess of multitude's general intellect. There is radical potential in the raising of consciousness through information provision, or even in the provoking of laughter and other affective intensities, using the tools of digital media. These sites, though, are also the products of voluntarily contributed labour that provides useful taste-identifying information, even when that information does not easily lend itself to commodification – while I am yet to receive Marxist-related advertising on Facebook or Google, Amazon is certainly aware of my ideological tendencies. That Marx is sexting from inside the social factory says a great deal about digital media's absorption of the whole of life into capital and the dialectic this entails.

The ideas of the Autonomist Marxists – the centrality of immaterial labour, multitude and the social factory – are undoubtedly useful explanatory tools for understanding the political economy of digital media. However, in this literature there is a significant and surprising gap. It is in this space that we find the Digital Housewife. Studies linking the social factory to consumer labour in digital media typically draw on an assumption that this context has emerged as part of recent trends towards information-intensive industries and consumer capitalism. Yet this ignores a long history of the inclusion of life-processes into the economics and organisational logics of capital in the form of domestic work and other arenas of social reproduction. For a long time, models for understanding these dynamics have been provided by feminist theorists whose work has firmly placed domestic labour (affective, immaterial reproductive work) in the heart of capitalism, both socially and economically. These models, however, have been elided from thinking about immaterial labour and the social factory and in their application to digital media. The Digital Housewife does not appear in this chapter because the obvious connections between immaterial labour, social reproduction, domestic work and capital have not been made. In the following chapter, I will trace this marginalisation of feminist thinking in contemporary Marxist approaches and the limitations of contemporary applications of the social factory concept. The intention is not to discard the concepts of the social factory, immaterial labour or multitude, but to change the conceptualisation of their dynamics, expanding the definition of what constitutes productive activity and so to interrogate more holistically how consumers contribute to capitalism.

In this project to centralise feminist thinking and the figure of the Digital Housewife, I have support from "Marx's" own sexting. (see Figure 1.1 overleaf). "Marx" begins with the usual heteronormative greeting "hey girl," quoting his own, very problematic statement that "social progress may be measured precisely by the social position of the fair sex (plain ones included)." In this "sext" he goes on to add that this is a "stupid addendum" added to an otherwise sound observation, made "in order to score some cheap laughs from engels. male homosocial bonding at its worst, really." But he concludes with a useful rallying cry: "let's fight this lazy misogynistic bullshit together by taking seriously the proposition that gender and race must be central to any theory of socialism." However flippant and absurd this "quote," it nevertheless speaks to the intentions that animate this book: to take seriously the proposition that gender must be central to understanding digital media and to reconceive the theories about consumer labour in ways that reflect that centrality. This work begins in the next chapter.

September 14, 2013

hey girl,

11 notes

Vulgar Marxist Sextarianism.

Hunting in the morning.
Fishing in the afternoon.
Sweet loving all night long.

Sext the Central Committee!

Search

Blog Tools

Archive
RSS

"social progress may be measured precisely by the social position of the fair sex (plain ones included)" is a stupid addendum i added to a solid observation in order to score some cheap laughs from engels. male homosocial bonding at its worst, really.

let's fight this lazy misogynistic bullshit together by taking seriously the proposition that gender and race must be central to any theory of socialism.

Figure 1.1 Screenshot of *Sexts from Marxists*, 14 September 2013 (reprinted with permission).

References

Amin, Ash, ed. 1997. *Post-Fordism: A Reader.* Oxford: Blackwell.

Andrejevic, Mark. 2002. "The Work of Being Watched: Interactive Media and the Exploitation of Self-disclosure." *Critical Studies in Mass Communication* 19 (2): 230–248.

Ang, Ien. 1991. *Desperately Seeking the Audience.* London: Routledge.

Armstrong, Arthur and John Hagel III. 1996. "The Real Value of On-line Communities." *Harvard Business Review* 74 (3): 134–41.

Barbrook, Richard. 1998. "The High-tech Gift Economy." *First Monday* 3 (12). doi:http://dx.doi.org/10.5210/fm.v3i12.631.

Barbrook, Richard and Andy Cameron. 1996. "The Californian Ideology." *Science as Culture* 26: 44–72.

Barnett, Emma and Amanda Andrews. 2010. "AOL Merger was 'The Biggest Mistake in Corporate History' Believes Time Warner Chief Jeff Bewkes." *The Telegraph*, September 28. http://www.telegraph.co.uk/finance/newsbysector/mediatechnolo-gyandtelecoms/media/8031227/AOL-merger-was-the-biggest-mistake-in-corpor ate-history-believes-Time-Warner-chief-Jeff-Bewkes.html.

Bell, Daniel. 1973. *The Coming of Post-industrial Society: A Venture in Social Forecasting.* New York: Basic Books.

Berardi, Franco "Bifo". 2007. "Schizo-economy." Translated by Michael Goddard. *SubStance* 36 (1): 75–85.

Caraway, Brett. 2011. "Audience Labor in the New Media Environment: A Marxian Revisiting of the Audience Commodity." *Media, Culture and Society* 33 (5): 693–708.

Castells, Manuel. 1996. *The Rise of the Network Society: The Information Age: Economy, Society and Culture Vol. 1.* Oxford: Blackwell.

Cleaver, Harry. 1979. *Reading Capital Politically.* Sussex: Harvester Press.

Cohen, Nicole S. 2008. "The Valorization of Surveillance: Towards a Political Economy of Facebook." *Democratic Communiqué* 22 (1): 5–22.

Douzinas, Costas. 2010. "The Greek Tragedy." *Critical Legal Thinking*, November 17. http://criticallegalthinking.com/2010/11/17/the-greek-tragedy/.

———. 2013. *Philosophy and Resistance in the Crisis.* Cambridge: Polity Press.

Dyer-Witheford, Nick. 1999. *Cyber-Marx: Cycles and Circuits of Struggle in High-technology Capitalism.* Urbana and Chicago: University of Illinois Press.

Dyer-Witheford, Nick and Greig de Peuter. 2009. *Games of Empire: Global Capitalism and Video Games.* Minneapolis: University of Minnesota Press.

EA Spouse. 2004. "EA: The Human Story." *Live Journal*, November 10. http://ea-spouse.livejournal.com/274.html.

Farzad, Roben. 2014. "Google at $400 Billion: A New No. 2 in Market Cap." *Bloomberg Business*, February 12. http://www.bloomberg.com/bw/articles/2014-02-12/google-at-400-billion-a-new-no-dot-2-in-market-cap.

Fuchs, Christian. 2008. *Internet and Society: Social Theory in the Information Age.* London: Routledge.

———. 2009. "Information and Communication Technologies and Society: A Contribution to the Critique of the Political Economy of the Internet." *European Journal of Communication* 24 (1): 69–87.

———. 2014a. *Social Media: A Critical Introduction.* London: Sage.

———. 2014b. *Digital Labour and Karl Marx.* Oxon: Routledge.

Gorz, André. 2010. *The Immaterial.* Translated by Chris Turner. London: Seagull Books.

Green, Lelia. 2001. "The Work of Consumption: Why Aren't We Paid?" *M/C Journal* 4 (5). http://journal.media-culture.org.au/0111/Green.php.

Gregg, Melissa. 2011. *Work's Intimacy.* Cambridge: Polity Press.

Griffen-Foley, Bridget. 2004. "From Tit-Bits to Big Brother: A Century of Audience Participation in Media." *Media Culture & Society* 26 (4): 533–548.

Grove, Robert, Michael S. Malone and Patrick Dillion. 2001. "The Little People vs. America Online." *Forbes*, February 19. http://www.forbes.com/asap/2001/0219/060.html.

Halavais, Alex. 2009. *Search Engine Society.* Cambridge: Polity Press.

Hardt, Michael and Antonio Negri. 2000. *Empire.* Cambridge, Massachusetts: Harvard University Press.

———. 2005. *Multitude.* London: Penguin.

———. 2009. *Commonwealth.* Cambridge, Massachusetts: Harvard University Press.

Harvey, David. 1990. *The Condition of Postmodernity.* Massachusetts: Blackwell.

Himanen, Pekka. 2001. *The Hacker Ethic and the Spirit of the Information Age.* London: Secker & Warburg.

Huws, Ursula. 2003. *The Making of a Cybertariat: Virtual Work in the Real World.* New York: Monthly Review Press.

Ilouz, Eva. 2007. *Cold Intimacies: The Making of Emotional Capitalism.* Cambridge: Polity Press.

Jhally, Sut and Bill Livant. 1986. "Watching as Working: The Valorization of Audience Consciousness." *Journal of Communication* 36 (3): 124–143.

Johnson, Tom. 2000. "That's AOL Folks." *CNN Money*, January 10. http://money.cnn.com/2000/01/10/deals/aol_warner/.

Johnson, Joel. 2014. "Oculus Grift: Kickstarter as Charity for Venture Capitalists." *Valley Wag*, March 26. http://valleywag.gawker.com/oculus-grift-kickstarter-a s-charity-for-venture-capita-1551921517.

Kelly, Kevin. 1998. *New Rules for the New Economy: 10 Radical Strategies for a Connected World.* New York: Penguin.

Kenney, Martin. 2003. "What Goes Up Must Come Down: The Political Economy of the US Internet Industry." In *The Industrial Dynamics of the New Digital Economy*, edited by Jens Froslev Christensen and Peter Maskell, 33–55. Cheltenham: Edward Elgar.

Kirchner, Lauren. 2011. "AOL Settled With Unpaid 'Volunteers' for $15 Million." *Columbia Journalism Review*, February 10. http://www.cjr.org/the_news_fron-tier/aol_settled_with_unpaid_volunt.php?page=all.

Lash, Scott. 2007. "Power after Hegemony: Cultural Studies in Mutation?" *Theory, Culture & Society* 24 (3): 55–78.

Lazzarato, Maurizio. 1996. "Immaterial Labor." In *Radical Thought in Italy: A Potential Politics*, edited by Paolo Virno and Michael Hardt, 132–146. Minneapolis: University of Minnesota Press.

Lotringer, Sylvére. 2007. "In the Shadow of the Red Brigades." In *Autonomia: Post-political Politics*, edited by Sylvére Lotringer and Christian Marazzi, 2nd ed., v–xvi. Translated by John Johnston. Los Angeles: Semiotext(e).

Lotringer, Sylvére and Christian Marazzi, eds. 2007. *Autonomia: Post-political Politics.* 2nd ed. Los Angeles: Semiotext(e).

Manzerolle, Vincent. 2010. "Mobilizing the Audience Commodity: Digital Labour in the Wireless World." *ephemera* 10 (3/4): 455–469.

Marazzi, Christian. 2011. *Capital and Affects: The Politics of the Language Economy.* Translated by Giuseppina Mecchia. Los Angeles: Semiotext(e).

Margonelli, Lisa. 1999. "Inside AOL's 'Cyber-sweatshop'." *Wired* 7 (10). http://www.wired.com/wired/archive/7.10/volunteers.html.

Marshall, P. David. 1997. "The Commodity and the Internet: Interactivity and the Generation of the Audience Commodity." *Media International Australia* 83: 51–62.

Marx, Karl. 1973. *Grundrisse: Foundations of the Critique of Political Economy.* Translated by Martin Nicolaus. London: Penguin. Originally published 1939.

———. 1976. *Capital: A Critique of Political Economy. Volume 1.* Translated by Ben Fowkes. London: Penguin. Originally published 1867.

Marxist Cats. n.d. Tumblr blog. http://marxist-cats.tumblr.com/.

Marxists Internet Archive. n.d. https://www.marxists.org/.

Marxwear. n.d. Tumblr blog. http://marxwear.tumblr.com/.

Napoli, Philip M. 2010. "Revisiting 'Mass Communication' and the 'Work' of the Audience in the New Media Environment." *Media, Culture & Society* 32 (3): 505–516.

Negri, Antonio. 1989. *The Politics of Subversion: A Manifesto for the Twenty-first Century.* Translated by James Newell. Cambridge: Polity Press.

————. 1991. *The Savage Anomaly: The Power of Spinoza's Metaphysics and Politics*. Translated by Michael Hardt. Minneapolis: University of Minnesota Press.

Pepitone, Julianne. 2012. "Facebook Trading Sets Record IPO Volume." *CNN.com* May 18. http://money.cnn.com/2012/05/18/technology/facebook-ipo-trading/index.htm.

Petersen, Søren Mørk. 2008. "Loser Generated Content: From Participation to Exploitation." *First Monday* 13 (3). doi:http://dx.doi.org/10.5210/fm.v13i3.2141.

Postigo, Hector. 2003. "Emerging Sources of Labor on the Internet: The Case of American Online Volunteers." *International Review of Social History* 48: 205–223.

————. 2009. "American Online Volunteers: Lessons from an Early Co-production Community." *International Journal of Cultural Studies* 12 (5): 451–169.

Raymond, David. 2001. "True Value." *Forbes*, February 19. http://www.forbes.com/asap/2001/0219/060s02.html.

Roscoe, Timothy. 1999. "The Construction of the World Wide Web Audience." *Media Culture & Society* 21 (5): 673–684.

Rose, Nikolas. 1999. *Powers of Freedom: Reframing Political Thought*. Cambridge: Cambridge University Press.

Ross, Andrew. 2009. *Nice Work if You Can Get It: Life and Labor in Precarious Times*. New York: New York University Press.

————. 2013. "In Search of the Lost Paycheck." In *Digital Labor: The Internet as Playground and Factory*, edited by Trebor Scholz, 13–32. New York: Routledge.

Sexts from Marxists. n.d. Tumblr blog. http://sextsfrommarxists.tumblr.com/.

Shapiro, Carl and Hal R. Varian. 1999. *Information Rules: A Strategic Guide to the Network Economy*. Boston, Massachusetts: Harvard Business School Press.

Shimpach, Shawn. 2005. "Working Watching: The Creative and Cultural Labor of the Media Audience." *Social Semiotics* 15 (3): 343–360.

Smythe, Dallas W. 2014. "Communications: Blindspot of Western Marxism." In *The Audience Commodity in a Digital Age: Revisiting a Critical Theory of Commercial Media*, edited by Lee McGuigan and Vincent Manzerolle, 29–53. New York: Peter Lang. Originally published 1977.

Socialist Meme Caucus. n.d. Facebook page. https://www.facebook.com/socialistmemecaucus.

Socialist Worker. n.d. http://socialistworker.org/.

Streeter, Thomas. 2011. *The Net Effect: Romanticism, Capitalism and the Internet*. New York: New York University Press.

Terranova, Tiziana. 2000. "Free Labor: Producing Culture for the Digital Economy." *Social Text* 18 (2): 33–58.

Tapscott, Don. 1998. "Introduction." In *Blueprint to the Digital Economy: Creating Wealth in the Era of e-Business*, edited by Don Tapscott, Alex Lowy and David Ticoll, 1–16. New York: McGraw-Hill.

Thorburn, Elise Danielle. 2012. "A Common Assembly: Multitude, Assemblies, and a New Politics of the Common." *interface* 4 (2): 254–279.

Tronti, Mario. 1973. "Social Capital." *Telos* 17: 98–121.

Van Couvering, Elizabeth. 2008. "The History of the Internet Search Engine: Navigational Media and the Traffic Commodity." In *Web Search: Multidisciplinary Perspectives*, edited by Amanda Spink and Michael Zimmer, 177–206. Berlin: Springer-Verlag.

Venn, Couze. 2007. "Cultural Theory, Biopolitics, and the Question of Power." *Theory, Culture & Society* 24 (3): 111–124.

Virno, Paolo. 1996a. "The Ambivalence of Disenchantment." In *Radical Thought in Italy: A Potential Politics*, edited by Paolo Virno and Michael Hardt, 12–33. London: Routledge.

———. 1996b. "Notes on the 'General Intellect'." In *Marxism Beyond Marxism*, edited by Saree Makdisi, Cesare Casarino and Rebecca E. Karl, 265–272. London: Routledge.

———. 2004. *A Grammar of the Multitude*. Los Angeles: Semiotext(e).

Werry, Chris. 1999. "Imagined Electronic Community: Representations of Virtual Community in Contemporary Business Discourse." *First Monday* 4 (9). doi:http://dx.doi.org/10.5210/fm.v4i9.690.

Wölfl, Anita. 2005. *The Service Economy in OECD Countries: OECD/Centre d'Études Prospectives et d'Informations Internationales (CEPII)*. OECD Science, Technology and Industry Working Papers 2005/03. Paris: OECD Publishing. doi:http://dx.doi.org/10.1787/212257000720.

Wright, Steve. 2002. *Storming Heaven: Class Composition and Struggle in Italian Autonomist Marxism*. London: Pluto Press.

Zuboff, Shoshana. 1988. *In the Age of the Smart Machine: The Future of Work and Power*. USA: Basic Books.

Zwick, Detlev, Samuel K. Bonsu and Aron Darmody. 2008. "Putting Consumers to Work: 'Co-creation' and New Marketing Govern-mentality." *Journal of Consumer Culture* 8 (2): 163–196.

Zwick, Detlev and Janice Denegri-Knott. 2009. "Manufacturing Consumers: The Database as a Means of Production." *Journal of Consumer Culture* 9 (2): 221–247.

2 My Marxist Feminist Dialectic Brings All the Boys to the Yard

A Feminist Critique of the Social Factory

In 2007, I attended the Association of Internet Researchers conference in Vancouver. Roaming the streets on the evening prior to the event, I encountered a fellow researcher and a group of his doctoral students and we decided to go to dinner together. During the meal, the discussion turned to the topic of consumer labour that was increasing in prominence within the field, as well as having relevance in our respective research areas. My colleague began waxing lyrical about the importance of understanding this activity through Autonomist Marxist paradigms and particularly through the concept of immaterial labour. He then declared: "This is the first time that capitalism has *ever* exploited this labour." I frowned my disagreement, asserting instead that capitalism has in fact *always* needed this labour as it has *always* needed to be reproduced through immaterial labour, particularly in the realm of the domestic sphere. Despite support from a female colleague at the table, my idea was summarily dismissed, much to my annoyance.

I chose not to pursue the point during this social event, but as I engaged with other teaching and research projects over the following years, this conversation remained in my mind. The refusal to recognise the sphere of social reproduction, domestic work and the stubborn insistence on the novelty of the social factory niggled at me. Years later, when I finally had the opportunity to return to the topic, I discovered little had changed. Despite the growing array of literature exploring consumer labour and drawing on Autonomist thinking in its interrogation of digital media economics, scant regard was being paid to conceptualising the relationship between online consumer activity and socially meaningful reproductive labour such as domestic work. When I began probing this literature for its conceptualisation of "production," it was very difficult to find any references to the terms "social reproduction" or to the kinds of reproductive activity Marx recognised as necessary to the maintenance and reproduction of capital. The situation was even worse when I tried to find meaningful connections between feminist theorising of domestic labour (as a key site for social reproduction) and affective/immaterial labour more generally. This link barely existed in the literature beyond token citations, despite what I thought was an obvious relationship between them.

In connecting the concept of the social factory to Marxist feminist perspectives on (re)-productive domestic labour, this chapter is, effectively, a belated response to that colleague. It seeks first to challenge the pervasive idea of the novelty of the social factory, offering instead studies of domestic labour by various Marxist feminists and cultural Marxists that show the long history of the incorporation of sociality, affect and care into capitalist economics. Rather than exploring the immaterial labour of contemporary capitalism as emblematic of a profound shift in the mode of accumulation, this chapter argues instead for exploring it as a continuation of existing forms of exploitation, agency and, importantly, subjectivation. It documents feminist perspectives on domestic work that view immaterial labour, the social factory and, consequently, the labour of digital media consumers as an ongoing articulation of capitalist socioeconomics.

Moreover, in demonstrating the importance of the reproductive sphere to capitalism, it emphasises the social functions of consumer labour in capitalism, rather than only the economic. An additional goal is to explain how studies into feminised labour and feminist approaches to defining productive activity more generally have been elided from the expanding explorations of immaterial labour and its economic role. It offers a close critique of key ideas from *Autonomia* described in the previous chapter, not because they are inapplicable to the context of digital media, but because they do not incorporate an existent body of work relating to domestic work and social reproduction, and in doing so, reproduce patriarchal relations. They also limit the nuance and critical capacity of their critique.

In effect, this chapter fleshes out the background that links domestic work, feminist thinkers and digital media and so gives legitimacy to the metaphor of the Digital Housewife that animates this book. The title – "My Marxist Feminist Dialectic Brings All the Boys to the Yard" – is drawn from a meme I first encountered on the Facebook page of the *Socialist Meme Caucus*. I find it amusing for its play with the pop song by Kelis, but also a very useful framing device for my argument. It articulates the point of this book, which is to explore the tools Marxist feminists have in their "yard" and what happens when we bring these to bear upon contemporary labouring practices. This chapter is shameless advocacy for this approach – it wants to bring all the "boys" to adopt this perspective – not merely as a model for thinking about digital media, but in order to centralise feminist ideas to debates about work more broadly.

The Novelty of the Social Factory

As documented in the previous chapter, the influence of Autonomist Marxism has led to a focus on the incorporation of immaterial labour and immaterial products into capitalism. Coupled with this is the suffusion of capitalist logics throughout the whole of life, as work incorporates inalienable and social aspects of an individual and communities such as affect, communicative capacity and cognition. This is the social factory. However, there are very valid criticisms to be made of the reality behind the trends toward the immaterialisation of labour identified by Hardt and Negri. Rather than productivity gains being an effect of an increase in service work, Federici (2011, 61) argues instead that, "the force driving the world economy has been international capital's ability to throw on the global labor-market masses of expropriated peasants and housewives, that is, immense qualities of non-contractual labor, exponentially increasing the rate of surplus extraction." She also goes on to question the autonomy granted to workers when placed against the evidence of the exhausting labour conditions associated with industries relying heavily on immaterial labour such as the creative/cultural industries. These jobs are not necessarily highly paid given the long hours involved and they come with labour cycles exposing workers to risk of burn-out, constant reskilling and a perpetual focus on informal networking outside of work hours (de Peuter 2011; Gill 2011; Gill and Pratt 2008; Kotamraju 2002; Neff et al. 2005).

More important for this analysis at the moment though, is Federici's criticism of the idea that the collapsed distinction between productive and unproductive work associated with the social factory is a fundamentally new formation of labour. The blurring of boundaries between work that can be appropriated by capital and that which is "life" is often represented as a novel experience emerging from relatively recent changes in the mode of accumulation. For instance, Negri insists that in contemporary capitalism "we have seen how work processes have shifted from the factory to society thereby *setting in motion* a truly complex machine" (1989, 92; emphasis added). This phrase is also cited by Terranova (2000) in her original "free labour" argument. Her later revision to that article also states: "Subscribing to the Autonomists' thesis of the social factory meant rejecting the separation between production and consumption and hence arguing that the production of value could *no longer* be confined to the spaces and times of waged work" (2013, 52; emphasis added). She then goes onto describe "a *new* kind of exploitation – that which concerns the immaterial commons of cultural and technical production" (2013, 53; emphasis added).

Lazzarato (1996) specifically associates immaterial labour with post-Fordist, post-industrial economies and in particular with the "great transformation" of the 1970s which diminished the necessity of manual labour in the developed world through processes of automation and offshore production. Berardi describes how throughout "the history of capitalism the body was disciplined and put to work while the soul was left on hold, unoccupied and neglected" (2009, 115). This, he says, was the situation until the post-industrial context of the "last decades of the twentieth-century" where now even the soul is in the service of capital (2009, 116). In *Signs and Machines*, Lazzarato's (2014) valuable engagement with the processes of capitalist subjection as described by Deleuze and Guattari, also refers repeatedly to "modern-day capitalism" and firmly implies a specific contemporary context for these processes. Similarly McKenzie Wark notes the "wake-up call for educated people in the overdeveloped world" that "what we do has *finally* been proletarianized" (2013, 74; emphasis added). This is because what "were formerly qualities of private, affective and intimate life are *now* the kinds of labor that can be commodified" (2013, 74; emphasis added).

Primitive Accumulation and the Social Factory

The assertions of the novelty of the social factory that have crept into under-standings of immaterial labour imply that until recently there have been spaces unnecessary to capitalist accumulation and, therefore, outside of its logics. It also suggests that it is only a contemporary phenomenon that immaterial labour has been incorporated into the machinery of capitalism, or captured by its measures. There is the implication that through recent technological change, but particularly digitisation, we have moved into an epoch with a new mode of production that uniquely requires the saturation of life with economic logic.

This, however, does not hold up to historical scrutiny. Marx may have argued that the real subsumption of everyday life was a logical telos of capitalism, but this is not only associated with a particular advanced form of capitalism as implied by various theorists working in the Autonomist tradition. Marx describes capitalism as more than an economy. It is, rather, a particular mode of production, "a historically variable relation between a particular production of material existence, and a particular social order, including forms of consciousness" (Read 2003, 4). Capitalism is not only the economic base and its particular relations of production, but also the ideologically charged superstructure of family, religion, law, media, etc., where the particular relations of the base are legitimated, reproduced and given the veneer of necessity (Gramsci 1992; Althusser 2008). This has been the case since the inception of the capitalist mode of production.

Jason Read (2003) reminds us that, from the outset, capitalism required a certain disposition from worker and capitalist alike, suggesting the pervasive influence of capitalist logics well beyond the nascent factory gates. Marx says, "in order that the owner of money may find labour-power on the market as a commodity, various conditions must first be fulfilled" (1976, 270). Key of these conditions is that the capitalist must find a "free" worker who has pos-session of his/her labour-capacity and thus also of his/her person. The exis-tence of this "free worker," able and willing to sell his/her labour-power as a commodity, is thus the precondition for capital as well as the end-result of the emergence of the capitalist mode of production: it is both cause and effect, necessary and contingent. However, for workers to consider themselves "free" and be able to abstract and sell their labour requires the re-organisation and transformation of social relations, but more importantly their normalisation. "For a new mode of production such as capital to be instituted it is not suffi-cient for it to simply form a new economy, or write new laws, it must institute itself in the quotidian dimensions of existence – it must become habit" (Read 2003, 36). The interpellation of subjects oriented towards the particular kinds of work-relations associated with capitalism is therefore necessary to the grounding and continuity of the capitalist mode of production. This requires social and cultural institutions that manage a population towards particular goals. It requires a social factory.

To point to the importance of social and cultural mechanisms for disciplining subjectivity in the history of capitalism is not to propose an interminable "chicken or the egg" argument, attempting to decipher which is the originating cause. Rather, it is to describe the mutually constitutive relationship between production and reproduction – between economic and social organisation – in the development and ongoing maintenance of any economic system. There is no viability to exploitative production relations without the inscription of subjectivities who attribute legitimacy to that relation and the existence of mechanisms by which to reproduce that subject both as a biological and a social entity. What is required are technologies of bio-power "present at every level of the social body and utilized by very diverse institutions" (Foucault 1998, 141) that produce a subject who is as much a part of the productive circuits of capital as the manufactured commodities and raw materials of the production process. These dynamics are in evidence in the example of the company town (see *Reproductive Labour and the Company Town* below) marked by the deliberate construction of social milieux conducive to producing and sustaining appropriate class relations and individual subjectivities.

Marx says: "The maintenance and reproduction of the working class remains a necessary condition for the reproduction of capital" so that "the working class, even when it stands outside the direct labor process, is just as much an appendage of capital as the lifeless instruments of labour are" (1976, 718–719). This is the definition of the "real subsumption" Autonomist Marxists ascribe to the social factory – the conditions where subjectivity is made productive – but it is clearly not specific to contemporary communicative capitalism, nor indeed to capitalism per se. "The conditions and limits of a mode of production, everything that causes the dissolution of one and the formation of another, necessarily pass through the production of subjectivity" (Read 2003, 62). Consequently, to propose the social factory as a novel set of conditions, or to refer to the real subsumption of individuals' subjectivities into value-generating mechanisms as a uniquely contemporary economic relation, becomes untenable.

Reproductive Labour and the Company Town

When the concept of the social factory is refocused on mechanisms of social reproduction a very concrete example emerges: the company town. Often associated with industrialised manufacturing, but particularly with Fordism, company towns exemplify the suffusion of "the whole of life" into a capitalist and often a specific corporate logic. They are more than just an arrangement of building materials but experiments in forming society, culture and individuals in terms desirable to corporations. As Andrew Herod summarises, "they are concrete examples of what I am here calling "spatial engineering" – the deliberate manipulation of the landscape – for purposes of social engineering" (2011, 21).

The company town has a long history across the developed industrial world. It tends to be traced to the interventions of eighteenth century British industrialists such as spinner Richard Arkwright and porcelain manufacturer Josiah Wedgewood who developed towns to house workers for their newly centralised production facilities. It is, however, possible to track the idea back to fourteenth-century Ghent where tracts of housing were developed for weavers (Herod 2011). Company towns demonstrate David Harvey's (2006) point that the success of the capitalist mode of accumulation requires fixing the landscape in ways that efficiently bring workers and raw materials together. Company towns also function as a colonising force in the expansion of capital, the obvious example of which is the spectacular failure of Henry Ford's Brazilian social experiment Fordlandia. Ford told the *Washington Post* in 1931 that in building this city in the middle of the Amazon his plan was not only to cultivate rubber but "the rubber gatherers as well" (cited in Grandin 2010, 5).

Important for this analysis is that the company town inevitably draws attention to the importance placed on social reproduction at a biological and sociocultural level by capitalist enterprise. The company town incorporates reproductive labour into its logics in a variety of ways. For industrialists, the provision of housing in order to provide appropriate sanitation and therefore hygiene was important in producing healthy labouring bodies, while the clustering of employees and their families with shared cultural and educational resources was intended to produce social milieux appropriate to their economic function. Consumption was directed and limited by company control over the local store, with workers often paid in company scrip that could only be redeemed for the proscribed goods available at this retailer. The better quality of company-supplied housing provided an aspirational push to conform to the norms of temperance, frugality and industry that facilitated home ownership (Johnson 1971). On the other hand, the segregation of middle and lower-management housing from that of blue-collar workers that occurred in some towns ensured that malign influences associated with the working class could not spread more widely. Berardi (2009) suggests that incorporation of "the soul" is a feature of contemporary labour, but this was also overtly incorporated into the company town's logics. Companies built churches of various denominations in order to "provide workers with a moral foundation for peaceful labor relations" (Post 2011, 114). In designing Bournville in the late 1800s, the Quaker George Cadbury insisted that each cottage have a garden complete with trees and flowers in the hope that "doing God's work in the garden would prove more satisfying to workers than doing Satan's bidding in the pub" (Dellheim 1987, 20).

The development of an appropriate habitus was not always left to chance. The provision of formal and informal education for adults and children, including the education of girls in appropriate domestic management, was a powerful normalising tool. The Ford factory infamously deployed its

(Continued)

"Sociological Department" through Dearborn and Detroit to offer education and surveillance of the "most intimate corners of Ford workers' lives, including their sex lives" (Grandin 2010, 38). This served the purposes of "Americanising" the largely immigrant workforce of the factory, as well as disciplining all workers into appropriate modes of consumption, sobriety and propriety. By 1914, Ford was known not only for his automobile assembly but also for assembling workers (Grandin 2010, 34).

It is important to emphasise that despite their manufactured qualities and their use in controlling the labour force, real communities emerge and continue to develop in company towns and that corporate control is never total. Despite both positive and negative reinforcement, company town residents continued to drink and carouse, to consume too much or too little, and failed to adopt appropriate middle-class attitudes. The failure of Fordlandia could in part be ascribed to the effective resistance of the indigenous workforce that refused to absorb the structured patterns of work/life imposed upon them by the Fordist regime (Esch 2011; Grandin 2010). Social and living arrangements in company towns are both imposed upon and created by those who live them (Esch 2011) such that they are mutually constitutive.

Nevertheless, these spaces clearly demonstrate the long history of the extension of the factory outside the walls and show the re-organisation of cultural, interpersonal and biological functions – the full range of human activities involved in producing and reproducing the labouring subject – in line with the dictates of capital. They make visible the everyday mechanisms by which we are made and re-made as subjects in the image of capital.

Moreover, company towns are not mere historical footnotes but continue in various forms as concentrations of industries change the social, cultural and physical qualities of a place. Remote mining communities in Australia are one such example, but we could take as an example the re-organisation of physical infrastructure, culture and employment opportunities for existing residents of the docklands and Liberties areas in Dublin through the state-sponsored introduction of digital media and high finance companies such as Google (MacLaran and Kelly 2014; Moore 2002; Newenham 2015). The aggregation of particular classes of workers and/or industries has had a transforming, and often negative, effect on the local urban environment and the lived experience of all residents. Indeed, this is the premise of Richard Florida's (2002; 2003) influential idea of the "creative class" that advocates for transformation of cultural and physical environments, not only as an effect of the migration of particular kinds of creative industries, but also as a tool to attract those industries and their workers. Whether by design or accident, the company rarely ends at the factory walls.

Domestic Labour and the Capitalist Mode of Production

What is missing from the construction of the social factory in Autonomist Marxism is the already necessary role of the various arenas of social reproduction within capitalist economies. This is a peculiar omission because, as Negri himself points out, today productive labour is "no longer 'that which directly produces capital', but that which reproduces society" (1996, 157). These arenas include the law, civil society infrastructures, the education system and religion but, importantly, also the family and the privatised domestic sphere. These are the sites in which the labouring body and, I would stress, the labouring self are produced and reproduced and so are vital to the maintenance of capitalism. They are fields that have long been structured by capitalist ideals, and in turn have served to suture individuals into that ideological framework as well. The family and the feminised domestic sphere have been of particular focus for Marxist feminists interested in understanding the relationship between the subordination of women and capitalism.

The domestic arena has typically been considered "unproductive" and outside of capitalist relations, and indeed has often been posited as the sanctuary from their brutal commodity logics. For feminists however, it is an important locus for activity historically done by women, as well as being central to the construction of female subjectivity under capitalism. Marxist feminist thinking has, therefore, often focussed on sites of social reproduction, interrogating their role in capital in a manner that contradicts the representation of the social factory and the exploitation of immaterial labour as a novel social condition. Like the company town, the history of domestic work in reproducing society can serve as a model for how the social factory functions and thus as a model for understanding consumer labour. To do this, though, it is important to explain the particular ways in which Marxist feminists have theorised the role of reproductive labour.

Silvia Federici's (2004) *Caliban and the Witch*, in which she documents the emergence of market-based capitalism from feudalism, is a useful resource here. As she articulates it, the shift to a capitalist mode of production involved a wholesale re-organisation of social relations that divested certain work traditionally done by women from the arena of waged labour, and separated out private and public spaces of production. This restructuring of socio-economics contributed to the subordination of women by drawing on and systematising organisational structures associated with patriarchal authority (Hartmann 1979a; 1979b; Alessandrini 2012; Dalla Costa and James 1975; Engels 2010; Fortunati 1995; Mies et al. 1988; Vogel 2013; Zaretsky 1976).

Federici describes a period of primitive accumulation associated with the enclosure movements involving the expropriation and privatisation of "the commons" – land traditionally held as a shared good by the people and where animals could be grazed, crops grown and livelihoods maintained. With this land no longer available, it became necessary for workers to purchase goods that hitherto they had been able to grow, harvest or make using common resources. Submission to a wage-relation was the inevitable consequence. At the same time, economic growth also required the expansion of land ownership into newly colonised parts of the world, increasing the range of available resources, and thus potential commodities, as well as access to a new population of workers who could be indentured as slaves. This period of primitive accumulation associated with the emergence of market capitalism, Federici says, also consisted of "an immense accumulation of labor-power – 'dead labor' in the form of stolen goods, and 'living labor' in the form of human beings made available for exploitation" (2004, 64). This period of primitive accumulation violently demanded the subordination of subjects to its logic.

What Federici also documents throughout this period is the increasing separation of work involved in the production of goods from that associated with the reproduction of the health, well-being and life of people. In the shift to a wage relation, the unity of production and reproduction was broken. When one is no longer labouring to produce use-values to sustain the family, but is instead working for the abstraction of wages, the work that is valued becomes only that which earns an income. A conceptual distance emerges between that which is considered economically and socially valuable and that which reproduces individuals and the family, often manifesting as the physical distance between the home and the industrial context where this newly defined productive work takes place. This process differentiated work along gendered lines. In doing so, "the economic importance of the repro-duction of labor-power carried out in the home, and its function in the accu-mulation of capital became invisible, being mystified as a natural vocation and labeled 'women's labor'" (Federici 2004, 74–75).

Federici designates the creation of the full-time housewife in the nine-teenth century, driven by the shift to more intensive, heavy industrial work that required "a leap in the investment made in its reproduction" (Federici 2011, 62), as the culmination of this re-organisation of labour. Nancy Folbre also tracks changing attitudes towards household labour during this period, citing a "new enthusiasm for female domesticity" (1991, 464). This intensi-fication of the sexual division of labour, she says, inexorably linked women to reproductive and specifically domestic labour that was considered outside of accumulation and therefore remained unpaid. This increased women's economic dependence, generating a regime of chronic poverty, allowed the use of the male wage to control women's activity, and rendered women invisible as workers. Importantly, it also placed the woman's labour and her body as a reward for the working man, using them to reduce the effects of alienation and exploitation found in his labour, thereby pacifying the workforce. Women, men and their social and interpersonal relations were fundamentally remade in these processes.

What is more, this division between production and reproductive labour – ultimately between the sphere of paid work and the private world of domestic labour – was no mere side-effect of capitalism. In the same way as the expansions of colonialism allowed for the accumulation of living labour, so too did the removal of domestic labour from compensation. As Federici says, "capital accumulation feeds upon an immense amount of unpaid labor; above all it feeds upon the systematic devaluation of reproduc-tive work that is translated into the devaluation of large sectors of the world proletariat" (2011, 71; Bernería 1999; Mies et al. 1988). The process of differentiating labour based on sex that has had such negative consequences for women and other subaltern social groups, has enabled the accumulation of unpaid labour that, as I will explain more thoroughly in the next section, is necessary for securing profit in capitalism.

Consequently, the "unique process of social degradation" (Federici 2004, 75) that has made women's work "invisible" is as fundamental to capitalist accumulation as the development of the "free" subject described by Read. It also constitutes a powerful form of social engineering, producing a set of social and interpersonal relations, and ultimately individual subjectivities, fundamentally marked by the dictates of capital. Federici's study thus reveals that production and reproduction have always been necessarily intertwined, with the designation of one forming the other. Viewed from this feminist perspective, to claim any novelty for the incorporation of "the whole of life" into capitalism is even less convincing.

Domestic Work's Immaterial Labour and the Social Factory

This history of domestic work also begins to reveal the centrality of immaterial labour to the capitalist system, not least because its differentiation from that which is deemed productive and compensated is integral to establishing a properly capitalist mode of production. Marxist feminist interpretations of domestic labour assert that reproductive work is, in fact, a productive force that contributes meaningfully within market economics (for instance Ferber and Nelson 1993; Folbre 2001; Fortunati 1995; Mies et al. 1988; Picchio 1992). However, because of its association with generating socially embedded use-values rather than exchange-value, in orthodox Marxist thinking such labour is typically designated as "unproductive" (Dalla Costa and James 1975, 33). The privileging of strictly monetised exchange in capitalist systems and in critical thought has downgraded the importance of non-monetised production, viewing such activity as mere exchanges of fuzzy well-being that, by virtue of being beyond measure of the legitimised instruments, are not central to economic nor political calculation (Adkins 2009; Adkins and Jokinen 2008). However, as Federici's history indicates, the reproduction of the labouring body and the labouring subject that occurs in domestic settings, and that this work remains formally uncompensated, is an essential cog in the capitalist system.

As Fortunati (1995; Dalla Costa and James 1975; Federici 2004; 2012) argues, domestic work is productive because it contributes to the generation of surplus-value. If capitalism necessarily requires the production, reproduction and maintenance of effective labouring bodies because they have use-value for capital, then it requires services to generate that product. Domestic labour is one of those necessary services. The construction of the modern bourgeois family with its patriarchal centre (Engels 2010; Zaretsky 1976) is the mechanism by which the male worker – head of the household, breadwinner – is freed from the necessity to undertake the work required to reproduce his own labour. His capacity for production thus also contains the female production capacity expended on his reproduction. Consequently, when this worker exchanges his labour-power for wages, what he sells is not only the "socially necessary labor time supplied by the male worker himself within the process of production, it also contains the socially necessary housework labor time required to produce the labor-power itself" (Fortunati 1995, 84).

The productivity of the waged thus relies on the productivity of the domestic labourer. But when it is an *unpaid* workforce that is reproducing the labour-power instantiated in the body and subjectivity of each worker, then domestic work becomes linked to surplus. As will be explained in more detail in the next chapter, when supplied by an unpaid housewife, the maintenance of health, nutrition and hygiene of the labourer is supplied to the capitalist below cost, thereby becoming an additional source of value and increasing the relative surplus generated by any individual worker. This economic reality is tacitly endorsed by the calculation of the exchange-value of labour-power – the "natural" price of labour – based upon that which is necessary to reproduce that worker and, in the "family wage," his family who are the next generation of workers (Marx 1976, 270–280; Picchio 1992). As Dalla Costa and James put it, the exploitation of wageless domestic work offers the worker the freedom "to 'earn' enough for a woman to reproduce him as labor power" (1975, 34).

Domestic Work's Value Beyond Economics

However, the role of domestic labour in supporting capitalism is not only its economic contribution. The importance of domestic work to the economy also lies in the centrality of its product – labour-power – to all capitalist systems. This significance is tacitly recognised in the widespread disciplining of women into appropriate attitudes towards the kinds of domestic work that would produce workers appropriate for the needs of capitalism. Barbara Ehrenreich and Deirdre English (2005; Folbre 1991) document at least two centuries of shifting advice to women about better domestic management offered in popular culture, specific etiquette literature and in the education sector in the form of domestic science programmes. Through this literature, women were exposed to direct advice on appropriate regimes of cleanliness, personal deportment, child-rearing and expressions of sexual desire, as well as models of inappropriate behaviour to serve as cautionary tales. The inculcation of these norms allowed the woman to become "a repressive figure, disciplinarian of all the members of the family, ideology and psychologically" whose role it was to "discipline the children who will be workers tomorrow and on the other hand discipline the husband to work today" (Dalla Costa and James 1975, 47–48). Not only were women's subjectivities shaped by these texts, by extension so were the subjectivities of those in their care.

Today's disciplining mechanisms are less didactic than those documented by Ehrenreich and English and they articulate a historically specific ideal subject. In contemporary neoliberal contexts, where overt impositions of authority have become illegitimate, self-help literature has arguably taken on the role of re-shaping the individual citizen into the entrepreneurial subject of advanced liberal capitalism who, as described by Virno (1996), is open to the precariousness, intensity and affective costs of contemporary labour. Nevertheless, Ehrenreich and English's argument suggests that over many centuries there have been identifiable and pervasive infrastructures shaping identity and practices toward capitalist ends. To absorb the entire subject into capitalist logics is thus in no way new or specific to the contemporary moment. This suggests that the regulation of a social factory and the incorporation of "the soul," as Berardi (2009) would have it, have been fundamental to capitalism from the outset. Moreover, the extent of this disciplining indicates that domestic work's role is not a mere addendum to the important business of capitalism. This should be no surprise to most women who, marked as Other and suffering regulation and oppression both violent and subtle in all spheres of life, have always experienced the personal as both political and economic.

Expanding Definitions of Work

As Weeks summarises (2007; Alessandrini 2012; Cameron and Gibson-Graham 2003), the expansion of the critical account of labour developed by second wave feminists does not only include studies that describe the role of reproductive work in the realm of formally defined, productive labour. It includes studies like that of Arlie Hochschild (2003) into the affective qualities of industrialised service and/or white-collar labour. This ground-breaking analysis of the role of emotional responses and their regulation in various industries involving public contact demonstrated that affect, or at least the sustained simulation of affect, was a core aspect of the labour in these sectors. From the ever-smiling flight attendants whose highly controlled emotional responses are central to the customer experience, to the bill collectors who are required to withhold affective intimacy, industry profits emerge from the ways in which workers manage their own emotions and those of others. Hochschild's study not only recognised the centrality of affective energies in paid, industrialised contexts but also importantly asserted that this work is a generator of value.

Her work "allowed us to take emotion out of the invisible realm of the private and the social and put it into an analysis of the labour process, recognising it as an important contribution to a profitable product" (Bolton 2009, 73). Hochschild's analysis challenged the limited definition of productive activity in ways that also apply to much domestic labour. It has been particularly useful for generating holistic accounts of the labour involved in various kinds of feminised industries, but particularly care work. It is also important in its assertion that there are real, personal consequences of its incorporation into capitalism. For instance, in her study of live-in migrant nannies and maids, Bridget Anderson (2003) describes the difficulty for these women in maintaining boundaries around their paid and unpaid contributions to the personal lives of the families for whom they work, and also the impact on their sense of belonging when returning to their home country. To identify that "the heart" is also at stake in the waged workplace complicates understandings of the nature of work.

The types of work described in Marxist feminist interpretations of domestic labour and in Hochschild's analysis are cognitive, communicative and richly affective – the immaterial labour of Hardt and Negri's reckoning. But they also include the biological aspects of labour constituted in orthodox thought as "unproductive" or, at worst, natural (Barker 2005; Mies 1988). Analysis of sex work and biological reproduction – perhaps the original bio-power exploited by capitalism – and their role in sustaining the social and economic fabric of capitalism has been important to feminists in ways that do not register in Autonomist Marxist theories. To include these functions under the rubric of immaterial labour would, at first glance, seem contradictory as they are defined very much by their physical materiality. However, as Sharon C. Bolton's criticism of Hardt and Negri's use of the term affective labour explains, their refusal to address the embodied nature of all kinds of work is due to an emphasis on the "top end" of the labour market, "producing a tidy white, middle-class analysis" rather than the "front-line service jobs that involve large amounts of emotion work" (2009, 75). This ensures that menial, physical and emotional care work typically done by women, and its often messy materiality, continues to be invisible within analysis of contemporary labour. While Hardt and Negri fail to adequately acknowledge it, because it includes the affective, the concept of immaterial labour also involves the work of bodies. To include "natural" physical labour in calculations of immaterial labour, and thus into the assessment of productive, value-generating and exploited activity, is thus an important complication of Hardt and Negri's thesis.

Taken together, these intertwined conceptualisations of the nature of work that "expand the category of labor to include more of its gendered forms" (Weeks 2007, 233) constitute a complex interrogation of immaterial labour, even though this remains little acknowledged. Feminist interrogations of domestic labour, and in particular their identification of its crucial role throughout the history of capitalism, thus raise two important points of dissent from the discussion of the social factory by *Autonomia* theorists. First, they suggest that there has never been a space outside of capitalism that has only recently been absorbed into late capitalism as implied in dominant uses of Autonomist Marxist approaches. The history of capitalism, but particularly the exclusion of women's work from economic calculation and the subsequent effects on social, familial and intersubjective power, shows the incorporation of life into capitalist commerce at its outset. This may not have been successful, or may have been effected crudely at times, but it has always been integral to capitalism. From a feminist perspective, the history of capitalism is a history of a social factory.

The second point is that if the social factory is merely the conditions of capitalism then it is no surprise that immaterial processes and objects have a central place within contemporary capitalism; they always have. There certainly has been an intensification of the importance placed upon these activities in work practices and in the spreadsheets that determine economic value for corporations, and perhaps a naturalisation that diminishes the need for (symbolic) violence to maintain discipline in relation to this dynamic. Nevertheless, this does not mean that there has been the introduction of an entirely new paradigm of work. What is important about *Autonomia's* theorisations then, is not that they map the emergence of a novel form of labour exploitation. It is that they demonstrate the remarkable continuity of capitalist socioeconomics, with their key contribution being merely the re-statement of the capital relations already understood by feminists and experienced in the everyday life of women. The "sudden recognition" that Wark refers to in experiencing the social factory is, perhaps, merely the realisation that white, heterosexual, able, cis-men are also subjects of capitalism. These empowered, autonomous, agential subjects of history are the only ones who could find novelty in digital media's social factory. For everyone else, it is business as usual.

What feminist arguments about domestic labour point out then is that the re-organisation of familial, interpersonal and affective relations is integral to capitalist societies. This is important to recognise because the activity of the domestic sphere such as caring, health maintenance and sexual activity is too often placed outside of market relations in a mythic past in order to service claims that the politics of the social factory can be readily over-turned, achieving a return to a fabled state of un-alienated autonomy. As will be explored in later chapters, this is particularly pertinent to the study of digital media for similar claims are often made about the politics of the reciprocal gift-giving that occurs between consumers. For now, though, the expansion of the history of the social factory performed by the feminist analyses explored here has two functions. It first refuses the novelty of such work, placing it in an established economic and material context of exploitation. Second, given the close relationship between immaterial labour, the social factory and digital media documented in the previous chapter, it opens up the analogy between the immaterial labour of digital media and domestic work, allowing Marxist feminist analytical insights into domestic work to become useful tools for prising open that context in relation to digital media. It establishes the Digital Housewife as the obvious metaphor for analysing consumer labour.

Where Did All the Women Go?

Recognition of the continuity of immaterial labour's role within capital means that it is possible, indeed essential, to use theoretical frameworks that have already explored the economic and social significance of such work. This leads inexorably to all the feminist thinkers discussed above who worked diligently, not only to demonstrate how household management and caring for children and the aged actually constituted work, but also to identify the particular qualities of this labour and its economic function. Yet, in discussion of the contemporary social factory and immaterial labour it is quite common to only see a brief, perhaps token, mention of feminist researchers such as Federici, Dalla Costa, James and Fortunati who, in the words of Kathi Weeks, "opened the door to a new conceptualization of the structure of capitalist social production, to which the category of the social factory was an early contribution" (2011, 123).

Even when making some connection to feminist theorising, the arguments of these theorists are typically not developed in a meaningful way, except perhaps in *Digital Labour and Karl Marx* (2014) where Fuchs spends some time discussing the concept of "housewifisation" as described by Maria Mies et al. (1988). This is a rare application of feminist ideas though. Even Hardt's article "Affective Labor" (1999), the text that most overtly speaks to the importance of feminist analysis in understanding contemporary capital, cites only a few specific sources, preferring instead to ventriloquise arguments by unknown feminists and not to fully explain or use their explanatory power. This problem is compounded in his later work with Negri that, although demonstrating more complexity in its historicisation of immaterial labour than appears in many later applications of their ideas, slips inexorably into statements of novelty and a limited exploration of feminist conceptualisations of labour. This is particularly vexing given the important role played by feminist thinking in expanding the definition of labour that is central to the theories of Autonomist Marxism (Cuninghame 2008). Federici (2006, n.p.; McRobbie 2010) notes that in paying only "lip service" to feminist thought, the dominant approach in contemporary Autonomist Marxist critique

> ignores, bypasses, one of the most important contributions of feminist theory and struggle, which is the redefinition of work, and the recognition of women's unpaid reproductive labor as a key source of capitalist accumulation. In redefining housework as WORK, as not a personal service but the work that produces and reproduces labor power, feminists have uncovered a new crucial ground of exploitation that Marx and Marxist theory completely ignored. All of the important political insights contained in those analysis [sic] are now brushed aside as if they were of no relevance to an understanding of the present organization of production.

The epochalisation inherent to dominant uses of the concept of the social factory continues the elision of feminised, domestic work from the understanding of labour and labour practices (Bernería 1999; Cuninghame 2008;

Federici 2004; McRobbie 2010; Mies et al. 1988). The implication that capitalism has historically impacted *only* within the walls of the factory denies the already social labour of women, and men, which has contributed directly and indirectly to capitalist relations. For many women, whose negotiation of the labyrinthine emotional, physical and fiscal demands of combining unpaid and paid work is long-standing and ongoing, the social factory lacks the novelty ascribed to it here. It is not new that power exerts itself through living matter, the emblematic evidence of which lies in the various forms for policing, suppressing and manipulating women's bodies and particularly their biological reproductive function that has served the interests of capitalism over centuries. To assert otherwise is to restate the capitalist logic that differentiates productive and unproductive labour, men's and women's work, in order to generate a standing reserve of living labour whose inputs, because entirely unpaid, are entirely surplus. To fail to recognise the role of social reproduction is to re-assert the exploitative logic at the heart of capitalism.

The elision and/or marginalisation of feminist research into domestic work in interrogations of immaterial labour is therefore surprising and discomforting. But this is made even more notable given the "feminisation" or, as Mies et al. (1988) call it, the "housewifisation" of labour in contemporary capital. This is not only in the sense of the increasing inclusion of women as paid workers and the rising importance of services in economic systems. It also because of the "soft feminine skills" of flexibility and constant adaptability demanded within current employment systems; what Lisa Adkins (2001; 2002) calls the "cultural feminisation thesis" in which both men and women are increasingly called upon to perform the "aesthetics of femininity" in the workplace. As Cristina Morini says, "in cognitive capitalism precariousness, mobility and fragmentation become constituent elements of the work of all persons irrespective of gender. The model advanced is pliable, hyper-flexible and in this sense it draws on the *baggage of female experience*" (2007, 4; emphasis in original).

The slippage between work and leisure time typical of the increasing number of people "working from home" in informationalised industries is also an experience common to women for whom the house has always been a site of work (Gregg 2008; Gregg 2011). As Mies et al. (1988) remind us, unpaid domestic work is also socially, politically and economically coerced as well as being isolated and unorganised and so resembles the precarious work of high-technology capitalism as well as the violent slavery of extractive industries in the developing world. It is work that is "not protected by trade unions or labour laws, that is available at any time, for any price" and so serves today as a useful model in "a political strategy to break the power of the organized (male) proletariat" (1988, 10). Indeed for Mies et al. (1988), the proletarian is "dead" as the centre of labour, replaced by the life-long housewife and the principles of domestic work that orient the economy to unpaid and unfree labour. Feminisation thus marks the structural and simultaneous over- and under-employment that are the conditions of work in today's global neoliberal economy. "Work is being redefined as both literally female and feminized, whether performed by men or women. To be feminized is to be made extremely vulnerable; able to be disassembled, reassembled, exploited as reserve labour force; seen less as workers than as servers; subjected to time arrangements on and off the paid job that make a mockery of a limited work day; leading an existence that always borders on being obscene, out of place" (Haraway 1991, 166).

Yet despite the obvious potential of research into the "baggage" of women's labour to illuminate the specificity of contemporary labour practices, the long history of thinking into feminised, affective labour remains little considered. This is particularly true of the study of digital media which, as David Staples (2007) points out, is haunted by the "spectre" of domestic work and feminist thought. That studies in this area rarely draw overtly upon its rich analytical insights (Alessandrini 2012; McRobbie 2010; Weeks 2007) is the legacy of Autonomist Marxism's marginalisation of feminist perspectives. Indeed, in my field of Media Studies, it often seems as if immaterial labour was only "invented" when it moved out of the kitchen and onto the Internet.

A generous reading of this situation would argue that the long schism between orthodox Marxist frameworks, that trace subordination to class relations, and feminist approaches, that identify women's oppression in patriarchy, is the cause of the failure to integrate these approaches. Obvious weaknesses in the interrogation of women's experience in the socialist tradition and the inability of "economist" approaches to explain issues of sexuality and the constancy of male domination over time (Barrett 1980; Eisenstein 1979), coupled with rising pessimism about the effectiveness and achievements of socialist initiatives at a global level, caused feminist movements and theorists since the 1970s to shy away from utilising Marxist frameworks (Arruzza 2013; Hartmann 1979a). As Lise Vogel (2013, 2) describes, "some socialist feminists became persuaded that Marxism could not be transformed or extended by means of the application of feminist insight. They suggested, moreover, that such a goal is not only unattainable but betrays women's liberation to the demands of socialism."

As feminists moved away from debates about domestic labour, at the same time most orthodox "Marxists simply disregarded the debate, neither following nor participating in it" (Vogel 2013, 195). The absolute primacy of class struggle – the assumption that revolution within the mode of production would adequately address all issues of social dominance, including those within personal and family life – has been widespread in many socialist and communist organisations (Zaretsky 1976). With the apparent incompatibility between their goals and the definitions of what constitutes struggle, it is perhaps possible that neither Marxists nor feminists were able to see the utility in each other's approaches, leading to the limited application of feminist approaches in theorisation of labour drawing on Autonomist paradigms.

A more critical reading would, however, map the novelty ascribed to the social factory onto a long history of the marginalisation of domestic work in dominant academic and activist conceptualisations of labour (Bernería 1999; Folbre 1991). This marginalised work also includes that of mostly female, feminist labour scholars and activists. Their insights often do not register in the pantheon of great thinkers because their subject matter – domestic labour – is not considered important due to a peculiar re-inscription of the logic of capitalism that designates it as "unproductive" and therefore not relevant to interrogations of capitalist labouring. This has the effect of making women politically invisible, reifying the role of domestic work and pushing women's concerns out of economic and political calculations except when they are waged workers (Picchio 1992, 110). The other related reason is because the particular conditions of oppression feminists document are considered to be "mere" bourgeois, post-structuralist identity politics and therefore a side-line to the "real issue" of transforming or overturning class relations. Despite a long history of engagement with "the woman-question," including in the work of Marx and Engels (Brown 2013; Folbre 1993; Vogel 2013), the subordination of feminist concerns is also a feature of socialist politics.

However, as Judith Butler (1997) reminds us, the politics of repression and resistance based on sexuality, gender, race or disability or indeed any other politics not grounded in class, are never "merely cultural." There are real material causes and effects of the marginalisation of self-valorised expressions of identity by subordinated social groups. To dismiss these as only the manifestation of non-productive, and therefore unimportant, cultural sensibilities is to silence the materiality of those groups' experiences. It is to maintain a definition of productive labour that is exclusive and in doing so to ascribe importance and meaningful political agency to the actions attributed to only a select group of society. It is to privilege white, heterosexual men's labouring experiences over those of other people in ways that reproduce capital's exploitation of those groups. To explore immaterial labour and the social factory without a meaningful engagement with feminist views on reproductive work is thus theoretically unsound and also profoundly misogynist.

The Marxist feminist theories drawn upon here and developed in following chapters avoid this problem as they work from the unity of the historical materialist and economic insights of orthodox Marxism, radical feminists' emphasis on gender oppression and include engagement with the arenas of social reproduction (culture). This framework offers a route out of the impasse associated with these supposedly conflicting paradigms. This is the approach advocated by Vogel (2013; Barker 2005; Skeggs 2014) who situates women's oppression in the reproduction of labour-power in the overall context of capitalist social reproduction. Maintaining such a focus on the material sources of oppression "counters an idealist tendency within the Left, which trivializes the issue of women's oppression as a mere matter of lack of rights and ideological chauvinism. Second, socialist-feminists' special concern with psychological and ideological issues, especially those arising within the family, stands opposed to the crudities of an economic-determinist interpretation of women's position, also common within the socialist movement" (Vogel 2013, 31). More importantly, it re-centres feminist interpretations of labour, refusing their relegation solely to the realm of "culture" where their critical capacity is misrecognised.

The framework I am adopting is important beyond the identification of a viable theoretical paradigm for understanding consumer labour in digital media. The elision of feminist perspectives from interpretations of immaterial labour "hides the continuing exploitation of women's unpaid domestic labor and makes the struggles that women are waging on the terrain of reproduction invisible" (Federici 2011, 58). While it is not directly engaging with women's political struggles over labour, one goal of this project is to ensure that domestic work is brought to the forefront of current thinking about immaterial labour, which will hopefully allow for greater recognition of this struggle. By overtly shining a spotlight on feminist frameworks for understanding labour, the real struggles of actual women may also be brought into relief. These politics and a complex combination of both cultural and economic Marxism are what a Marxist feminist dialectic brings to the yard.

Re-Enter the Digital Housewife

With their long association with the politics of the social factory, feminist perspectives on domestic work thus seem uniquely placed to provide insight into the social factory and consumer labour. This link becomes clear in Fortunati's criticism of the current state of debate on the nature of immaterial labour that she says has "completely ignored the material labor of the domestic sphere (cleaning the house, cooking, shopping, washing and ironing clothes) and above all, ignored the labor done in order to produce individuals (sex, pregnancy, childbirth, breastfeeding and care), as well as the other fundamental parts of the immaterial sphere (affect, care, love, education, socialization, communication, information, entertainment, organization, planning, coordination, logistics)" (2007, 144). The equation Fortunati makes here between immaterial labour and social reproduction I have also made in articulating the figure of the Digital Housewife. As I suggested in the introduction, the latter part of her statement depicting the work of the "immaterial sphere" neatly describes the types of work associated with the labour of consumers in digital media contexts – in young women posting critical interpretations of Ophelia to YouTube (O'Neill 2014); in expressing social solidarity by retweeting a friend's humorous message; in coordinating a political event on Facebook; in sharing your favourite paint sample on Pinterest, to cite merely a few examples. These are the practices associated with generating and maintaining social cohesion or dependency, as well as generating the intellectual and creative commons shared by all users.

Consumer labour is akin to domestic labour not only because it is unpaid and occurs outside of formal factory walls in what is ostensibly free time. It is also akin to it because it is a site of social reproduction: a site for the making and re-making of the social, affective, ideological and psychological states of being that (may) accord with appropriate capitalist subjectivities. This is the work of the Digital Housewife who, it should be reiterated, is not a woman, but the non-gender-specific unpaid worker involved in the feminised sphere of social reproduction in digital media.

The Digital Housewife thus bears the very particular relationship to capitalism as domestic workers for s/he generates products that contribute economic value by providing free content and user data. S/he also works within the social factory, generating immaterial products that can be associated with inalienable use-values but which may nevertheless be integral to the reproduction of capital. Both consumer labour in digital media and domestic work are simultaneously inside and outside of capitalism, manifesting the dialectical qualities that Hardt and Negri associate with multitude and which have been aligned with the networked politics of the Internet. This dialectic and the insights that can be generated into its politics by feminist perspectives about domestic work are described in the next chapter. It picks up a central debate in the field of digital media – that between those who describe the alienating qualities of consumer labour and those who reference the empowering, agential qualities of this work. The following chapter will demonstrate the insights that can be generated by viewing such labour through the prism of domestic work.

References

Adkins, Lisa. 2001. "Cultural Feminization: 'Money, Sex and Power' for Women." *Signs* 26 (3): 669–695.

———. 2002. *Revisions: Gender and Sexuality in Late Modernity*. Buckingham: Open University Press.

———. 2009. "Feminism After Measure." *Feminist Theory* 10 (3): 323–339.

Adkins, Lisa and Eeva Jokinen. 2008. "Introduction: Gender, Living and Labour in the Fourth Shift." *NORA – Nordic Journal of Feminist and Gender Research* 16 (3): 138–148.

Alessandrini, Donatella. 2012. "Immaterial Labor and Alternative Valorisation Processes." *feminists@law* 1 (2): 1–28.

Althusser, Louis. 2008. *On Ideology*. London: Verso. Originally published 1971.

Anderson, Bridget. 2003. "Just Another Job? The Commodification of Domestic Labour." In *Global Woman: Nannies, Maids and Sex Workers in the New Economy*, edited by Barbara Ehrenreich and Arlie Russell Hochschild, 104–114. London: Granta Books.

Arruzza, Cinzia. 2013. *Dangerous Liaisons: The Marriages and Divorces of Marxism and Feminism*. Wales: Merlin Press.

Barker, Drucilla K. 2005. "Beyond Women and Economics: Rereading 'Women's Work'." *Signs: Journal of Women in Culture and Society* 30 (4): 2,189–2,209.

Barrett, Michéle. 1980. *Women's Oppression Today: Problems in Marxist Feminist Analysis*. London: Verso.

Berardi, Franco "Bifo". 2009. *The Soul at Work: From Alienation to Autonomy*. Translated by Francesca Cadel and Giuseppina Mecchia. LA: Semiotext(e).

Bernería, Lourdes. 1999. "The Enduring Debate over Unpaid Labour." *International Labour Review* 138 (3): 287–309.

Bolton, Sharon C. 2009. "The Lady Vanishes: Women's Work and Affective Labour." *International Journal of Work Organisation and Emotion* 3 (1): 72–80.

Brown, Heather A. 2013. *Marx on Gender and the Family: A Critical Study*. Chicago: Haymarket Books.

Butler, Judith. 1997. "Merely Cultural." *Social Text* 15 (3–4): 265–277.

Cameron, Jenny and J. K. Gibson-Graham. 2003. "Feminising the Economy: Metaphors, Strategies, Politics." *Gender, Place and Culture* 10 (2): 145–157.

Cuninghame, Patrick. 2008. "Italian Feminism, Workerism and Autonomy in the 1970s: The Struggle Against Unpaid Reproductive Labour and Violence." *Amnis: Revue de Civilization Contemporaine Europes/Amériques* 8. http://amnis.revues.org/575.

Dalla Costa, Mariarosa and Selma James. 1975. *The Power of Women and the Subversion of the Community*. 3rd edition. London: Falling Wall Press.

Dellheim, Charles. 1987. "The Creation of a Company Culture: Cadburys, 1861–1931." *The American Historical Review* 92 (1): 13–44.

de Peuter, Greig. 2011. "Creative Economy and Labor Precarity: A Contested Convergence." *Journal of Communication Inquiry* 35 (4): 417–425.

Ehrenreich, Barbara and Deirdre English. 2005. *For Her Own Good: Two Centuries of the Experts' Advice to Women*. 2nd edition. New York: Anchor Books. Originally published 1978.

Eisenstein, Zillah R. 1979. "Developing a Theory of Capitalist Patriarchy and Socialist Feminism." In *Capitalist Patriarchy and the Case for Socialist Feminism*, edited by Zillah R. Eisenstein, 5–40. New York: Monthly Review Press.

Engels, Friedrich. 2010. *The Origin of the Family, Private Property and the State*. London: Penguin. Originally published 1884.

Esch, Elizabeth. 2011. "Whitened and Enlightened: The Ford Motor Company and Racial Engineering in the Brazilian Amazon." In *Company Towns in the Americas: Landscape, Power and Working-class Communities*, edited by Oliver J. Dinius and Angela Vergara, 91–110. Athens, Georgia: University of Georgia Press.

Federici, Silvia. 2004. *Caliban and the Witch: Women, the Body and Primitive Accumulation*. New York: Autonomedia.

———. 2006. "Precarious Labour: A Feminist Viewpoint." Lecture at Bluestockings Radical Bookstore, New York, October 28. *In the Middle of the Whirlwind*. https://inthemiddleofthewhirlwind.wordpress.com/precarious-labor-a-feminist-viewpoint/.

———. 2011. "On Affective Labor." In *Cognitive Capitalism, Education and Digital Labor*, edited by Michael A. Peters and Ergin Bulut, 57–73. New York: Peter Lang.

———. 2012. *Revolution at Point Zero: Housework, Reproduction and Feminist Struggle*. Oakland, California: PM Press.

Ferber, Marianne A. and Julie A. Nelson, eds. 1993. *Beyond Economic Man: Feminist Theory and Economics*. Chicago: University of Chicago Press.

Florida, Richard. 2002. *The Rise of the Creative Class … and How It's Transforming Work, Leisure, Community, & Everyday Life*. New York: Basic Books.

———. 2003. "Cities and the Creative Class." *City and Community* 2 (1): 3–19.

Folbre, Nancy. 1991. "The Unproductive Housewife: Her Evolution in Nineteenth Century Thought." *Signs* 16 (3): 463–484.

———. 1993. "Socialism, Feminist and Scientific." In *Beyond Economic Man: Feminist Theory and Economics*, edited by Marianna A. Ferber and Julie A. Nelson, 94–110. Chicago: University of Chicago Press.

———. 2001. *The Invisible Heart: Economics and Family Values*. New York: The New Press.

Fortunati, Leopoldina. 1995. *The Arcane of Reproduction: Housework, Prostitution, Labour and Capital*. Translated by Hilary Creek. New York: Autonomedia.

———. 2007. "Immaterial Labor and its Machinization." *ephemera* 7 (1): 139–157.

Foucault, Michel. 1998. *The Will to Knowledge: The History of Sexuality Volume 1*. Translated by Robert Hurley. London: Penguin. Originally published 1976.

Fuchs, Christian. 2014. *Digital Labour and Karl Marx*. Oxon: Routledge.

Gill, Rosalind. 2011. "'Life as a Pitch': Managing Self in New Media Work." In *Managing Media Work*, edited by Mark Deuze, 249–262. London: Sage.

Gill, Rosalind and Andy Pratt. 2008. "In the Social Factory? Immaterial Labour, Precariousness and Cultural Work." *Theory, Culture & Society* 25 (7–8): 1–30.

Gramsci, Antonio. 1992. *The Prison Notebooks Vol I–III*. Translated by Joseph A. Buttigieg and Antonio Callari. New York: Columbia University Press. Originally published 1975.

Grandin, Greg. 2010. *Fordlandia: The Rise and Fall of Henry Ford's Forgotten Jungle City*. London: Icon Books.

Gregg, Melissa. 2008. "The Normalization of Flexible Female Labour in the Information Economy." *Feminist Media Studies* 8 (3): 285–299.

———. 2011. *Work's Intimacy*. Cambridge: Polity Press.

Haraway, Donna J. 1991. *Simians, Cyborgs, and Women: The Reinvention of Nature*. London: Free Association Books.

Hardt, Michael. 1999. "Affective Labor." *Boundary 2* 26 (2): 89–100.

Hartmann, Heidi. 1979a. "Capitalism, Patriarchy and Job Segregation by Sex." In *Capitalist Patriarchy and the Case for Socialist Feminism*, edited by Zillah R. Eisenstein, 206–247. New York: Monthly Review Press.

———. 1979b. "The Unhappy Marriage of Marxism and Feminism: Towards a More Progressive Union." *Capital & Class* 3 (2): 1–33.

Harvey, David. 2006. *Spaces of Global Capitalism: Towards a Theory of Uneven Geographical Development*. London: Verso.

Herod, Andrew. 2011. "Social Engineering Through Spatial Engineering: Company Towns and the Geographic Imagination." In *Company Towns in the Americas: Landscape, Power and Working-class Communities*, edited by Oliver J. Dinius and Angela Vergara, 21–44. Athens, Georgia: University of Georgia Press.

Hochschild, Arlie. 2003. *The Managed Heart: Commercialization of Human Feeling*. Berkeley and LA: University of California Press. Originally published 1983.

Johnson, William R. 1971. "The Kohlers of Kohler: Acculturation in a Company Town." *History of Education Quarterly* 11 (3): 219–248.

Kotamraju, Nalini P. 2002. "Keeping Up: Web Design Skills and the Reinvented Worker." *Information, Communication and Society* 5 (1): 1–26.

Lawton, Philip, Enda Murphy and Declan Redmond. 2014. "Neoliberalising the City 'Creative-class' Style." In *Neoliberal Urban Policy and the Transformation of the City: Reshaping Dublin*, edited by Andrew MacLaran and Sinéad Kelly, 189–202. London: Palgrave Macmillan.

Lazzarato, Maurizio. 1996. "Immaterial Labor." In *Radical Thought in Italy: A Potential Politics,* edited by Paolo Virno and Michael Hardt, 132–146. Minneapolis: University of Minnesota Press.

———. 2014. *Signs and Machines: Capitalism and the Production of Subjectivity.* Los Angeles: Semiotext(e).

MacLaran, Andrew and Sinéad Kelly eds. 2014. *Neoliberal Urban Policy and the Transformation of the City: Reshaping Dublin.* London: Palgrave Macmillan.

Marx, Karl. 1976. *Capital: A Critique of Political Economy Volume 1.* Translated by Ben Fowkes. London: Penguin. Originally published 1867.

McRobbie, Angela. 2010. "Reflections on Feminism, Immaterial Labour and the Post-Fordist Regime." *New Formations* 70: 60–76.

Mies, Maria. 1988. "Social Origins of the Sexual Division of Labour." In *Women: The Last Colony,* edited by Maria Mies, Veronika Bennholdt-Thomsen and Claudia Von Werlhof, 67–95. London: Zed Books.

Mies, Maria, Veronika Bennholdt-Thomsen and Claudia Von Werlhof. 1988. *Women: The Last Colony.* London: Zed Books.

Moore, Niamh. 2002. "From Indigenous Industry to Foreign Finance: The Changing Face of Dublin Docklands." *Land Use Policy* 19 (4): 325–331.

Morini, Cristina. 2007. "The Feminization of Labour in Cognitive Capitalism." *Feminist Review* 87: 40–59.

Neff, Gina, Elizabeth Wissinger and Sharon Zukin. 2005. "Entrepreneurial Labour Among Cultural Producers: 'Cool' Jobs in 'Hot' Industries." *Social Semiotics* 15 (3): 307–334.

Negri, Antonio. 1989. *The Politics of Subversion: A Manifesto for the Twenty-first Century.* Translated by James Newell. Cambridge: Polity Press.

———. 1996. "Twenty Theses on Marx: Interpretation of the Class Situation Today." In *Marxism Beyond Marxism,* edited by Saree Makdisi, Cesare Casarino and Rebecca E. Karl, 149–180. London: Routledge.

Newenham, Pamela, ed. 2015. *Silicon Docks: The Rise of Dublin as a Global Tech Hub.* Dublin: Liberties Press.

O'Neill, Stephen. 2014. *Shakespeare and YouTube: New Media Forms of the Bard.* London: Bloomsbury.

Picchio, Antonella. 1992. *Social Reproduction: The Political Economy of the Labour Market.* Cambridge: Cambridge University Press.

Post, Christopher W. 2011. "The Making of a Federal Company Town: Sunflower Village, Kansas." In *Company Towns in the Americas: Landscape, Power and Working-class Communities,* edited by Oliver J. Dinius and Angela Vergara, 111–133. Athens, Georgia: University of Georgia Press.

Read, Jason. 2003. *The Micro-politics of Capital: Marx and the Prehistory of the Present.* Albany: State University of New York Press.

Skeggs, Beverley. 2014. "Value Beyond Value? Is Anything Beyond the Logic of Capital?" *British Journal of Sociology* 65 (1): 1–20.

Socialist Meme Caucus. n.d. Facebook page. https://www.facebook.com/socialistmemecaucus.

Staples, David. 2007. "Women's Work and the Ambivalent Gift of Entropy." In *The Affective Turn: Theorizing the Social,* edited by Patricia Ticineto Clough with Jean Halley, 119–150. Durham: Duke University Press.

Terranova, Tiziana. 2000. "Free Labor: Producing Culture for the Digital Economy." *Social Text* 18: 2, pp. 33–58.

————. 2013. "Free Labor." In *Digital Labor: The Internet as Playground and Factory*, edited by Trebor Scholz, 33–57. New York: Routledge.

Tronti, Mario. 1973. "Social Capital." *Telos* 17: 98–121.

Virno, Paolo. 1996. "The Ambivalence of Disenchantment." In *Radical Thought in Italy: A Potential Politics*, edited by Paolo Virno and Michael Hardt, 12–33. London: Routledge.

Vogel, Lise. 2013. *Marxism and the Oppression of Women: Toward a Unitary Theory*. Chicago: Haymarket Books. Originally published 1983.

Wark, McKenzie. 2013. "Considerations on a Hacker Manifesto." In *Digital Labor: The Internet as Playground and Factory*, edited by Trebor Scholz, 67–75. New York: Routledge.

Weeks, Kathi. 2007. "Life Within and Against Work: Affective Labor, Feminist Critique, and Post-Fordist Politics." *ephemera* 7 (1): 233–249.

————. 2011. *The Problem with Work: Feminism, Marxism, Antiwork Politics, and Postwork Imaginaries*. Durham: Duke University Press.

Zaretsky, Eli. 1976. *Capitalism, the Family, and Personal Life*. London: Pluto Press.

3   Who Says Facebook Friends Are Not Your Real Friends? Alienation and Exploitation in Digital Media

One of my friends often shares inspirational messages on Facebook. The following image was uploaded in May 2014.

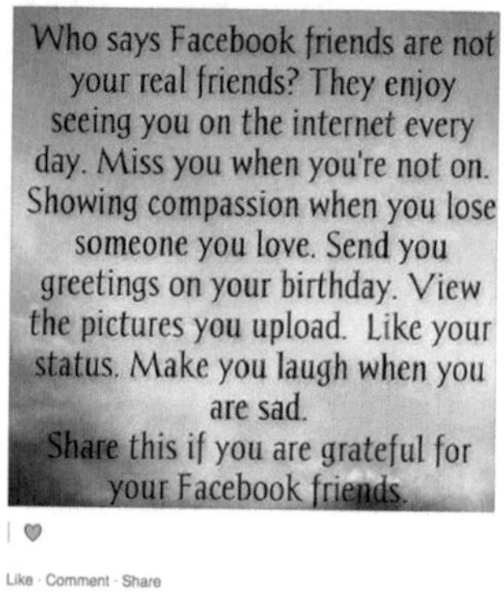

Figure 3.1 Screenshot of my Facebook newsfeed, May 2014.

It is easy to mock this post for its mawkish sentimentality, grammatical and semantic errors and for its unappealing aesthetic. But this image nevertheless captures an important aspect of the experience of commercial digital media sites – they are rich with meaningful and powerful sociality, affect and sharing of knowledge. My own experience of using social networking sites includes valuable articulations of political resistance, education and social interactions that would challenge any construction of them as alienated activity. Living in Ireland, I maintain connections with family and friends in Australia by using a variety of commercial media. I have also built entirely new, very meaningful social connections through Facebook and the site serves as an important resource for sharing information and organisation within my political activism networks.

However, in the previous chapters I have documented how feminist perspectives on domestic work can be aligned with various Marxist analyses of digital media economics to suggest that the kinds of exchanges we have on these sites are diminished by their status within the circuits of capital. From this perspective, our Facebook friendships are primarily part of a regime of exploitation and alienation with attendant consequences for society, culture and the agency of individual citizens. Digital media sites are almost perfect examples of the social factory and so are implicated in a politics that saturates our lives with the relentless abstractions of consumer capitalism. This post, though, insists the contrary. It states that such exchanges are indeed manifestations of inalienable friendship, generating various socially embedded and affective intensities that are assumed to be destroyed in capitalist contexts such as commercial digital media.

This Facebook post then speaks of the conundrum of trying to understand consumer labour in digital media from a Marxist perspective: how do we reconcile the political and economic critique with the lived experience of social, cultural and individual agency? Like domestic work, consumer labour is both exploited and a site that serves myriad other socially meaningful functions. In the literature on digital media though, these two positions are typically constructed as mutually exclusive, forming a field animated by binaries. First, there is the schism between claims that consumer labour is productive, and therefore exploited, and claims that assert it is unproductive labour and therefore outside regimes of exploitation. The other binary is that between those who define such exchanges as a form of alienation and those who attribute agency and empowerment to them. If we are to understand consumer labour it is vital then that we navigate a path through these arguments. That is the work of this chapter.

In keeping with the thematic of this book, though, these debates will be explored through the lens of feminist perspectives on domestic work. This chapter will expand the key argument that associates consumer labour with the generation of surplus and, through that, regimes of exploitation. It provides an overview of how these arguments have been articulated within the field of Internet research, drawing heavily on the work of Christian Fuchs (2008; 2014b) whose framing of consumer activity as exploited work is particularly influential. It will then explore the political critique connecting exploitation to regimes of alienation (see Cleaver 1979 for clarification about the distinction between political economy and political readings of Marx). Each of these arguments will be set against alternative perspectives that challenge this framing of consumer labour drawn from Marxist critiques and cultural studies of user activity. Most importantly though, a range of feminist perspectives will also be mobilised throughout this analysis, used at times to support claims for the economic role of consumer labour and at other times to support claims for the inalienable qualities of this work.

The point of this chapter is therefore twofold. First it is to document an important debate within the field of Internet research, generating a comprehensive account of Marxist economic logic in the process. Its second goal is to indicate what feminist perspectives can add to this debate. Rather than being used to settle the dispute between alienation and agency, feminist theorising will be mobilised in this chapter to trouble the binary and to argue for thinking about consumer labour as a hybrid activity that may be exploited, alienating work at the same time as it is agential and socially meaningful. The argument in this chapter is that it is only through such a position, a model for which will be outlined in the following chapter, that we can come to understand how our Facebook friends can be our real friends.

Understanding Capitalist Accumulation

The Autonomist Marxist argument that digital media consumers' labour is alienated stems initially from an economic interpretation of this work as exploited, which is then overlaid with a political critique. The economic argument begins with the fundamental logic of capitalist accumulation, which is to generate profit. It is worth describing this logic in some detail, not least because some of these terms will be drawn upon later, before considering how it relates to the ideological critique. Marx's model of capitalist accumulation is that a capitalist buys the means of production – raw goods and factory equipment, for instance – and the labour-power of workers. These workers then transform and use the means of production to produce new commodities. These goods then enter the sphere of circulation, where value is realised as money profit, which can then be reinvested in the purchase of goods or labour, thereby re-entering the production process. Commodities consequently must be sold at prices higher than the investment costs – higher than the cost to the capitalist of purchasing the labour-power, raw materials, and other fixed costs of production and circulation.

For Marx (1976), human labour is the basis of any commodity's value because this value is a measure of what is added to raw materials through the labour required for its production. This includes the commodities of constant and fixed capital such as the technological machinery of production and raw materials that are themselves products of (accretions of) human labouring. For all commodities then, there is a generalised "socially necessary" amount of labour-time required for their production that is reflected in their economic value (Luxemburg 1951). Socially necessary labour-time is the basis for the calculation of the wage associated with labour, but it also includes the time involved in producing and reproducing the living labour in the first place. The socially necessary labour-time that goes into any product thus includes the time of production but also some time for reproduction (Picchio 1992).

Variations in the actual amount of labour-time required to produce goods manifest as a greater or lesser difference between the costs of production and the generalised value of the commodity and also its price when that value is translated into the monetary terms of the market. Any work provided below the cost of the socially necessary labour-time associated with the goods it produces generates profit. Reduction in the amount of paid labour-time incorporated into products, whether it is that instantiated in the raw materials and technologies of the production line (objectified or dead labour) or that of the physical and mental energy of their workers (living labour) is thus key to capitalist gain. This can occur by increasing the length of the working day, producing an absolute surplus. In contemporary capitalism though, this effect is typically achieved by increasing the speed or efficiency of production while wages and time at work are maintained at a steady level. This increases the number of commodities produced without an increase in costs. The extra production thus generated (or the value of goods beyond that needed to cover the costs of production) generates a relative profit. These are the basic economics of all capitalist industries.

In practice, this means that workers are typically not compensated for the full value generated by their production activity. Once a worker has produced goods of enough value to cover the costs of their employment and the cost of the other commodities involved in production, the value of what they produce is surplus to cost. It is through the generation of this surplus-value that labour is defined as productive. Take a worker capable of producing one widget an hour in an eight-hour working day, but who is only paid a daily wage that is the equivalent of the money realised by the sale of six widgets in the market. Consequently, even though engaged in labour for eight hours, the worker is only compensated for the products of six of those hours. The remaining two hours are, effectively, unpaid work and therefore generate surplus-value for the capitalist. The worker is thus involved in a structurally exploitative relationship in that s/he remains uncompensated for a significant component of his/her working day. The extra two hours of her/his time and energy only generates profits for the capitalist to reinvest in production or to accumulate. Unpaid labour-time is therefore a vital component of capitalist dynamics. It is also a vital component of the digital media economy.

User-Generated Content

As already noted in Chapter 1, digital media users contribute unpaid labour in two distinct, but inter-related ways. First, there are the material contributions of content such as that necessary to multimedia sharing sites such as YouTube, Tumblr, Flickr, Pinterest, Vimeo, Twitter and Facebook, etc. These contributions form the backbone of many contemporary digital media sites which function primarily as platforms for communication between users and which supply little to no content themselves. While paid employees develop and maintain the legal, technical and financial infrastructure of these sites, they are made up primarily of user-generated content (UGC). The term, UGC, has also been applied to those sites that draw on users for the creation of small-scale tools (app distributors) and those that rely on collaborative content such as Wikipedia or open source software development communities (McKenzie et al. 2012).

As documented in the AOL volunteers example in the previous chapter, such sites also rely on their users to manage and maintain the symbolic and affective dimensions of their platforms, including the policing of other users such as happens with Amazon or eBay seller ratings systems (Jarrett

2006). UGC is also an important tool for offline companies such as retailers who use competitions, consumer feedback and sharing of brand messages as organised aspects of their marketing strategies. For digital media companies, this devolution of site population, marketing and distribution to users significantly reduces their wage bill. Unlike traditional media firms, they do not have to pay salaries to their content producers or even the costs to subcontract out its production. By taking on this creative role without payment, users reduce the costs for these companies, thereby significantly increasing the amount of relative surplus-value that can be generated.

The actual revenues generated from this unmeasured and variously defined activity can be difficult to fathom, but nevertheless, some statistics on the prevalence of UGC can be illuminating. In its 2013 *Annual Report* (Facebook, Inc. 2013), Facebook listed only 6,337 employees at the end of December but 757 million daily active users for that same month. It is difficult to see how the company mission "to give people the power to share and make the world more open and connected" could be facilitated at a global scale with so few paid staff unless the company was drawing upon the engagement of its vast user-base. The use of consumers as unpaid content producers is a significant plank of a variety of digital media companies' economic structure and the wider digital economy (Petersen 2008).

Adam Arvidsson and Elanor Colleoni (2012; Foster 2007) provocatively extend our understanding of the ways in which users add value. They argue that for many digital media companies, profit is not primarily generated through advertising revenue. Rather, it is produced when these entities enter financial markets. Even after the NASDAQ crash in 2000, this has certainly been true of many digital media companies that have generated huge value in financial markets through public offerings or acquisitions, despite never having generated meaningful revenue. Google bought YouTube in 2006 for US$1.65 billion in shares despite the video sharing site having never generated a significant profit. Given that Google already had its own video streaming technology, the profit in this purchase lay in the brand and in user loyalty. What was purchased was the potential of its user base – at the time the site was registering 100 million video views per day, 72 million unique visitors per month and 46 per cent of the online video market in the US (Delaney 2006; *BBC News* 2006). In this context, value becomes abstracted from real processes or production, as captured in the concept of "brand value," which Arvidsson and Colleoni describe as "a convention that enables the interpretation of information about a company, so that a large share of the discrepancy between market and book value can be made sense of" (2012, 141).

In highlighting the importance of brand value, they emphasise the importance of consumer labour in the sphere of circulation, underscoring how the affective investment of consumers reduce the costs involved in the realisation of profit from consumer goods or in financial markets. As Harry Pitts (2015) argues, at the very least there is a metaphoric relationship between the costs of transporting consumer goods for sale (which must be lowered to increase relative surplus-value) and the work of consumers in "moving" themselves and others in the desire for and commitment to those goods. Divesting the costs of circulation to consumers is an important generator of relative surplus-value.

The Audience-Commodity

The other key means by which digital media consumers contribute to the generation of surplus-value is in the form of the audience-commodity. This method of exploitation has a complex relationship with Marxist frameworks and a fractious history as a theoretical paradigm that is integral to the binary being discussed in this chapter. As outlined in the introduction to this book, most commercial digital media companies gather the bulk of their revenues from advertising. Consequently, there are clear correspondences with the economic structures of commercial mass media such as television and radio. In the 1970s, these structures were usefully interrogated from a materialist perspective by Dallas Smythe (2014). His goal was to define the commodity form produced by mass, advertiser-supported communication systems. The product of media, he concluded, was not messages, information or images, but audiences and readerships.

In Smythe's analysis, the content of programming was merely an inducement to attract and sustain the attention of potential audiences. He argued that what advertisers buy when they purchase broadcast time for their products are "the services of audiences with predictable specifications who will pay attention in predictable numbers and at particular times to particular means of communication (TV, radio, newspapers, magazines, billboards, and third-class mail). As collectivities these audiences are commodities" (2014, 32). Ratings systems are thus mechanisms for capturing the activity of audiences as they watch or "audience" a media text similar to the mechanisms for measuring labour-time in industrial workplaces. Smythe subsequently argues that during their supposed leisure-time, audiences are doing the work of marketing, drawing meaning and value from advertising which assures the continued consumption of consumer goods. He famously notes that under monopoly capitalism, the non-sleeping time of most of the population is actually spent in the work of consumption, with the largest single block of "off-the-clock" time being that which is sold to broadcast advertisers. Smythe, it seems, also recognised the social factory in his analysis.

Based on Smythe's argument, we can read the time audiences spend engaged with media as an unpaid contribution to capitalist economics. This framework led Sut Jhally and Bill Livant (1986) to also describe watching television as working. However, they suggest that Smythe's argument functions mostly as an ideological critique, describing how the work of audiences is primarily about reproducing a consumer culture and public opinion supportive of existing capitalist state institutions, rather than being focused on the economic function of audiences to media industries. They shifted emphasis to this economic function. For Jhally and Livant, audience activity serves as the living labour that is "bought" as watching time by the media company for the nominal "wage" of media content, akin to the purchase of labour-power as labour-time. This commodity then enters another circuit where it is transformed again into the abstraction of ratings data that can then be valorised in the advertising marketplace and sold for more than the costs of producing the content that attracted the audience in the first place. They argue that there is a certain amount of necessary watching-time, the value of which to advertisers covers the costs of producing television content, but the rest remains surplus watching-time. Jhally and Livant's framework specifically spelled out the link between audience watching-time and uncompensated labour and consequently to the generation of surplus-value. In their thesis, it does not matter which meanings audiences are making, for what is important to the industry is the exchange-value of certain kinds of attention in the media marketplace.

The Digital Audience-Commodity

The audience-commodity thesis has not been without its controversies, particularly over the definition of consumption as "productive" in Marxist terms, but also because broadcast industries have changed dramatically through recent social and technological change leading to a decline in the importance of mass audience measurement systems (McGuigan and Manzerolle 2014). Nevertheless, Smythe's concept, and Jhally and Livant's extension of it, have been critical to understanding the contemporary media economy (Artz 2008; Napoli 2010). Digital media economics have been interpreted through the concept of audience commodification since the commercialisation of the web (Marshall 1997; Roscoe 1999). More recently, there has been a focus on tracing this commodification within the range of platforms associated with social media or "Web 2.0," with attention increasingly being paid to the specificity of valorisation processes in particular platforms (for example, Kücklich 2005 on gaming; Manzerolle 2010 on mobile media), particular user practices (De Kosnik 2013 on fandom) or for specific commercial providers (Cohen 2008 on Facebook; Lee 2011; 2014 on Google).

Christian Fuchs offers the most comprehensive interrogation of the ways in which the audience-commodity is generated in contemporary digital media. Across various works, but particularly in *Digital Labour and Karl Marx* (2014b), he applies Marxist labour frameworks to the entire value chain of the digital economy, from the conditions of coercive slavery experienced by many working in the extractive industries that provide the raw materials for digital devices, through manufacturing such as in Apple's outsourced factories in China (see also Sandoval 2013) to the work of end-product consumers that interests me here. The core of this aspect of his argument is that Internet users are productive forces in an industry driven by revenue from advertising.

Fuchs argues that if, like the media companies explored by Smythe, Jhally and Livant, the commodity produced by Internet platforms is user data, "then the process of creating these data must be considered to be value-generating labour" (2014b, 246). The logic is similar to that of broadcast media in that waged employees produce a social media platform that is made available to audiences or, in this case, users. Like media programming, these platforms are the lure to draw and maintain an audience. However, there is a second production process in which users create content or interact with the site in ways that produce the monetisable commodity that is "user-generated data, personal data, and transaction data about their browsing behaviour and communication behaviour" (2014a, 100). These data go on to generate revenue when they are sold to advertisers. The value of this product is almost entirely surplus as users are generally unpaid. Users are, therefore, productive labourers, generating value for the digital media companies whose products they use.

In the interactive, cybernetic context of digital media industries, the data about consumers that can be gathered are extensive. *All* interactions with a digital database – and all websites are merely an interface to a database of content and data capture systems (Manovich 2002) – leave traces that can be collated and commodified. Mark Andrejevic (2014) also suggests that there is a growing demand for more and more data about user activity. Not only does the malleability and scalability of digital data increase the capacity for data collection, storage and manipulation, it generates its own data as ads feed back more interactions that are folded into the monetisable dataset. "The upshot is that emerging advertising regimes are becoming ever more data-intensive, a fact which helps explain the demand for increasingly comprehensive information about audiences" (2014, 194).

Consequently, the commercial digital media system is saturated with mechanisms to collect user data: this system is almost entirely composed of sites for consumer labour. These data range from active inputs such as search terms, status updates, personalisation options or taste-identifying activity such as "liking" or "following" to more passive inputs such as clickstream data that measures how long an individual stays on a particular site, the geographic location of that user's IP address, through to dubious spyware systems that monitor keystrokes, caches and/or CPU inputs. These data are also collated across platforms, particularly those associated with a single parent company (such as the number of sites that can be accessed using a single Google+ account), or through the use of cookies – bits of data stored on a user's computer that "remember" previous activity and build up longitudinal records of that user's browsing and purchasing behaviour. The capacity of databases and interactive media for surveillance is extensive (Andrejevic 2002; 2007; 2010; 2011; 2013a; Fuchs 2010; Manzerolle and Smeltzer 2011; Poster 1995; Pridmore and Zwick 2011; Zwick and Denegri-Knott 2009; Zwick et al. 2008) and raises particular concerns about privacy and relations of control.

Googlenomics

At first glance, Google and the search industry seem an unlikely example to illustrate the incorporation of user activity into digital media's economic dynamics. The industry is driven by advertising revenue, but no more than any other sector. Social networking sites, such as Facebook, Twitter or Tumblr, would seem to offer richer inputs for exploitation and so be more obvious examples of the breadth of the industry's data capture mechanisms. Search, where user input returns in the form of advertising related to the terms they enter, seems particularly uninteresting by comparison. However, there is a complexity to the ways in which user data inform the valorisation practices of the industry, but particularly of Google, that warrants investigation.

As Van Couvering (2008) suggests, Google is centrally concerned with monetising user traffic rather than content creation, drawing income from the physical act of a user selecting an ad, or by the act of viewing websites and their attendant advertising. It is, therefore, uncompensated user activity that is integral to the generation of relative surplus by the company, evidenced by the fact that the more users interact with the site, the more data there are for Google to sell. The prices for these data are calculated by the amount advertisers are willing to pay either for a click on their advertisement – pay-per-click model – or for every 1,000 impressions – pay-per-view model akin to that of print and broadcast media – calculated by Google's automated auction system, AdWords (for more on the mechanics of Google's economics, see Halavais 2009; Lee 2011; 2014; McStay 2010, 48–54; Pasquinelli 2009; Vaidhyanathan 2011). To search is therefore productive, valorised activity. It is work.

Moreover as Fuchs points out, even when the data that are created by users are not directly monetised (for example, there may be no advertising market for certain search terms for instance), they are always potentially monetisable. All time spent searching through Google is "potential profit realization time" (2014b, 115). Google's searchers are producing the basic commodity that goes on to generate the almost staggering amount of advertising revenue the company generates – over US$59,000 million in 2014, which is just under 90 per cent of the company's entire revenues (Google Inc. 2014). This work is not waged, but is integral to the economics of one of digital media's most powerful businesses. But it is not the only way Google uses consumer labour.

Google's key technical innovation, which arguably gives rise to its dominant position in the market, is its PageRank algorithm. This algorithm weights and then lists search results based on the number and "quality" of the links to and from that page and so is shaped by user inputs. Each link generated by a user to another page on the web contributes to the ability of the search engine to identify the most popular results for this kind of query and therefore the results most likely to satisfy the user. Even though this system is weighted heavily to institutional authority (Diaz 2008; Halavais 2009; Reilly 2008), Google is still drawing on consumer labour in the form of "the wisdom of the crowds" in this algorithm.

More recently, the company has become focused on using personalisation systems that aggregate use information for a particular IP address or user profile, generating results and rankings that reflect the assumed desires and interests of that "individual" (Stalder and Mayer 2009; Zimmer 2008b). This personalisation is another important aspect of Google's success, providing not only results and advertising that are relevant to that user's geographic, socio-demographic, gender or other personal characteristics, but also mimicking the kinds of individualised, personal attention that transcends the clutter of mass media marketing (Rogers 2009). This is also a product of consumer labour. Every time I enter a search term into Google, I "teach" its algorithms more about my tastes and interests, helping it build maps of consumer desires on an individual and aggregative level, that allow it to better serve my needs and the needs of advertisers who want to sell to me. This particular work is not necessarily linked directly to profit-generation but to the effectiveness of the search engine and, consequently, the brand.

Consumer labour is also used in other ways. One of Google's key goals outlined in its 2013 Annual Report (Google Inc. 2013) is to develop natural language or semantic searching. These systems, though, increasingly rely on human intelligence to "teach" them natural language use. The Google Books project, for instance, is not only about making texts widely available but also about providing a corpus from which Google's systems can identify common semantic structures and word arrangements in order to understand human communication patterns (Hillis et al. 2013; Pariser 2011). To achieve this goal and to iron out inevitable problems using optical character recognition for translating analogue text, it also uses what Jonathan Zittrain (2008) calls "ubiquitous human computing," distributing some of its data processing throughout the web.

In 2009, Google acquired reCAPTCHA, a system designed by Luis von Ahn that works like a standard captcha code (where users replicate a distorted word image to prove that they are human actors) to aid in its ability to scan and encode these texts. The codes users are confronted with are words that are tangled by the Google Books scanning process or unclear numbers from Google Street View. Users submitting reCAPTCHA codes are teaching the systems more about natural language use and are therefore doing work that advances Google's global projects. They are not only achieving the immediate goal of translating the text, but the longer-term goal of building semantic search systems that will sustain the company and the dominance of its technologies in the field of search. They are offsetting costs of production – in this case the ongoing development of search engine technological capabilities – through their unpaid activity. Whether providing directly monetisable audience data, or being (unwittingly) involved in research and development in this way, users are integral to Google's creation of value now and into the future. To search is to work in really complex ways.

What is interesting is how the extensive capacity for monitoring, and subsequently monetising, all kinds of user activity relates to the generation of surplus-value. Users' time is productive not only when they are providing content, are being directly exposed to advertising as in pay-per-view models, or are interacting with an ad, as in the pay-per-click model used by Google.

All interactions produce information about users and it is the parsing of these data through algorithms that determines the monetary value of users (their price) to advertisers and marketers.

Furthermore, value is not always realised at the same time as the user interaction but is instead aggregated and re-purposed over time. A useful example is Twitter's "data-licensing" business where it sells user data in various forms to other social media analytics firms and/or companies seeking insight into what people are tweeting about their products. In 2014, this revenue stream generated US$35 million. While only 11 per cent of the company's total revenues (predominantly based on direct advertising within Twitter itself), this aspect of its business grew 90 per cent from the previous year (Kaye 2014). The various ways to extract revenue or generate surplus from user information means that "[a]ll hours spent online by users of Facebook, Google and comparable corporate social media constitute work time, in which data commodities are generated, and potential time for profit realization. The maximum time of a single user that is productive (i.e. results in data commodities) is 100% of the time spent online" (Fuchs 2014a, 115).

Unpaid Consumer Labour and Domestic Work

The analysis by Fuchs establishes that not only is consumer labour in digital media productive, it is also severely exploited. Because the work of contributing content, user data and brand value to commercial digital media platforms is unpaid and saturates all of life, it is almost entirely surplus. The relationship between user and digital media platform provider is thus profoundly exploitative. Fuchs emphasises this point: "The rate of exploitation (also called the rate of surplus value) measures the relationship of workers' unpaid work time and paid work time. The higher the rate of exploitation, the more work time is unpaid. Users of commercial social media platforms have no wages ($v = 0$). Therefore the rate of surplus value converges towards infinity. Internet prosumer labour is infinitely exploited by capital" (2014a, 111).

It is this connection with the generation of surplus-value through under-compensation, or indeed the absence of compensation, that most overtly links the labour of digital media consumers to the Marxist feminist interpretations of domestic work described in the previous chapter and therefore to the Digital Housewife. The costs of commodity production also include the costs of reproducing workers. Reducing the costs of producing and reproducing labouring bodies and subjects is thus a means of increasing surplus. As Antonella Picchio (1992) and Fortunati's (1995) descriptions of the connection between wages and reproductive work argue, reproducing the labourer by using unpaid labour increases the amount of relative surplus-value that can be generated by that labourer. Wages may rise slightly to incorporate the costs of sustaining the domestic worker as well, but they do not rise as much as would be needed if that reproductive work occurred under a contracted wage relation. By using the labour of the unpaid housewife, the socially necessary labour-time incorporated into commodities can be reduced, thereby increasing the differential between costs and the exchange-value of the goods produced.

Moreover, the value contained in the labour-power produced by domestic workers is much greater than their direct exchange-value in the wage market, for it involves the production and reproduction of children and the domestic worker as well (Fortunati 1995, 84). Like the context where users' contributions are of value beyond their immediate sale to advertisers, regimes of unpaid domestic work are an invaluable tool for building a social fabric supportive of capitalism, generating a steady, viable workforce. Digital media consumers thus have a similar relationship to capital as unpaid domestic workers. They are both engaged in ostensibly voluntary and socially meaningful work that serves a similar economic function of reducing the costs of production either in the immediate sense or over the longer term. Also, for both kinds of workers, their contributions to capital are almost entirely surplus-value. The Digital Housewife is profoundly exploited.

Productive and Exploited?

Thus far, I have tracked the Marxist economic logic by which consumers of digital media are said to generate surplus and can therefore be defined as both productive and involved in an exploitative relationship with media companies. However, for some theorists it is fallacious that the activity of consumers constitutes exploited labour based upon their interpretation of Marxist concepts or the audience-commodity thesis. These arguments feed into one of the binaries being critiqued in this inquiry: that between productive and unproductive labour.

A key focus of those who challenge the consumer labour thesis is that such work occurs outside a formal wage relation and so the labour-theory of value does not apply (Comor 2014; Green 2001). Edward Comor (2014, 247–248) asks, "how can media capitalists economically exploit something they do not formally own (or even rent); the time and labor of the audience or prosumer? And, for that matter, how can television viewers or online prosumers themselves sell what they do not formally own; their watching time, watching power or, more generally, their knowledge?" Without the formal wage relation to define a context of exploitation, the difficulty Comor sees is how to categorise "the exploited." The category becomes so expansive as to be meaningless.

More importantly, the lack of quantification associated with viewing or online activity means that it cannot be abstracted. It remains concrete labour-power rather than labour-time, the "legal and economic category that is expressed and materialized through the wage labor contract" (2014, 255). It is therefore not productive and consequently not exploited in the terms used by Marx. Furthermore, for Comor, money, labour and value are hopelessly intertwined. For manufactured goods to have value for the capitalist, they must be articulated in terms of money. Because in his interpretation the kinds of knowledge and affective intensities generated by users and audiences merely stimulate production and cannot be understood in abstract monetary terms, they are not linked to the realisation of profit. He summarises: "Unwaged concrete prosumer labor therefore cannot *itself* produce surplus value and, as such, the digital prosumer's assumed economic exploitation also is false" (2014, 258).

There are quite a few variations on the theme that the types of work undertaken by digital media users do not qualify as productive work based on close readings of Marxist theory. As with Comor, these arguments often critique the concept of the audience-commodity. Micky Lee (2014), for instance, suggests that online labour is not productive because it does not transform natural resources into goods. This, he says, is certainly the case for watching television programming but even, he says, the act of clicking on an ad does not change the ad and so does not generate surplus. Göran Bolin (2011) and Eileen R. Meehan (1984) argue that it is not users who produce the audience-commodity but those employed in ratings companies who transform viewer activity into a marketable commodity. The core of these arguments is debate over the particular formal structures that incorporate user activity into the economics of particular media organisations and, subsequently, whether these structures constitute an exploitative relationship.

In documenting some limitations of Smythe's thesis, Brett Caraway (2011) argues that what Smythe is describing is not productive labour, but a process of rent. "The media owner rents the use of the medium to the industrial capitalist who is interested in gaining access to an audience. The rental may be either for time (broadcasting) or space (print). It is the job of the media owner to create an environment which is conducive to the formation of a particular audience" (2011, 701). Matteo Pasquinelli similarly describes Google's use of user data within its PageRank algorithm as a form of "cognitive rent" – a "*parasitic* income an owner can earn just by possessing an asset" (2009, 158; emphasis in original). As such it is not formally productive because, even though it can be related to profit, this profitability is not connected to the generation of surplus-value through exploitation of labour but is, instead, exploitation of a natural resource such as land. For Caraway, though, the point is more specific to media production. Any surplus or profit of media industries is generated by those who work in media production, marketing and advertising as it is they who are responsible for the commodities that actually realise value. Moreover, while we may consider audience meaning-making and their consumption activity as work for capital, this remains a creative process. He notes: "Especially in the context of digital public goods there is cause for considerable skepticism of the extent to which capital is truly in exclusive control of this process" (2011, 702).

Domestic Work and Exploitation

For all their theoretical complexity and the specific and subtle differences between them, these arguments lack validity when viewed through

Marxist feminist lenses. This perspective first challenges emphasis on formal wage-relations as a requirement for defining productive work and the existence of an exploitative relationship. To insist that productive labour is only that which is waged implies that "wage-ability" is inherent to the nature of activity and that this is always recognised in the market. However as feminist thinking about domestic work argues, what is waged is a product of patriarchal social relations and is historically specific – hence the claims of the wages for housework movement (Dalla Costa and James 1975). Folbre (1991), for instance, documents the shift across the nineteenth century from categorising women involved in family care work as being productive to classifying them as "dependents" in a variety of national census.

Today unpaid work remains an underestimated and mostly unmeasured part of national economies. Labour force, GNP and income statistics, as Lourdes Bernería points out, are skewed toward markets, so that "'work' has been defined, both in theory and in conventional statistics, as a paid economic activity linked to the market" (1999, 288; Lynch et al. 2009, 21–22). This excludes the informal, volunteer and subsistence sectors and, importantly, domestic labour from formal definitions of work and, therefore, of labour for which it is sensible to offer a wage. To insist upon the existence of a wage relation to define labour, as do many critics of the digital media consumer labour thesis, is to deny the important role played by work in these unpaid sectors in sustaining the economy at a macro-level, reproducing individuals and groups at a social level and in the generation of surplus. It draws on a definition of what is "wage-able" labour that is an arbitrary and contingent construct. Consequently, because certain kinds of audience activity are not currently waged does not mean that they are not implicated in capitalist production.

Linked to this is the assertion that formal contracts do not define productivity and exploitation. This is firstly a misplaced criticism in the context of digital media, for its consumers typically do have an explicit contract – the End User Licence Agreement (EULA) – that effectively spells out the user's alienation from the products of their labour (Humphreys 2008). In any case, to insist upon a formal contract as a marker of contribution to economics presupposes "contract-ability" as inherent to certain kinds of work and not a contingent product of capitalist social relations that profit from the exclusion of certain kinds of labour. Such work could be placed under contract and/or be waged, but historically specific social, political and economic norms dictate otherwise (Zelizer 2005; 2011). Picchio's (1992) history of the Poor Laws describes how maintaining and sustaining domestic work as unpaid and (ostensibly) voluntary is an important part of state economic policies. There is, she says, "no interest in changing the social organization based on a division of labour between waged work and wageless housework and between men and women. Savings on the costs of reproduction are so crucial that wages for the work of reproduction are avoided wherever possible, with consequent gains in social control because of the greater insecurity inherent in women's wageless condition within the family" (1992, 85). Furthermore, obfuscation of the social/sexual contract (Pateman 1988) that underpins heteronormative marriage is necessary to maintain the illusion that domestic work is "natural," thereby sustaining its appearance as a purely social exchange and not one inherent to capitalism. Limits on what is "contractable" normalise the exploitative, patriarchal dynamics heterosexual marriage articulates (Fortunati 1995).

The critique that user activity is not involved in the realisation of profit is also troublesome. All forms of production have variously complex value chains so that it is often unclear how one form of activity contributes to the overall accumulation of capital. In some stages of a particular industry's value chain, capital may be spent on raw materials, at another on fixed capital, in others on wages, in yet another on transport and advertising. Each of these has a different relationship to value and its materialisation as money (and capital) and may involve different sets of workers involved in different kinds of productive activity. Individuals also play different roles – at one instance, the capitalist is selling goods, in the other, consuming goods. Proximity to the realisation of monetary value is also different for different workers. One set of workers may produce a microchip that is subsequently taken to another part of the plant where it is combined with other commodities produced in the factory and assembled into a mobile phone. It is the phone that is sold to consumers, not the microchip, yet it would be absurd to suggest that the microchip workers are not productive. It seems similarly absurd to suggest that, because digital media consumers and housewives are producing what functions as fixed capital (Lee 2014) in the form of content, raw data or labour-power that requires transformation to become monetisable, they are not implicated in a capitalist value chain.

Furthermore, consumers are not inert in the digital media production economy as Lee (2014) suggests. Rather, they do perform material transformations through their activity. To use his example, it is true that clicking on advertisement may not alter the interface, but it does transform the underlying data structure which then goes on to be further transformed in the production process, becoming monetisable audience data. The clicking on a link by a user is therefore an *essential* part of a long series of transformations of matter that are that industry's production circuit. As domestic work demonstrates, there may not always be a direct or obvious line between a particular activity and monetisation, but this does not mean that it is not part of the productive machinery of capital.

The insistence that the only work that is exploited is waged labour is, at the very least, androcentric. It implies that work that occurs outside the waged relation is "natural" labour and part of "natural" social relations, mystifying the capitalist and patriarchal origins described in the previous chapter. It also draws a tenuous link between biology and the capacity for certain kinds of labour, and so has been used to justify and perpetuate the continued exploitation of women and other subaltern groups (Barker 2005;

Fortunati 1995; Mies 1988). As Selma James writes in her introduction to *The Power of Women and the Subversion of the Community*: "When previously so-called Marxists said that the capitalist family did not produce for capitalism, was not part of social production, it followed that they repudiated women's potential *social power*. Or rather, presuming that women in the home could not have social power, they could not see that women in the home produced" (Dalla Costa and James 1975, 10; emphasis in original). Most of the theorists critiquing the idea that consumer labour in digital media is formally exploited perform a similar differentiation. They draw on Marx's distinction between concrete and abstract labour with the assumption that concrete labour satisfies needs alone and is somehow outside of the social relations of capitalism. They do not reflect on how unwaged, immaterial (and therefore concrete) labour like domestic work is nevertheless bound into capitalist circuits and social structures. The labour that society pays a wage for is a social construct that does not, in fact, define the importance of that work to capitalist accumulation.

What this feminist-led argument means for understanding digital media consumers is that we can disregard arguments that deny its productive and therefore exploited character. They are based on a fundamentally flawed framework for understanding value production as well as the distribution of social power. To argue that there is no direct connection between certain kinds of activities and productivity because they lack a direct and formal relationship to monetisation shows a narrow understanding of capitalist economies and their scope. The Digital Housewife here leads us to recognition of the productivity and exploitation of digital media consumers.

Use-Value, Exchange-Value and Alienation

That the labour of consumers, and domestic workers, is formally exploited is merely the basis of the more important critical argument that users suffer alienation in their digitally mediated exchanges. To understand this aspect of the argument requires explication of the Marxist concepts of use-value and exchange-value and how these relate to the concept of alienation. In Marx's thinking, all commodities have both use-value and exchange-value. The use-value of a good is, formally, the amount of socially necessary labour-time instantiated within it, but defined in political terms, goods with use-value are primarily "objects of appropriation and consumption, things to be used to satisfy ... needs" (Cleaver 1979, 92). The term is generally used to define the functional significance of goods as they are directly used to build the fabric of life (from food to more symbolically meaningful objects). Use-values are, consequently, grounded in social, cultural and interpersonal contexts.

Exchange-values, on the other hand, are defined by the capitalist class, and are an abstract calculation of that which can be realised in the marketplace. They are the key focus of capitalists who have no real interest in the uses of the goods produced in their factories, caring only that they are able to circulate in ways that generate surplus. The use-value of a car may be understood as its capacity to get me from A to B or, using a more formal economic definition, the amount of labour-power incorporated in its production and the production and extraction of all the raw materials from which it is manufactured. The exchange-value though is the amount paid to purchase this car, which includes the surplus-value associated with labour exploitation across its production and circulation processes that will be reinvested in the production process.

The possession of both use-values and exchange-values by goods are not unique to capitalist societies, but it is in capitalism that exchange-values come to dominate use-values. This is a central plank of the political critique of this mode of accumulation. As Comor summarises, particularly in Marx's early works "the essence of humanity is its engagement in the act of self-creation" (2010, 439). People who are unable to actively perform this self-making and in doing so initiate the conditions of their existence, become instead a passive object of external processes and as such are alienated from their own humanity. In industrialised labour this occurs because workers produce goods over which they have no control, defined by their exchange-value and not their use-value to individuals as would be the case in a subsistence or barter economy. Capitalism alienates people from the products of their labour (the alienation of things), turning these objects into something that is alien to them in its ends and functions. In this context, the more someone works, the more s/he become dominated by the "world of objects" (Swingewood 1975, 91) his/her labour has produced.

This is not to forget that the key commodity workers produce is their own labour-time, the conversion of the use-values of their instantiated labour-power to the commodity of labour-time. This conversion, which is at the base of the capitalist mode of accumulation, is the prime example of capitalism's alienating logic. Waged work is "not performed to satisfy needs. Instead, for workers, the aim is to gain the means (the wages) required to satisfy needs through subsequent purchases" (Comor 2010, 442). In waged labour, workers' essential humanity as defined by their ability to create the conditions of their existence, including their work, is no longer under their control. When performed under capitalist conditions, labour that otherwise has use-value to the worker becomes part of the machinery that perpetuates alienation. It becomes instrumental, forced rather than emergent, exterior to the subject's identity and needs, denying self-actualisation and "stunting" the worker's faculties, "inducing misery, exhaustion and mental despair" (Swingewood 1975, 91).

Alienation and Digital Media

This formal concept of alienation can be applied to the labour of digital media consumers. The commodification of user data is a process that is opaque at the level of the interface and shaped by unknown and unknowable algorithms. The governance of these sites and decision-making about features and future directions rarely involves the participation of users, except as a reaction against these sites, as evidenced in certain consumer complaints about Facebook (Bates 2008; Grimmelmann 2008; Ionescu 2009). Users also have no control over how and why digital media platforms will use the data they input, a logic typically enshrined in the EULAs that must be agreed to upon joining most sites (Humphreys 2008). Coupled with the exploitative nature of this labour, this means users are alienated from the processes of production and the products their interactions generate.

Moreover, like the ratings measurement systems and demographic categorisations of television criticised by Ien Ang (1991; Poster 1995), the commodification of data reduces the rich socially and culturally embedded use-values of user activities to a pre-determined, pre-structured form that fails to be representative of those users and their needs. Once it becomes an alienated commodity in the form of demographic information, user activity is no longer serving the purposes of self-realisation, but also can actively be used in ways that work against the interests of those users, for instance to invade their privacy and for surveillance.

Smythe (2014) raised similar concerns about broadcast media. The commodification of non-work, reproductive viewing time was an extension of the alienation of workers from the means of production. Time outside of work, and therefore outside of capitalist exchange-relations, that workers would otherwise use to produce and consume use-values important for the creation of individual and social identity is colonised by the requirement to continue adding value to commercial goods through the act of watching and consuming. Moreover, and this is Smythe's main critique, in exposing audience members to advertising and the underlying logic of consumption it espouses, television viewing also serves to reproduce the same capitalist logic that forms the basis of the audience's oppression.

For Fuchs, the argument about the alienating effects of labour exploitation is richer and focussed at a societal level. He locates the digital media economy in the dialectic between the cooperative gift economy associated with the Internet's early phase and the commodified, competitive logics associated with informational capitalism. He argues that self-realisation of people (Marx's "species-being") can only emerge from socially embedded cooperative processes, involving common ownership of the means of production and the products of that production. Here he draws on Marx and Engels' concept of freedom that he says is not based in individual possession of the means of production. Rather it is constituted by "freedom from scarcity and domination and as a community of associated individuals that provides wealth, self-ownership, self-realization of human faculties, and self-determination for all" (2008, 163). He goes on to add: "Based on such a concept of freedom, a free culture doesn't only mean that digital knowledge can be freely used but that it also isn't exchanged for money as a commodity but provided for free" (2008, 163).

Fuchs' position is based on the particularity of the information good that emerges from cooperative social relations and which is common to all. He sees such social relations in the open source movements and hacker cultures of the Internet, but also in the general practices of digital media in which it is the collective and cooperative labour of users that create meaning. However, in contemporary capitalist contexts, information and user data has become a commodity (Fuchs 2008, 164–5). For Fuchs, the tragedy of the digital media sector is this subsumption of both the inherent use-values of informational goods, such as user data and affect, and the cooperative production processes of the networked information economy under the commodity logic (see also Kostakis and Stavroulakis 2013). When information becomes primarily exchange-value, users become alienated both from the process and the product of their knowledge and, consequently, society is no longer free. According to a Marxist politics, by alienating users from their own social interactions, products and processes, the commodification of user activity takes away from individual citizens the tools for building and sustaining subjectivities grounded in alternative, less exploitative social relations. In this way, as suggested by Jhally and Livant (1986) in relation to television, consumer exploitation in digital media reflects and embodies the whole economy.

Agency, Pleasure and Inalienability in Digital Media

Compared to the arguments against exploitation, criticisms of this alienation thesis are not so easy to overturn and are, in fact, supported by a variety of feminist critiques. These arguments are less directly concerned with digital media consumers' exploitation as an economic effect, but rather challenge the political argument that such work is alienating and alienated and so detrimental to the social fabric (Ritzer and Jurgenson 2010). These are predominantly cultural critiques, often drawing on ethnographic research or user studies that reveal that consumer activity is not experienced as exploitative. These studies suggest that consumer labour is often highly pleasurable for users and is oftentimes a source of social agency that is disruptive of commodity logics. There is an extraordinary diversity of studies about the mediation of self and community through commercial media technologies, and with decades of Cultural Studies scholarship as the backdrop, it would be futile to document them all here in order to establish this argument. Rather, I will pick out a few critiques that speak directly against the exploitation/alienation thesis and which contend, as suggested by my friend's inspirational post noted at the opening of this chapter, that Facebook friends *are* real friends.

One strand of these arguments picks up on the question of coercion and voluntarism to counter assertions of alienation. Often these rely on common-sense definitions of exploitation and therefore of resultant alienation. For instance, Andrejevic says, "the mere fact that someone benefits from the efforts of another does not, in itself, constitute exploitation" (2011,

91). David Hesmondhalgh (2010, 271) similarly asks, "are we really meant to see people who sit at their computers modifying code or typing out responses to TV shows as 'exploited' in the same way as those who endure appalling conditions and pay in Indonesian sweatshops?" The lack of coercion in the types of digital labour typically explored through the consumer labour thesis tends to refute its categorisation as an exploitative exchange (Andrejevic 2009). Terranova herself directly states that: "Free labor ... is not necessarily exploited labor" (2000, 48).

From a strictly economic perspective, these arguments do not convince as they do not address the generation of surplus from collective intelligence, and the question of coercion can often slip into the problem associated with waged contracts as evidence of productivity. Nevertheless, they raise an important point. The types of activity I am primarily interested in are not onerous, nor burdensome, and are typically activities that are freely entered into and for which the costs of refusal are negligible. The kinds of activities being discussed in this book are not necessary for subsistence as are other kinds of work (Andrejevic 2010). It is difficult to imagine how instagramming your breakfast or taking a *BuzzFeed* quiz to determine which *Star Trek* character you resemble or retweeting a pop star's latest selfie would be necessary for an individual's survival. Certainly there are some brutalised users in commercial digital media – gold farmers in MMOGs (massively multi-player online games), for instance – but these are typically workers who are formally contracted and waged and so are not involved in the kinds of labour being addressed here. From a political viewpoint, to describe Facebook users in the same terms as slave-labourers in blood diamond mines, Bangladeshi garment workers or manufacturers in Apple's outsourced plants across Asia seems insensitive and the height of hyperbole.

Moreover, the political argument loses validity when placed against the kinds of activities consumers are involved in while online. A greater capacity to participate in the development and maintenance of our cultural and symbolic fabric and to challenge the power of institutionalised gatekeepers such as state-run propaganda machines and commercial media companies is argued to be one of the empowering qualities of the contemporary media landscape (Andrejevic 2009; 2010; Castells 2007; Jenkins 2006a; 2006b; Rheingold 1994; Zimmer 2008a). Importantly, this agency is more than the ability to negotiate unique meanings or create unauthorised versions of texts. It also involves the capacity to produce the products of the industry itself. Even proprietary digital media platforms such as those discussed here generate products that are unfixed because they emerge from interactions by users on a mass scale. "Unexpected outcomes and developments emerge from having so many people contributing to the creation of the ongoing 'product'. Control of the text, so firmly in the hands of the author in a medium such as book (although control of meaning is another matter, of course) has slipped to some extent into the hands of users" (Humphreys 2008, 151).

It is the creative agency available within digital media that overtly speaks against the kinds of alienation described in the exploitation thesis. To participate in the production of culture and meaning as is enabled and fostered by interactive technologies is arguably to be involved in the self-production that facilitates full human and social flourishing in Marx's reckoning. At the level of individuals and small groups, there are many studies documenting the role of digital media communication in the development and maintenance of cooperative social relations and self-actualisation, the very antithesis of the alienation thesis (for example, Baym 2010; Boellstorff 2008; Miller 2011; Poletti and Rak 2014; Turkle 1995). Unlike in commercial media, the user who is actively engaged in production does not see the products of that activity as somehow separate and oppositional to his or her interests. The capacity for today's media use to (appear to) be unalienated – to resemble the "vernacular creativity" (Burgess 2006) that can be associated with society prior to the differentiation of production and consumption in capitalism – is crucial to understanding the social and cultural importance of the Internet. The dis-alienation of cultural production has long been the promise of digital media. Even while this may be a utopian wish, it nevertheless articulates some of the experience of today's commercial web.

Rather than being alienated from their products, users may best be described as co-creators (Banks 2002; 2013; Zwick et al. 2008), with at least some degree of control, agency and/or profit within the productive activity of the sector. Banks and Humphreys (2008) describe how users involved in modding for Auran Games articulate a power, albeit one different from that associated with industrial capital's waged labourers. The "user creators" in this study are depicted as "quite competent and canny participants" (2008, 405) in the economic exchanges that take place in the context of their game production, manifesting agency to resist, change and negotiate their shifting "working" arrangements. The transformations of labour that emerged from these discussions show the emergence of meaningful agency for users, partly shaped by the voluntary nature of this work as opposed to the quasi-voluntary nature of waged work in the capitalist system. That some of these users also consciously parlayed their unpaid involvement into paid employment further suggests a complex relationship to capital. Banks and Humphreys (2008, 413) do take pains to point out that this is not an equitable power relationship, but their study demonstrates an investment and control within the production process that suggests there is far more than the exploitation of user labour-power in these practices. "User-led labour," they conclude, "is an agent of change that unsettles existent industrial knowledge regimes" (2008, 416).

John Banks and Mark Deuze (2009; Banks 2013; Banks and Humphreys 2008; Andrejevic et al. 2014) advocate exploring the question of consumer labour's exploitation through users' self-identification rather than abstract theorising using concepts from industrialised labour. They suggest that theorists describing consumer labour in terms of exploitation ascribe a passivity or naivety to users that is not representative of users' actual motivations for, and understandings of, their online activity. If attention is brought to the meanings amateur cultural workers bring to their work and the compensations they find there, the claim of alienation becomes less tenable. This work is often highly passionate (Postigo 2009), pleasurable and constitutive of social relations, technical skills and cultural capital through which users counter the alienating qualities of this labour and of capitalist society more generally.

Nancy Baym and Ron Burnett's (2009) empirical study of Swedish independent music fans' online contributions to building and sustaining the sector explores some of these dynamics. They found that although in this work there were costs to the fans, primarily of their time, there was also a complex system of rewards and compensations for their activities, defined by the cultural context of their fandom. The most important of these rewards was the ability to build relationships with bands or to contribute meaningfully to the cultural domain by building audiences for them. Some of these fans recognised the potential for their work to be economically valuable to record labels but actively spoke against framing their activity in terms of work. They referred instead to its intrinsic pleasures, implying that to consider it in the terms used to understand industrialised wage labour would diminish the meaningful qualities and/or overstate the importance of their work to the success of the bands. Socially embedded rewards were the key products of these users' involvement.

Similar findings occur in Green and Jenkins (2008), Light et al. (2012), Malaby (2006), Milner (2009) and Postigo (2009) to name merely a few studies that emphasise the moral economies of digital media and the importance of non-fiscal compensation. In their study of social networking sites, Paul Dourish and Christine Satchell (2011, 34) argue that these platforms need to be considered as spaces for social interaction that "entail reciprocal responsibilities and forms of social sanction that manifest themselves as moral and emotional pressures." This in turn suggests that inalienable use-values, rather than alienated and alienating commodities, remain at the heart of consumer labour.

In emphasising the inalienable use-values generated by such work, studies such as these point to a central problem of the user-exploitation thesis: it reduces meaningful social relations to, and solely to, its economic value. As Benkler (2006) points out, in the networks that produce our information and cultural commons there is great deal of non-market production. The exploitation thesis, however, generally fails to acknowledge that there may be economies other than the fiscal in which these practices have value (Spivak 1985). Banks and Humphreys (2008) insist that the activities of users circulate within symbolic, social and cultural economies in which "value" is predominantly constituted in terms other than the abstraction of "labor-time" (Alessandrini 2012; Arvidsson 2009; Hearn 2010; Morini and Fumagalli 2010). Thomas Malaby (2006) similarly argues for the inclusion of cultural capital in understanding the value systems of synthetic worlds such as MMOGs. While forms of capital accrued in these economies *may* be converted into economic capital, they are also forms of currency in their own right, the possession of which affords power and agency to the possessor in specific realms. To make blanket assertions of exploitation is to "ignore how much these other forms of capital matter in the well being of well rounded humans" (Baym and Burnett 2009, 23). All of this suggests that inalienable use-values such as pleasure, social solidarity and the general intellect are products of consumer labour as much as the audience-commodity. The presence of these tools for self-actualisation suggests that users are not primarily or solely alienated by and from their labour for digital media industries.

Work and Play in the Games Industry

The games industry is not an inconsequential media sector. According to data released by the Entertainment Software Association, in 2014 the industry directly employed more than 42,000 people in the US and added US$6.2 billion to US GDP (Siwek 2014). In the same year, consumers spent US$22.41 billion on video games, hardware and accessories (Entertainment Software Association 2014). There is clearly money in gaming. It is also a sector that has come under scrutiny for the exploitation of its paid workforce (for example Bulut 2015; Deuze et al. 2007; Dyer-Witheford and de Peuter 2009; EA Spouse 2004; Gill 2011; Gill and Pratt 2008; Harvey and Fisher 2013; Neff et al. 2005; Prescott and Bogg 2011). The work in this sector, while culturally valorised as "cool" because of the inalienable creative expression it allows (or demands), is also typified by long, socially inhospitable hours, gender imbalance and precariousness due to extensive use of project-based, temporary employment contracts and outsourcing. But when it comes to the exploitation of those contributors outside of a formal wage relation, the politics become less clear.

Much of the games industry's revenues come from sales of its software and hardware, but it nevertheless draws on the unpaid labour of consumers in a variety of ways. "The paid work teams of corporate developers – the A Web – thus becomes only the core of a diffuse swirl of creativity – the B Web – that includes unpaid creators, test subjects, expert informants and volunteer labour" (Dyer-Witheford 2005, n.p.). Users serve as beta-testers of games software, re-design and adapt game systems (modding), offer feedback that can drive innovation or be members of fan communities who promote games and create and sustain relationships that ultimately build brand value (Humphreys 2004; Kücklich 2005; Taylor 2006). Most importantly, in some online games involving multiplayer interactions, users provide the game play and social interaction that constitutes "the game". Sony may provide the hardware or EA Games the software that generates the sphere of play, but it is other gamers that add value and meaning to this experience. Gamers also work when they are exposed to in-game advertising, where they produce the audience-commodity (Andrejevic 2009; Glass 2007). Gamers thus contribute to the profits of the industry in material and immaterial ways. They increase surplus and so are productive workers within the digital media economy. They are, as T.L. Taylor (2006, n.p.) puts it, "central productive agents."

This relationship is exploitative at an economic level but can also be understood as alienating. Nick Yee describes MMOG players: "About half of these players have a full-time job. Every day, many of them go to work and perform an assortment of clerical tasks, logistical planning and management in their offices, then they come home and do those very same things in MMORPGs [massively multiplayer online role-playing game]" (2006, 69). For some gamers in Yee's study, the obligations associated with team playing meant they experienced their play as an obligation and "a second job," one for which they paid the game company a monthly subscription fee. For these gamers, work and fun become blurred as it does for paid employees like testers (Bulut 2015). It becomes what Julian Kücklich (2005; 2009) terms "playbour." This means that gamers are no longer using their leisure for autonomous self-actualisation outside of capitalist norms.

Yee (2006, 70) further suggests that the social obligations established between players and the staggering of rewards throughout a game "train us to become more industrious gameworkers" and thereby perpetuate the extraction of value from play. The self-expression and self-actualisation of play becomes incorporated into capitalist dynamics such that we can "regard the labor of play laborers as a form of biopolitical labor" (Kücklich 2009, 344). Players also have little to no control over game design and governance, or over the fate of communities they may have been instrumental in creating within a game space. These remain copyright to the game company and may be deleted or mined for data without consultation (Humphreys 2008; Kücklich 2009). These descriptions associate the work of gamers with capitalist exploitation, but particularly with its alienating effects in relation to products and self-actualisation.

But there is significant opposition to this characterisation of gamers' activities. John Banks (Banks 2002; 2013; Banks and Deuze 2009; Banks and Humphreys 2008; Banks and Potts 2010) has been a vociferous critic of the alienation thesis, preferring instead to think of users as involved in a process of co-creation. Game developers, such as those in Casey O'Donnell's (2009) study, often have an extensive history of game play and fandom before and during their tenure as paid workers, and have often used this experience to secure paid employment and attendant social mobility. Gamers have also been recognised as engaged in creative collaborative practice, as well as the development of community and self-actualisation (Kolo and Baur 2004). Nick Dyer-Witheford (2005; Banks 2013; Kow and Nardi 2010; Postigo 2003) also points out that the alienating effects of commodity production in gaming are contested by cheating, hacking, piracy, subversive modding and political protests inside game worlds. He says that through these "reappropriations and transgressions" interactive play is potentially associated with the "supersession of capital," for it "demonstrates the corrosive force with which contemporary biopower undermines cognitive commodification" (Dyer-Witheford 2005, n.p.).

(Continued)

In practice then, the alienation from self-actualisation and from other workers associated with capitalist exploitation may not be experienced by gamers, and moreover, the political effects of these may be curtailed by the very attempts to harness the general intellect that make it exploitative. The nature of gaming therefore cannot be captured by a binary in which alienation and exploitation are set against self-actualisation and cooperative sociality: a binary between work and play. It must be understood as both.

Feminism and the Inalienable

Arguments that advocate for the agency and meaning of digital media consumer labour accord with some radical feminist positions that suggest that it is inappropriate to approach certain kinds of activity using concepts derived from the market, arguing instead for a different (feminised) register in which to valorise behaviour. Key among these activities is intimate, domestic and care work over which there is much "anxiety" about whether it should, or can, ever be linked to organised labour (Meagher 2002; Cameron and Gibson-Graham 2003). For instance, feminist economist Nancy Folbre (2001) makes a claim for the retention of "family values," defined as conveying the ideas of love, obligation and reciprocity, across a variety of spheres linked to the domestic. In effect, she is asking that a certain level of altruism and "non-market" values be, or perhaps remain, the basis of the economic system of domestic work both in analysis and in lived reality. In *The Outsourced Self* (2012), Arlie Hochschild documents similar concerns about the alienation that occurs when otherwise intimate relationships such as care work become commercialised and are re-shaped by market values in ways that have destructive impacts on society, offering an implicit appeal for alternative valorisation systems. For Kathleen Lynch and Judy Walsh (2009, 35; Lynch 2007) love, care and solidarity are "vital for human self-preservation and self realisation, both collectively and individually." They then go on to generate a taxonomy of different kinds of caring labour, differentiated by the degree of interdependency and mutuality they demand and consequently their capacity to be commodified.

Implicit in these types of arguments is the idea that certain kinds of activity have social importance outside, and typically *only* outside, market relations and so should only be measured by the values of those contexts. Indeed, often these products, and the inputs that generate them, are immaterial and unmeasurable, particularly in terms of the clock time associated with waged labour (Adkins 2009; Marazzi 2007; Lynch and Walsh 2009, 38). They are typically only made visible through their instantiation in individuals or social practice. For example, the nurturing of a child produces a responsible, caring adult, while generating a sense of solidarity between people may result in shared political commitment within a social group. Like the social products of esteem and affect associated with digital media user practice, the activities of intimate care work have inalienable and non-commodifiable products that must be encountered as such in order to retain their substance. Lynch (2007, 563) says these kinds of work "all involve relations of dependence and interdependence, relations of giving and receiving; they are other-centred to a greater or lesser degree. Because they have an other-centred dimension to their character, they cannot be entirely marketised without undermining their care or solidarity purposes." When these use-values are experienced, as empirical analysis suggests they are in the work of digital media consumers, the activities *must* be outside of market logics. Consequently, to apply concepts such as the labour theory of value, and subsequently exploitation, to the kinds of socially meaningful work undertaken by consumers can be read as a serious category error.

While I have rarely encountered user studies that drew extensively on this particular branch of feminist economics, and there are issues with some underlying essentialism of this paradigm, empirical studies of users identify the production of inalienable products *within capital*. The weight of evidence is that consumers *do* experience gift-like social relations and encounter inalienable use-values based in reciprocity and mutuality in their online interactions. Consequently, these use-values are a key product of consumer activity as they are for the domestic or care worker. Christine Delphy and Diana Leonard say: "The fact that the family continues to coexist with a capitalist economy does not prove it serves the latter, still less that it serves *only* the latter" (1992, 33; emphasis added). The same is true of digital media consumer activity. Thus, in all the studies of the cultures of digital media users documented in this section we find a range of Digital Housewives at work generating vital inalienable commodities such as labour-power and social solidarity for themselves and others from within the very heart of capitalism.

To dismiss the inalienable outcomes of this labour in favour of those products like the audience-commodity that have overt exchange-value is to omit an important aspect of this activity and to perpetuate the androcentric bias that acknowledges only certain kinds of activity as productive and/ or meaningful (England 1993). It is to centralise the masculinised, isolated figure of "economic man" and to ignore the interdependency of all activity, including waged work (Ferber and Nelson 1993; Folbre 1994; Lynch 2007). A purely economic framework inexorably draws our attention to that which is alienating and socially destructive, rather than allowing view of the ways in which this activity also builds and sustains the lives of individual users and the social and cultural fabric. If generating the field of social relations is credited with importance, as suggested by these kinds of feminist interrogations, then the findings that describe the production of inalienable affect, social solidarity and agency within the practices of commercial digital media become a meaningful counterpoint to assumptions about consumer alienation.

Cyborgs, Post-Humans and the Hybridity of Consumer Labour

It would seem then that feminist critiques don't offer a solution or clear path through debates about the qualities of consumer labour. They can be used to support claims for the productivity and exploitation of digital media consumers but also to undermine the political argument that this constitutes alienation. While weighing heavily on one side of the productive/unproductive binary, feminist critiques then counterpose this with support for the other side of the binary in relation to the alienation thesis. As these dualisms are inextricably linked, it would seem then that feminist thought has not been helpful at all, failing to move the argument any further along. I would suggest, though, that highlighting this stalemate is the greatest insight supplied by feminist critiques. They demonstrate that binaries are fundamentally unhelpful in understanding the complexity of economically significant but socially important labour such as domestic work or digitally mediated social interaction. This is an important position to take in relation to consumer labour and is decidedly feminist in its outlook. Rather than merely recapping the debates explored above then, the conclusion of this chapter will instead tease out this final contribution of feminist perspectives to how we might understand consumer labour in digital media.

What criticisms of the alienation thesis have not addressed is the residual humanism of Marx's perspective. The concept of alienation, as Weeks explains, evokes a "given self, our estrangement from which constitutes a compelling crisis" (2007, 244). This subject, though, is not universal, nor transcendent. Rather, it accords with the humanist subject, carrying the attendant exclusions of that paradigm. Informed by feminist, queer and post-colonial perspectives, Rosi Braidotti (2013) argues that humanism places the figure of a white, European, heterosexual, able-bodied cis-male at the centre of thinking, as exemplified in da Vinci's Vitruvian Man. This paradigm, Braidotti says, draws on a subjectivity "equated with consciousness, universal rationality, and self-regulating ethical behaviour" (2013, 15) for whom perfectibility is defined in terms of "autonomy and self-determination" (2013, 23). This is arguably the subject about whom Marx draws his arguments, particularly in his earlier works, and whose tragedy is the alienation generated by capitalism (Eisenstein 1979).

However for women, and all other people mobilised as "other" in order to maintain this myth of "the One," such a state of autonomy and singularity has never been attributed nor achieved. As Eisenstein says, Marx did not see that the hierarchical sexual ordering of society "made species life unavailable to women" (1979, 9). Consequently, the pre-lapsarian state of unity, self-determination and autonomy that exists outside of capitalist exploitation in Marxist thought – in the commons that Fuchs imagines for instance – has not really existed in practice and certainly never conceived as a reality for many people (Chodorow 1978; Hekman 1992; Pateman 1988). This chimes with my critique of the novelty of the social factory made in Chapter 2 where the idea that until recently there was a space outside of capitalist relations is recognised as a gendered assumption. To claim such a space requires an autonomous agency historically denied to women.

Nor is such a state necessarily desirable. The condition of unitary wholeness is contrary to the relational identities and other-oriented caring practices from which women have historically drawn their agency and meaning and which are often found in cultures that do not draw on Western European paradigms of individuality. However, the position of other is not wholly desirable either, as it is a subordinated, subjugated identity that is too fractured to act effectively. As Haraway (1991, 177) says: "To be One is to be autonomous, to be powerful, to be God; but to be One is to be an illusion, and so to be involved in a dialectic of apocalypse with the other. Yet to be other is to be multiple, without clear boundary, frayed, insubstantial. One is too few, but two are too many." To take up the claims for or against alienation, then, is to re-inscribe the androcentrism, racism, ableism and heterosexism of the One and "his" other or to produce an untenable framework for action.

What, then, would a feminist perspective argue to be done? The use of the quote from Haraway's famous "Cyborg Manifesto" would suggest that rather than attempt to resolve the debate between alienation and agency, what is required is a hybrid position in which attention is paid to both the alienating and agential aspects of user practice and how they intertwine. Just as her cyborgs exist in the "spiral dance" between human and non-human, technology and biology, civilisation and nature, male and female, masculine and feminine, so too the labour of consumers and housewives exists between alienation and agency. Calls for such an approach have emerged in the literature on digital media, albeit not from a strictly feminist perspective (Banks and Humphreys 2008 for instance). Discussing arguments against the exploitation thesis, Andrejevic (2013b) points out that it is not clear that the Marxist interpretation of consumer labour as exploitation is incompatible with the persistence of pleasure and real meaningful sociality in its products and social relations, suggesting some means of integrating these aspects in analysis. Bolin (2011, 71) similarly argues for seeing the work of consumers as a "both-and" activity that "the user engages in, benefits from, and values the use of and an activity that is then used by others for other ends and whereby other value forms are generated."

What is called for, particularly for Marxist critique, is a model for understanding how such work can be simultaneously generative of use-values such as affect *and* calculable as exchange-value and how those qualities intersect. This demands a tool to explain the mechanisms of consumer labour in a manner that moves away from determining whether or not a particular practice is exploited or not, productive or not, alienating or not. It calls for a tool that allows us to understand labour where a key output is not always a commodity, but which is nevertheless incorporated into capital. What is needed is a model of consumer labour that allows for work that is integral to the generation of surplus but is also richly meaningful and replete with inalienable use-values, that can examine key outputs that are commodities but also socially meaningful use-values and that recognises both the economic and the social role of this work. More than this though, it must articulate a critical framework that does not rely on a subject who sits outside and beyond the social logics his (the gendered term is used advisedly) activity manifests. Outlining such a model is the work of the next chapter where Leopoldina Fortunati's (1995) phased model of capitalist incorporation of domestic work is explored. It is through such a model that we can finally understand how the Digital Housewife can have real friends on Facebook.

References

Adkins, Lisa. 2009. "Feminism After Measure." *Feminist Theory* 10 (3): 323–339.
Alessandrini, Donatella. 2012. "Immaterial Labor and Alternative Valorisation Processes." *feminists@law* 1 (2): 1–28.
Andrejevic, Mark. 2002. "The Work of Being Watched: Interactive Media and the Exploitation of Self-disclosure." *Critical Studies in Mass Communication* 19 (2): 230–248.
———. 2007. *iSpy: Surveillance and Power in the Interactive Era.* Kansas: University Press of Kansas.
———. 2009. "Exploiting YouTube: Contradictions of User-generated Labor." In *The YouTube Reader*, edited by Pelle Snickars and Patrick Vonderau, 406–423. Stockholm: National Library of Sweden.
———. 2010. "Surveillance and Alienation in the Online Economy." *Surveillance & Society* 8 (3): 278–287.
———. 2011. "Social Network Exploitation." In *A Networked Self: Identity, Community and Culture on Social Network Sites,* edited by Zizi Papacharissi, 82–101. New York: Routledge.
———. 2013a. "Exploitation in the Data Mine." In *Internet and Surveillance: The Challenges of Web 2.0 and Social Media*, edited by Christian Fuchs, Kees Boersma, Anders Albrechtslund and Marisol Sandoval, 71–88. Oxon: Routledge.
———. 2013b. "Estranged Free Labor." In *Digital Labor: The Internet as Playground and Factory*, edited by Trebor Scholz, 149–164. New York: Routledge.
———. 2014. "'Free Lunch' in the Digital Era: Organization is the New Content." In *The Audience Commodity in the Digital Age: Revisiting a Critical Theory of Commercial Media*, edited by Lee McGuigan and Vincent Manzerolle, 193–206. New York: Peter Lang.
Andrejevic, Mark, John Banks, John Edward Campbell, Nick Couldry, Adam Fish, Alison Hearn and Laurie Oullette. 2014. "Part 2: Labor – Participations: Dialogues on the Participatory Promise of Contemporary Culture and Politics." *International Journal of Communication* 8: 1,089–1,106.
Ang, Ien. 1991. *Desperately Seeking the Audience.* London: Routledge.
Artz, Lee. 2008. "Media Relations and Media Product: Audience Commodity." *Democratic Communique* 22 (1): 60–74.
Arvidsson, Adam. 2009. "The Ethical Economy: Towards a Post-capitalist Theory of Value." *Capital & Class* 3 (1): 13–29.

Arvidsson, Adam and Elanor Colleoni. 2012. "Value in Informational Capitalism and on the Internet." *The Information Society* 28 (3): 135–150.

Banks, John. 2002. "Games as Co-creators: Enlisting the Virtual Audience – a Report from the Net Face." In *Mobilising the Audience,* edited by Mark Balnaves, Tom O'Regan and Jason S. Sternberg, 188–212. St Lucia, Queensland: University of Queensland Press.

———. 2013. *Co-creating Videogames.* London: Bloomsbury Academic.

Banks, John and Mark Deuze. 2009. "Co-creative Labour." *International Journal of Cultural Studies* 12 (5): 419–431.

Banks, John and Sal Humphreys. 2008. "The Labor of User Co-creators: Emergent Social Network Markets." *Convergence* 14 (4): 401–418.

Banks, John and Jason Potts. 2010. "Co-creating Games: A Co-evolutionary Analysis." *New Media & Society* 12 (2): 253–270.

Barker, Drucilla K. 2005. "Beyond Women and Economics: Rereading 'Women's Work'." *Signs* 30 (4): 2,189–2,209.

Bates, Claire. 2008. "Facebook Fury: One Million Users Protest at Re-design of Social Networking Site." *The Daily Mail,* September 11. http://www.dailymail.co.uk/sciencetech/article-1053525/Facebook-fury-One-million-users-protest-design-social-networking-site.html.

Baym, Nancy. 2010. *Personal Connections in the Digital Age.* Cambridge, UK: Polity Press.

Baym, Nancy and Ron Burnett. 2009. "Amateur Experts: International Fan Labour in Swedish Independent Music." *International Journal of Cultural Studies* 12 (5): 433–449.

BBC News. 2006. "Google Buys YouTube for $1.65bn." October 10. http://news.bbc.co.uk/2/hi/business/6034577.stm.

Benkler, Yochai. 2006. *The Wealth of Networks: How Social Production Transforms Markets and Freedom.* New Haven: Yale University Press.

Bernería, Lourdes. 1999. "The Enduring Debate Over Unpaid Labour." *International Labour Review* 138 (3): 287–309.

Boellstorff, Tom. 2008. *Coming of Age in Second Life.* Princeton, NJ: Princeton University Press.

Bolin, Göran. 2011. *Value and the Media: Cultural Production and Consumption in Digital Markets.* Farnham, Surrey: Ashgate.

Braidotti, Rosi. 2013. *The Posthuman.* Cambridge, UK: Polity Press.

Bulut, Ergin. 2015. "Playboring in the Tester Pit: The Convergence of Precarity and the Degradation of Fun in Videogame Testing." *Television and New Media* 16 (3): 240–258.

Burgess, Jean. 2006. "Hearing Ordinary Voices: Cultural Studies, Vernacular Creativity and Digital Storytelling." *Continuum: Journal of Media & Cultural Studies* 20 (2): 201–214.

Cameron, Jenny and J. K. Gibson-Graham. 2003. "Feminising the Economy: Metaphors, Strategies, Politics." *Gender, Place and Culture* 10 (2): 145–157.

Caraway, Brett. 2011. "Audience Labor in the New Media Environment: A Marxian Revisiting of the Audience Commodity." *Media, Culture and Society* 33 (5): 693–708.

Castells, Manuel. 2007. "Communication, Power and Counter–power in the Network Society." *International Journal of Communication* 1: 238–266.

Chodorow, Nancy. 1978. *The Reproduction of Mothering.* Berkeley: University of California Press.

Cleaver, Harry. 1979. *Reading Capital Politically.* Sussex: Harvester Press.

Cohen, Nicole S. 2008. "The Valorization of Surveillance: Towards a Political Economy of Facebook." *Democratic Communiqué* 22 (1): 5–22.

Comor, Edward. 2010. "Digital Prosumption and Alienation." *ephemera* 10 (3/4): 439–454.

———. 2014. "Value, the Audience Commodity, and Digital Prosumption: A Plea for Precision." In *The Audience Commodity in the Digital Age: Revisiting a Critical Theory of Commercial Media*, edited by Lee McGuigan and Vincent Manzerolle, 245–265. New York: Peter Lang.

Dalla Costa, Mariarosa and Selma James. 1975. *The Power of Women and the Subversion of the Community.* 3rd edition. London: Falling Wall Press.

Deighton, John and Leora D. Kornfeld. 2012. *Economic Value of the Advertising-Supported Internet Ecosystem.* Interactive Advertising Bureau, September. http://www.iab.net/research/industry_data_and_landscape/economicvalue.

De Kosnik, Abigail. 2013. "Fandom as Free Labor." In *Digital Labor: The Internet as Playground and Factory*, edited by Trebor Scholz, 98–111. New York: Routledge.

Delaney, Kevin J. 2006. "Google in Talks to Buy YouTube for $1.6 billion." *Wall Street Journal*, October 7. http://www.wsj.com/news/articles/SB116014813857884917.

Delphy, Christine and Diana Leonard. 1992. *Familiar Exploitation: A New Analysis of Marriage in Contemporary Western Societies.* Cambridge, UK: Polity Press.

Deuze, Mark, Chase Bowen Martin, and Christian Allen. 2007. "The Professional Identity of Gameworkers." *Convergence: The International Journal of Research into New Media Technologies* 13 (4): 335–353.

Diaz, Alejandro. 2008. "Through the Google Goggles: Sociopolitical Bias in Search Engine Design." In *Web Search: Multidisciplinary Perspectives*, edited by Amanda Spink and Michael Zimmer, 11–34. Berlin: Springer-Verlag.

Dourish, Paul and Christine Satchell. 2011. "The Moral Economy of Social Media." In *From Social Butterfly to Engaged Citizen: Urban Informatics, Social Media, Ubiquitous Computing and Mobile Technology to Support Citizen Engagement*, edited by Marcus Foth, Laura Forlano, Christine Satchell and Martin Gibbs, 21–37. Cambridge, Massachusetts: MIT Press.

Dyer-Witheford, Nick. 2005. "Cognitive Capitalism Contested: The Class Composition of the Video and Computer Game Industry." Available from *libcom.org.* http://libcom.org/library/cognitive-capital-contested-nick-dyer-witheford.

Dyer-Witheford, Nick and Greig de Peuter. 2009. *Games of Empire: Global Capitalism and Video Games.* Minneapolis: University of Minnesota Press.

EA Spouse. 2004. "EA: The Human Story." *Live Journal*, November 10. http://ea-spouse.livejournal.com/274.html.

Eisenstein, Zillah R. 1979. "Developing a Theory of Capitalist Patriarchy and Socialist Feminism." In *Capitalist Patriarchy and the Case for Socialist Feminism*, edited by Zillah R. Eisenstein, 5–40. New York: Monthly Review Press.

England, Paula. 1993. "The Separative Self: Androcentric Bias in Neoclassical Assumptions." In *Beyond Economic Man: Feminist Theory and Economics*, edited by Marianne A. Ferber and Julie A. Nelson, 37–53. Chicago: University of Chicago Press.

Entertainment Software Association. 2014. *2015 Essential Facts about the Computer and Video Game Industry*. http://www.theesa.com/wp-content/uploads/2015/04/ESA-Essential-Facts-2015.pdf.

Facebook, Inc. 2013. *Annual Report*. https://materials.proxyvote.com/Approved/30303M/20140324/AR_200747/#/6/.

Ferber, Marianne A. and Julie A. Nelson, eds. 1993. *Beyond Economic Man: Feminist Theory and Economics*. Chicago: University of Chicago Press.

Folbre, Nancy. 1991. "The Unproductive Housewife: Her Evolution in Nineteenth Century Thought." *Signs* 16 (3): 463–484.

———. 1994. *Who Pays for the Kids? Gender and the Structures of Constraint*. London: Routledge.

———. 2001. *The Invisible Heart: Economics and Family Values*. New York: The New Press.

Fortunati, Leopoldina. 1995. *The Arcane of Reproduction: Housework, Prostitution, Labour and Capital*. Translated by Hilary Creek. New York: Autonomedia.

Foster, Robert J. 2007. "The Work of the New Economy: Consumers, Brands, and Value Creation." *Cultural Anthropology* 22 (4): 707–731.

Fuchs, Christian. 2008. *Internet and Society: Social Theory in the Information Age*. London: Routledge.

———. 2010. "Web 2.0, Prosumption and Surveillance." *Surveillance & Society* 8 (3): 288–309. http://library.queensu.ca/ojs/index.php/surveillance-and-society/article/view/4165.

———. 2014a. *Social Media: A Critical Introduction*. London: Sage.

———. 2014b. *Digital Labour and Karl Marx*. Oxon: Routledge.

Gill, Rosalind. 2011. "'Life as a Pitch': Managing Self in New Media Work." In *Managing Media Work*, edited by Mark Deuze, 249–262. London: Sage.

Gill, Rosalind and Andy Pratt. 2008. "In the Social Factory? Immaterial Labour, Precariousness and Cultural Work." *Theory, Culture & Society* 25 (7–8): 1–30.

Glass, Zachary. 2007. "The Effectiveness of Product Placement in Video Games." *Journal of Interactive Advertising* 8 (1): 23–32.

Google Inc. 2013. *Annual Report 2013*. http://www.sec.gov/Archives/edgar/data/1288776/000128877614000020/0001288776-14-000020-index.htm.

———. 2014. *Annual Report 2014*. http://www.sec.gov/Archives/edgar/data/1288776/000128877615000008/goog2014123110-k.htm.

Green, Lelia. 2001. "The Work of Consumption: Why Aren't We Paid?" *M/C Journal* 4 (5). http://journal.media-culture.org.au/0111/Green.php.

Green, Joshua and Henry Jenkins. 2008. "The Moral Economy of Web 2.0: Audience Research and Convergence Culture." *Confessions of an ACA-Fan: The Official Weblog of Henry Jenkins* March 18. http://henryjenkins.org/2008/03/the_moral_economy_of_web_20_pa.html.

Grimmelmann, James. 2008. "Saving Facebook (September 3, 2008). NYLS Legal Studies Research Paper No. 08/09-7." *Iowa Law Review* 94: 1,137–2,009.

Halavais, Alex. 2009. *Search Engine Society*. Cambridge, UK: Polity Press.

Haraway, Donna J. 1991. *Simians, Cyborgs, and Women: The Reinvention of Nature*. London: Free Association Books.

Harvey, Alison and Stephanie Fisher. 2013. "Making a Name in Games." *Information, Communication and Society* 16 (3): 362–380.

Hearn, Alison. 2010. "Structuring Feeling: Web 2.0, Online Ranking and Rating, and the Digital 'Reputation' Economy." *ephemera* 10 (3/4): 421–438.

Hekman, Susan. 1992. "The Embodiment of the Subject: Feminism and the Communitarian Critique of Liberalism." *Journal of Politics* 54 (4): 1,098–1,119.

Hesmondhalgh, David. 2010. "User-generated Content, Free Labour and the Cultural Industries." *ephemera* 10 (3/4): 267–84.

Hillis, Ken, Michael Petit and Kylie Jarrett. 2013. *Google and the Culture of Search.* New York: Routledge.

Hochschild, Arlie. 2012. *The Outsourced Self: Intimate Life in Market Times.* New York: Metropolitan Books.

Humphreys, Sal. 2004. "Commodifying Culture – It's Not Just about the Virtual Sword." In *Proceedings of the Other Players conference,* Copenhagen, Denmark, December 6–8, edited by Jonas Heide Smith and Miguel Sicart. Copenhagen: IT University Copenhagen.

———. 2008. "Ruling the Virtual World: Governance in Massive Multiplayer Online Games." *European Journal of Cultural Studies* 11 (2): 149–171.

Ionescu, Daniel. 2009. "Facebook Redesign Revolt Grows to 1.7m." *PCWorld,* March 23. http://www.pcworld.com/article/161752/facebook_users_against_redesign.html.

Jarrett, Kylie. 2006. "The Perfect Community: Disciplining the eBay User." In *Everyday eBay: Culture, Consumption and Collecting Online,* edited by Ken Hillis, Michael Petit and Nathan Epley, 107–122. New York: Routledge.

Jenkins, Henry. 2006a. *Fans, Bloggers, and Gamers: Exploring Participatory Culture.* New York: New York University Press.

———. 2006b. *Convergence Culture: Where Old and New Media Collide.* New York: New York University Press.

Jhally, Sut and Bill Livant. 1986. "Watching as Working: The Valorization of Audience Consciousness." *Journal of Communication* 36 (3): 124–143.

Kaye, Kate. 2014. "Twitter Earnings Signal Healthy Data-Revenue Growth." *Ad Age,* July 31. http://adage.com/article/datadriven-marketing/twitter-s-data-revenue-grows/294402/.

Kolo, Castulus and Timo Baur. 2004. "Living a Virtual Life: Social Dynamics of Online Gaming." *Game Studies* 4: 1. http://www.gamestudies.org/0401/kolo/.

Kostakis, Vasilis and Stelios Stavroulakis. 2013. "The Parody of the Commons." *Triple C: Communication, Capitalism, Critique* 11 (2): 412–424.

Kow, Yong Ming and Bonnie Nardi. 2010. "Who Owns the Mods?" *First Monday* 15 (5). http://ojs-prod-lib.cc.uic.edu/ojs/index.php/fm/article/view/2971/2529.

Kücklich, Julian. 2005. "Precarious Playbour: Modders and the Digital Game Industry." *fibreculture* 5. http://five.fibreculturejournal.org/fcj-025-precarious-playbour-modders-and-the-digital-games-industry/.

———. 2009. "Virtual Worlds and Their Discontents: Precarious Sovereignty, Governmentality and the Ideology of Play." *Games and Culture* 4 (4): 340–352.

Lee, Micky. 2011. "Google Ads and the Blindspot Debate." *Media, Culture and Society* 33 (3): 433–447.

———. 2014. "From Googol to Guge: The Political Economy of a Search Engine." In *The Audience Commodity in the Digital Age: Revisiting a Critical Theory of Commercial Media,* edited by Lee McGuigan and Vincent Manzerolle, 175–191. New York: Peter Lang.

Light, Ben, Marie Griffiths and Sian Lincoln. 2012. "'Connect and Create': Young People, YouTube and Graffiti Communities." *Continuum: Journal of Media & Cultural Studies* 26 (3): 343–355.

Luxemburg, Rosa. 1951. *The Accumulation of Capital.* Translated by Agnes Schwarzschild. London: Routledge and Kegan Paul.

Lynch, Kathleen. 2007. "Love Labour as a Distinct and Non-commodifiable Form of Care Labour." *Sociological Review* 55 (3): 550–570.

Lynch, Kathleen, John Baker, Sara Cantillon and Judy Walsh. 2009. "Which Equalities Matter? The Place of Affective Equality in Egalitarian Thinking." In *Affective Equality: Love, Care and Injustice*, edited by Kathleen Lynch, John Baker and Maureen Lyons, 12–34. Basingstoke, Hampshire: Palgrave MacMillan.

Lynch, Kathleen and Judy Walsh. 2009. "Love, Care and Solidarity: What is and is Not Commodifiable." In *Affective Equality: Love, Care and Injustice*, edited by Kathleen Lynch, John Baker and Maureen Lyons, 35–53. Basingstoke, Hampshire: Palgrave MacMillan.

Malaby, Thomas. 2006. "Parlaying Value: Capital in and beyond Virtual Worlds." *Games and Culture* 1 (2): 141–162.

Manovich, Lev. 2002. *The Language of New Media.* Cambridge, Massachusetts: MIT Press.

Manzerolle, Vincent. 2010. "Mobilizing the Audience Commodity: Digital Labour in the Wireless World." *ephemera* 10 (3/4): 455–469.

Manzerolle, Vincent and Sandra Smeltzer. 2011. "Consumer Databases and the Commercial Mediation of Identity: A Medium Theory Analysis." *Surveillance & Society* 8 (3): 323–337.

Marazzi, Christian. 2007. "Rules for the Incommensurable." Translated by Giuseppina Mecchia. *SubStance* 36 (1): 11–36.

Marshall, P. David. 1997. "The Commodity and the Internet: Interactivity and the Generation of the Audience Commodity." *Media International Australia* 83: 51–62.

Marx, Karl. 1976. *Capital: A Critique of Political Economy Volume 1.* Translated by Ben Fowkes. London: Penguin. Originally published 1867.

McGuigan, Lee and Vincent Manzerolle, eds. 2014. *The Audience Commodity in the Digital Age: Revisiting a Critical Theory of Commercial Media.* New York: Peter Lang.

McKenzie, Pamela J., Jacquelyn Burkell, Lola Wong, Caroline Whippey, Samuel E. Trosow and Michael McNally. 2012. "User-generated Online Content: Overview, Current State and Context." *First Monday* 17 (6). doi:http://dx.doi.org/10.5210/fm.v17i6.3912.

McStay, Andrew. 2010. *Digital Advertising.* Basingstoke, Hampshire: Palgrave MacMillan.

Meagher, Gabrielle. 2002. "Is It Wrong To Pay For Housework?" *Hypatia* 17 (2): 52–66.

Meehan, Eileen R. 1984. "Ratings and the Institutional Approach: A Third Answer to the Commodity Question." *Critical Studies in Mass Communication* 1 (2): 216–225.

Mies, Maria. 1988. "Social Origins of the Sexual Division of Labour." In *Women: The Last Colony*, edited by Maria Mies, Veronika Bennholdt-Thomsen and Claudia Von Werlhof, 67–95. London: Zed Books.

Miller, Danny. 2011. *Tales from Facebook.* Cambridge, UK: Polity Press.

Milner, R. M. 2009. "Working for the Text: Fan Labor and the New Organization." *International Journal of Cultural Studies* 12 (5): 491–508.

Morini, Cristina and Andrea Fumagalli. 2010. "Life Put to Work: Towards a Life Theory of Value." Translated by Emanuele Leonardi. *ephemera* 10 (3/4): 234–52.

Napoli, Philip M. 2010. "Revisiting 'Mass Communication' and the 'Work' of the Audience in the New Media Environment." *Media, Culture & Society* 32 (3): 505–516.

Neff, Gina, Elizabeth Wissinger and Sharon Zukin. 2005. "Entrepreneurial Labour among Cultural Producers: 'Cool' Jobs in 'Hot' Industries." *Social Semiotics* 15 (3): 307–334.

O'Donnell, Casey. 2009. "The Everyday Lives of Game Developers: Experimentally Understanding Underlying Systems/Structures." *Transformative Works and Cultures* 2. http://journal.transformativeworks.org/index.php/twc/article/view/73.

Pariser, Eli. 2011. *The Filter Bubble: What the Internet is Hiding from You.* New York: Penguin.

Pasquinelli, Matteo. 2009. "Google's PageRank: Diagram of the Cognitive Capitalism and Rentier of the Common Intellect." In *Deep Search: The Politics of Search beyond Google,* edited by Konrad Becker and Felix Stalder, 152–162. Innsbruck: StudienVerlag.

Pateman, Carole. 1988. *The Sexual Contract.* Cambridge, UK: Polity Press.

Petersen, Søren Mørk. 2008. "Loser Generated Content: From Participation to Exploitation." *First Monday* 13: 3. doi:http://dx.doi.org/10.5210/fm.v13i3.2141.

Picchio, Antonella. 1992. *Social Reproduction: The Political Economy of the Labour Market.* Cambridge: Cambridge University Press.

Pitts, Frederick H. 2015. "Form-giving Fire": Creative Industries as Marx's 'Work of Combustion' and the Distinction Between Productive and Unproductive Labour." In *Reconsidering Value and Labour in the Digital Age,* edited by Eran Fisher and Christian Fuchs, 246–260. Basingstoke, Hampshire: Palgrave MacMillan.

Poletti, Anna and Julia Rak, eds. 2014. *Identity Technologies: Constructing the Self Online.* Madison: University of Wisconsin Press.

Poster, Mark. 1995. *The Second Media Age.* Cambridge, UK: Polity Press.

Postigo, Hector. 2003. "Emerging Sources of Labor on the Internet: The Case of America Online Volunteers." *International Review of Social History* 48: 205–223.

———. 2009. "American Online Volunteers: Lessons from an Early Co-Production Community." *International Journal of Cultural Studies* 12 (5): 451–169.

Prescott, Julie and Jan Bogg. 2011. "Segregation in a Male-dominated Industry: Women Working in the Computer Games Industry." *International Journal of Gender, Science and Technology* 3 (1). http://genderandset.open.ac.uk/index.php/genderandset/article/viewArticle/122.

Pridmore, Jason and Detlev Zwick. 2011. "Marketing and the Rise of Commercial Consumer Surveillance." *Surveillance & Society* 8 (3): 269–277.

Reilly, Paul. 2008. "'Googling' Terrorists: Are Northern Irish Terrorists Visible on Internet Search Engines?" In *Web Search: Multidisciplinary Perspectives,* edited by Amanda Spink and Michael Zimmer, 151–175. Berlin: Springer-Verlag.

Rheingold, Howard. 1994. *The Virtual Community: Homesteading on the Electronic Frontier.* New York: HarperCollins.

Ritzer, George and Nathan Jurgenson. 2010. "Production, Consumption, Prosumption: The Nature of Capitalism in the Age of the Digital 'Prosumer'." *Journal of Consumer Culture* 10 (1): 13–36.

Rogers, Richard. 2009. "The Googlization Question: Towards the Inculpable Engine?" In *Deep Search: The Politics of Search beyond Google*, edited by Konrad Becker and Felix Stalder, 173–184. Innsbruck: StudienVerlag.

Roscoe, Timothy. 1999. "The Construction of the World Wide Web Audience." *Media Culture & Society* 21 (5): 673–684.

Sandoval, Marisol. 2013. "Foxconned Labour as the Dark Side of the Information Age: Working Conditions at Apple's Contract Manufacturers in China." *Triple C: Communication, Capitalism, Critique* 11 (2). http://www.triple-c.at/index.php/tripleC/article/view/481.

Siwek, Stephen E. 2014. "Video Games in the 21st Century: The 2014 Report." Entertainment Software Association. http://www.ei.com/downloadables/Video_Games.pdf.

Smythe, Dallas W. 2014. "Communications: Blindspot of Western Marxism." In *The Audience Commodity in a Digital Age: Revisiting a Critical Theory of Commercial Media*, edited by Lee McGuigan and Vincent Manzerolle, 29–53. New York: Peter Lang. Originally published 1977.

Spivak, Gayatri Chakravorty. 1985. "Scattered Speculations on the Question of Value." *Diacritics* 15 (4): 73–93.

Stalder, Felix and Christine Mayer. 2009. "The Second Index: Search Engines, Personalization and Surveillance." In *Deep Search: The Politics of Search beyond Google*, edited by Konrad Becker and Felix Stalder, 98–115. Innsbruck: StudienVerlag.

Swingewood, Alan. 1975. *Marx and Modern Social Theory*. London: MacMillan Press.

Taylor, T. L. 2006. "Beyond Management: Considering Participatory Design and Governance in Player Culture." *First Monday* Special Issue No. 7. doi:http://dx.doi.org/10.5210/fm.v0i0.1611.

Terranova, Tiziana. 2000. "Free Labor: Producing Culture for the Digital Economy." *Social Text* 18 (2): 33–58.

Turkle, Sherry. 1995. *Life on the Screen: Identity in the Age of the Internet*. New York: Simon & Schuster.

Vaidhyanathan, Siva. 2011. *The Googlization of Everything (And Why We Should Worry)*. Berkeley: University of California Press.

Van Couvering, Elizabeth. 2008. "The History of the Internet Search Engine: Navigational Media and the Traffic Commodity." In *Web Search: Multidisciplinary Perspectives*, edited by Amanda Spink and Michael Zimmer, 177–206. Berlin: Springer-Verlag.

Weeks, Kathi. 2007. "Life Within and Against Work: Affective Labor, Feminist Critique, and Post-Fordist Politics." *ephemera* 7 (1): 233–249.

Yee, Nick. 2006. "The Labor of Fun: How Video Games Blur the Boundaries of Work and Play." *Games and Culture* 1 (1): 68–71.

Zelizer, Viviana A. 2005. *The Purchase of Intimacy*. New Jersey: Princeton University Press.

———. 2011. *Economic Lives: How Culture Shapes the Economy*. New Jersey: Princeton University Press.

Zimmer, Michael. 2008a. "Preface: Critical Perspectives on Web 2.0." *First Monday* 13 (3). http://firstmonday.org/ojs/index.php/fm/article/view/2137/1943.

———. 2008b. "The Gaze of the Perfect Search Engine: Google as an Infrastructure of Dataveillance." In *Web Search: Multidisciplinary Perspectives*, edited by Amanda Spink and Michael Zimmer, 77–99. Berlin: Springer-Verlag.

Zittrain, Jonathan. 2008. "Ubiquitous Human Computing." *Philosophical Transactions of the Royal Society* 366: 3,813–3,821.

Zwick, Detlev and Janice Denegri-Knott. 2009. "Manufacturing Consumers: The Database as a Means of Production." *Journal of Consumer Culture* 9 (2): 221–247.

Zwick, Detlev, Samuel K. Bonsu and Aron Darmody. 2008. "Putting Consumers to Work: 'Co-creation' and New Marketing Govern-mentality." *Journal of Consumer Culture* 8 (2): 163–196.

4 Gifts, Commodities and the Economics of Affect

The previous chapter laid out a challenge. When applied to consumer labour in digital media, Marxist and radical feminist perspectives on domestic work align themselves with claims that such work is productive and exploited, but also that it continues to, and indeed must, produce inalienable products. If the work of the Digital Housewife for Twitter, or Pinterest or Instagram can be interpreted both as a rewarding moment of socialisation and as an instance of exploited labour, how then can we make sense of it as a whole? How do we reconcile our exploitation as consumers of digital media with the fact that our Facebook friends are our real friends? The answer proposed in the previous chapter was to avoid resolving this issue at all, but instead to embrace its duality. It advocated assuming a certain hybridity in the work done by digital media consumers and to critique its political consequences accordingly. The challenge that was left was to identify an appropriate critical economic model to do just that.

The need for such a framework has become increasingly important with the growing emphasis on understanding affect and affective relations in economic systems (Negri 1999), but particularly in digital media's commercial contexts. This "affective turn" (Clough and Halley 2007; Gregg and Seigworth 2010; Liljestrom and Paasonen 2010) has encouraged a move from considerations of mediated representation to interrogation of how we are moved, physically, psychically and emotionally by mediated texts and technologies. Digital media is increasingly seen as a suite of spaces for the expression, cultivation and manipulation of emotion and desire beyond the rationality of cognition and language (Ash 2012; Benski and Fisher 2014; Hillis et al. 2015; Karatzogianni and Kuntsman 2012; Papacharissi 2015; Vincent and Fortunati 2009; Ze-ev 2004). Drawing on the work of Sara Ahmed (2004a; 2004b) in particular, interest is increasingly focussed on understanding the ebb and flow of relational intensities in our digitally mediated interactions. The connection of this paradigm to the labour of consumers is obvious in the typification of this work as "affective" in studies drawing on Autonomist Marxist frameworks, but also in the obvious sociality, self-construction and visceral pleasures generated by such activity and identified in so many empirical studies.

These studies of affect, though, tend to leave aside some important economic questions. What is not often emphasised is that affective intensities are actively exploited in the context of commercial digital media. Even then, the elusive qualities of affect and the difficulties in capturing it in economic mechanisms speak of the need for an analytical approach that embraces hybridity. This "Facebook story" that appeared as a "suggested post" in my newsfeed in 2014 demonstrates this point.

Figure 4.1 Screenshot of Facebook Stories advertisement, 5 September 2014.

Under the heading "the healing power of friends" and the quote "no-one should ever have to go through cancer alone," this story documents the important and rich affectivity expressed through and encountered in digital media platforms. Upon hearing of her cancer diagnosis, the woman in the image claims that the first person she told was Facebook: "meaning I told every single person I knew … I was still on the phone with my doctor when I typed the status update." The *Facebook Stories* page to which this links, and for which it is an advertisement, documents instance after instance of people using the site as a platform for the creation and maintenance of this kind of supportive sociality as well as for various kinds of economic and social advancement. The October 7, 2014 post links to a *mashable* news story titled "Aspiring Flight Attendants Turn to Facebook for Job Advice," whereas September 18, 2014 documents the use of Facebook by the family business Oscar Williams' Gourmet Cotton Candy to establish and build their trade.

The *Facebook Stories* page underscores the importance of looking at Facebook as a site for agency, self-actualisation and social empowerment. However, that this post is an advertisement for a corporate promotional page that arrived unbidden in my newsfeed and that it uses a profoundly intimate personal moment in that promotion tells another story. We have another example of Arvidsson and Colleoni's (2012) argument about the role of users in creating brand value mentioned in the previous chapter and another example of the exploitative logics of commercial digital media platforms. To use such a personal narrative for promotional purposes is, at the very least, distasteful. Consequently, the *Facebook Stories* ad co-locates affect and economics in a way that demands the integration of these logics. To understand this, and digital media consumer labour more generally, requires a mechanism for reconciling the alienating and actualising tendencies inherent to economically important and affectively rich work.

The solution to this problem is the crux of this book and, obviously then, the answer lies in Marxist feminist theories of domestic labour. Specifically, it is Leopoldina Fortunati's (1995) model of domestic work's incorporation into capital that provides an economic framework that respects the inalienable qualities and products of labour. This chapter will outline this model and its utility for thinking about consumer labour, but also for placing affect within the economy. I will first document the important roles played by affect, inalienable commodities and use-values in the digital economy. Links will then be made to the long history of exploring exchanges on the internet as examples of gifting practices, but the chapter will go on to complicate this analysis by challenging the binary between gifts and commodities that underpins these arguments. It will draw on ideas from consumer culture research and anthropology to restate the hybridity of what is produced in the digital economy, using this to further justify a model that explores the duality, mutability and contingency of discrete moments in the life cycle of labour and its products. It is from here that Fortunati's model of domestic work will emerge as a useful tool for understanding not only the production of affect in the digital economy, but consumer labour more generally.

Affect in the Digital Economy

Affect has a particular importance in contemporary economics. As the arguments of Autonomist Marxists (see Chapter 1) and other political economists suggest, products such as services, information and digital data have become increasingly pivotal to global economics. Relatedly, but with broader resonance, is the increasing amount of labour based in subjectivity – cognition, communication and sociality – in emerging fields of high-technology, marketing and design, but also in the labour practices of manufacturing and extractive industries where automation has changed the necessary skill set. Affective labour is one facet of immaterial labour as defined by Hardt and Negri (2000). They distinguish between the cognitive and communicative work associated with high-technology industries and the labour of "human contact and interaction" (2000, 292). They argue that this latter form of labour, while corporeal, is nevertheless immaterial "in the sense that its products are intangible, a feeling of ease, well-being, satisfaction, excitement, or passion" (2000, 293). This work is about the creation and manipulation of affective intensities.

The use of the term "affective labour" in this way is contested though (Gill and Pratt 2008). David Hesmondhalgh and Sarah Baker (2008) argue that, as Hardt and Negri use it, the term is too vague and does not account for differences within and between industries. They prefer to rely on Hochschild's concept of "emotional labour" which is more specifically focussed on the inducement or suppression of natural affective tendencies in order to evoke appropriate responses from customers. More feminist critiques such as Bolton's (2009) argue that to place affective labour under the rubric of the "immaterial" denies the materiality of this work, particularly when it is associated with domestic or care work (discussed in Chapter 2). Federici (2011) questions the use of the term to describe a general characteristic of post-Fordist work, arguing similarly to Bolton, that such a move amounts to an "ungendering" of affective labour by removing its connection to domestic work, women's history and feminist thought.

Nevertheless, in each of these criticisms remains tacit or explicit recognition that affective intensities are a key product of contemporary media work and, I would emphasise, of the kinds of labour undertaken by consumers. The importance of affect can be associated with the rise of branding, advertising and marketing where, as Lazzarato points out, the labour of consumers "gives form to and materializes needs, the imaginary, consumer tastes, and so forth, and these products in turn become powerful producers of needs, images, and tastes" (1996, 137). Branding is ultimately about claiming a unique symbolic space by establishing a system of referent linkages that is different from those of other products (McAllister 1996, 136–7). Successful brand advertising though, is about focusing on the advantage gained when tangible product characteristics are integrated with symbols, meanings, images and feelings from a culture to create a brand that is loved (Davidson 1992, 26–7; Hakim 2002). "Online branding guru" Martin Lindstrom suggests that: "Branding is about making your brand so personal you can't live without it" (2002, n.p.). What is central to brands then is the affective relationship between consumers and products/companies that generates market share. Brands are the affective capital of a company and also, as Arvidsson and Colleoni (2012) remind us, the product of consumer labour.

This deep investment in goods, service and symbols is particularly important in high-technology capitalism where, as Lury summarises, such objects are "characteristically open, question-generating and in the process of being defined" (2004, 123). Consequently, to make sense of them involves ongoing relationships with these objects. It is here that branding lies, but it is also the place of social media sites where our connection with a technology becomes inextricably muddled with our connection with those we communicate with through that system. ICTs and digital media platforms are increasingly understood as relational artefacts (King-O'Riain 2014; Sugiyama 2009) *to which* we relate but also *through which* we relate to others. The objects carry memories and are invested with meaning (Leder Mackley and Karpovich 2012), so that it is difficult to extract our "love" for a brand, platform or device from the intensity we feel for the relationships we maintain through them (van Doorn 2011, 540). Jane Vincent's study of the relationship users have to their mobile phones identified how these devices not only enable connections with intimates but how the device itself becomes "imbued with the strong emotion of love and affection between close family and friends" (2009, 188). She also documents how these users' phones have "become embedded in the representation of their self" (2009, 188; Sirisena 2012; Sugiyama 2009). Digital media is also associated with visceral and embodied responses that on many platforms manifest in regimes of self-disclosure so that these sites serve as "an archive of feelings" (Raun 2012).

Affective intensities may also be instigated by mediated interactions. For evidence of this latter dynamic, we can look toward the importance of pornography and "adult services" such as hook-up, webcam and dating sites to digital media economics and in terms of what people do online. Online pornography exemplifies the affective relations at the core of the commercial web. As Sharif Mowlabocus (2010) argues, amateur pornography video-sharing sites such as XTube embody much of the participatory ethos of "Web 2.0." They typically draw on user-generated content, crowdsourced knowledge in the form of folksonomies of video categories and, most importantly for the argument here, they also engender a sense of community through the use of user ratings, comments and liking. David Slayden (2010) suggests that such "communities of exchange" have been a feature of porn sites since the mid-1990s. The technological infrastructure of these sites encourages individual physical responses and phatic relations as much as commercial transactions, serving both as a facilitator of commerce and affect.

Moreover, the central point of pornography and sexual services on the web is to produce affective intensities. As Susanna Paasonen (2011) puts it, the point of online or offline porn, as well as dating sites and other sexual services, is to generate a "carnal resonance." Porn, she argues, is about somatic responses, the "somewhat involuntary moments of proximity with characters and bodily performances on the screen" (2011, 186), rather than a regime of identification and narrative immersion. Indeed, it is difficult to truly engage with what porn is and what it means without understanding its affective register. Porn that fails to affect us, fails.

Intensifying affective states and building affective connections is the essence of the work we do when using social media, which in turn places affect at the core of the digital economy. According to web analytics company Alexa (n.d.), search sites are the most popular on the web, based on their calculations that combine average daily visitors and page views over the period of a month. However, search is listed alongside various sites associated heavily with UGC, from Facebook, which is consistently ranked as the second most accessed site after Google, followed by YouTube, Wikipedia, Twitter, qq.com (China's portal for various social media services), Linkedin, Weibo, and Wordpress. Social media sites like these, as their name suggests, have a profound, if not dominant, phatic function and so are integrally associated with affect rather than instrumental or informational exchange (Miller 2008; Tufekci 2008). On such sites, users share content that affirms, contradicts or generates affective responses and relational intensities within interpersonal networks. This reliance on the phatic is what makes them social and, subsequently, meaningful. But it also places affect at their centre. As Mark Coté and Jennifer Pybus (2007) argue, these sites rely upon the constant writing and rewriting of relational subjectivities across and within networks based in relations of affinity and resistance. What then is "produced in these social and economic relations – indeed, what causes them to coalesce in the first place – is the production of affect" (2007, 95).

For users, these affective relationships are psychically, physically and emotionally valuable but they are also valuable to the provider. Affect "expressed through particular compositions of bodies which alter our capacity to act … helps forge relationships with consumers through new subjectivities and networked relations that have the potential to interpolate users for the various lifestyles and identities that are being produced on an on-going basis" (Coté and Pybus 2007, 96). This is certainly true of the dominant social media site, Facebook. Unlike some other commercial digital media platforms that only target advertising based on an individual's inputs, Facebook's databases also capture hits of the "like" button, through which users express approval or social solidarity, as well as information provided by other users within a particular friend network. By assuming taste affinities exist between friends, advertising is subsequently targeted to a user based on the aggregation of extensive data from across that individual's network. The "creation of social relations, or at least relations of affective proximity" (Arvidsson and Colleoni 2012, 144) by users becomes directly value-generating, and consequently, productive. Generation of affective intensities is thus integral not only to what we do as users on the site, but also to the economic model of the digital media industry.

Manipulating Affect

In 2014, the National Academy of Sciences of the United States of America published its regular proceedings. Like most academic publishing, this would usually not be noteworthy. However, this edition contained an article by Facebook scientist Adam Kramer, writing with Jamie Guillory and Jeffrey Hancock from Cornell University (Kramer et al. 2014, n.p.), that documented a study testing the existence of emotional contagion where "people transfer positive and negative moods and emotions to others". This large-scale study ($N = 689,003$) involved manipulating the algorithms controlling English-speaking users' Facebook newsfeeds for a week in 2012, changing the extent to which users encountered either positive or negatively coded emotional content. These users' own output was then analysed for the existence of negatively or positively coded language to determine whether or not it correlated with the changes in emotional tone of the user's newsfeed. The study concluded that "the emotions expressed by friends, via online social networks, influence our own moods, constituting, to our knowledge, the first experimental evidence for massive-scale emotional contagion via social networks, and providing support for previously contested claims that emotions spread via contagion through a network" (Kramer et al. 2014, n.p.).

The response to this study was swift and outraged. Published online before print on June 2nd, by the end of the month, a variety of online and more mainstream media outlets had published critical commentary (Grimmelmann 2014; Meyer 2014). A range of academics had communicated their concerns across various communication platforms including, ironically, Facebook (I am a member of the Great Facebook "Emotional Contagion" Study Event Facebook group for instance). The ethics of manipulating the affective intensities of users was of most concern. Katy Waldman (2014), writing in *Slate*, Katy Waldman (2014) questioned whether the study breached US federal law and human rights declarations, pivoting on the question of whether user acceptance of the Facebook EULA (End User License Agreement) actually constituted "informed consent." This became even more problematic as ongoing analysis suggested that Facebook's EULA did not include the potential for research until after the data set had been gathered, and there was a lack of clarity in the report about whether all participants in the study were over the age of eighteen (Hill 2014).

The question of research ethics was made particularly pertinent given the role played by academics from the state-funded Cornell University, whose Ethics Board later denied pre-approving this study (Sullivan 2014). For some academics, the key issue lay in methodological concerns about the validity of the data set and the tools used in its gathering (Grohol 2014; Matthews 2014; McNeil 2014). For others though, it was the problem of treating human subjects as if they were the same as the textual content that was the data set (see Gray 2014 for considered commentary). The potential personal, psychological and social consequences of this kind of experimental study was also of great concern.

The point of surveying this event here, though, is not to explore its methodological issues but to instead focus on it as a useful example of the centrality of affect in the digital economy. The outrage about this study and evidence of the ability to manipulate emotional states it demonstrates (no matter how flawed the evidence and data collection methods) show the importance of affective intensities to the site. In a Facebook post from the June 29, 2014, Adam Kramer explained the reason for Facebook wanting to undertake the study. "The reason we did this research is because we care about the emotional impact of Facebook and the people that use our product. We felt that it was important to investigate the common worry that seeing friends post positive content leads to people feeling negative or left out. At the same time, we were concerned that exposure to friends' negativity might lead people to avoid visiting Facebook. We didn't clearly state our motivations in the paper" (2014, n.p.). Faux concern for users aside, this post offers important insight. If the point of understanding user responses is to find ways of keeping them connected to the site, and presumably generating surplus through this ongoing connection, then the manipulation of affect is the core business of Facebook.

(Continued)

That affect *can* be a product of calculated intervention is important to emphasise. Like the affect associated with domestic work, the intensities associated with Facebook are individually experienced as inherently meaningful and organic, but may be part of a coercive infrastructure at a more structural level. There are, then, some important questions to be put to these mediators of our affective communities. Writing on the *Culture Digitally* blog, Tarleton Gillespie (2014) places actions such as this by Facebook in the context of an implicit promise, also made by search companies, dating sites and other kinds of social networking platforms, to be trustworthy conduits for our affective intensities. If Facebook and its unknown algorithms are responsible for how we feel, Gillespie asks, what obligations should be placed on these commercial sites to ensure the ethical management of our affective experiences?

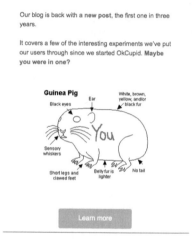

Figure 4.2 Screenshot of OKCupid email, 30 July 2014.

When only a few weeks after the Facebook controversy broke, dating site OKCupid could happily send the above email to its customers likening them to guinea pigs, the regulation of those who manage our digitally mediated interactions seems a pressing matter. If the controversy about Facebook's experiment does nothing else, it shows how seriously people are affected by their digitally mediated interactions and how seriously we should take the agendas of those who provide our social platforms.

In a web dominated by social media, affective intensities are a key outcome for users and producers alike. Even when information services such as news sites and transactional spaces such as Amazon or eBay are considered, it still remains difficult to dissociate affect from their functioning. Consumption decisions are rarely entirely rational. Anyone who has read the comments section on a news article will also recognise the persistence of affect in the networked public sphere or, as it has been described by Axel Bruns et al. (2011, 285; Bruns 2008; Paasonen 2015; Papacharissi 2010; 2015; Warner 2002), the "affective and emergent *publics*" of the Internet. There is much more than rationality in play in the consumption and production of information. For example, in their study of Twitter data from the 2011 Egypt uprisings, Zizi Papacharissi and Maria de Fatima Oliveira (2012, 276–277) describe a genre of "affective news" the function of which is not necessarily to share new information, but which is "characterized by mounting, emotive anticipation" and frequently shared "for the sake of opinion expression and release." While there are specialist uses of digital media sites and services that may defy categorisation as affective – I am thinking here of the rationalities of business to business communication as a potential example – the digital media of our banal, everyday practices cannot be so defined. Rather than merely a site of disembodied rationality, the Internet is a site for physical arousal, heightened emotion and the cultivation and maintenance of rich social relationships.

Affect, Use-Values and Gift Economies

Thus far though, I have not clearly defined affect or affective intensities, which is important to do if we are to locate them economically. In the work of Brian Massumi (2002), affect is understood as those sensory experiences of movement and feeling that are part of the social, cultural and psychological experience of individuals, but which lie beyond the directly signifying properties of discourse. It is differentiated from emotion for it is as an embodied intensity that is outside conscious articulation. Emotion, Massumi says, is "the sociolinguistic fixing of the quality of an experience" (Massumi 2002, 28), in effect the resolution of affect into something we recognise and can articulate. This resolution qualifies the intensity of the experience, inserting it into knowable, narratable meaning. Emotion is "intensity owned and recognized [whereas] affect is unqualified. As such, it is not ownable or recognizable" (Massumi 2002, 28). Affect is an autonomous energy, a state of potential that cannot be captured or confined within a body, perception or cognition without undergoing a fundamental transformation. It is inherently inalienable and so, to return to the language of Marx, can only be consumed (experienced) as use-value.

Sara Ahmed (2004b) makes the point that affect is relational, rather than objective, and therefore is intricately embedded in our sociality. The ways we feel about objects are not inherent to those objects themselves or to our interior state, but relate to our history of engagement with such objects. Like Massumi's description of emotion above, what we feel is mediated, involving a process of recognition bound up with what we already understand about those objects (2004b, 25). The impression we have of something – some object or some person – also impresses itself upon us, shaping our subjectivity and further emotional responses. Ahmed describes affect as circulating between and through bodies, signs and objects, gathering and losing intensity over time and repeated encounters. As an example of this dynamic, she uses hate speech and its creation of relations of difference and, consequently, of particular sensations of affinity or rejection between different bodies, signs and objects. What is important about Ahmed's work for us here is its emphasis on affective intensifications as a product of social relations.

Like domestic work as framed by the radical feminist perspectives, affect is inalienable and is bound to sociality as cause and effect. Similarly then, affect can only be produced and consumed outside of market relations. This is not to argue that it is does not have an economy. Indeed, Ahmed's analysis is informed by Marxist terms and she associates affect with the process of circulation and exchanges but these economies are not those of the market. The value she discusses is not fiscal surplus – the movement from money to commodity to money described by Marx – but hinges on the idea of affective value which accumulates in signs and bodies over time as affect circulates within and through them. The economics of affect are associated with the production and circulation of use-values. The model commonly used for describing such exchanges is gifting.

As famously described by Marcel Mauss' (2002) studies of pre-market societies, gift economies do not rely on abstract exchanges defined by impersonal contracts as is the case in capitalist systems. Rather, exchanges are predominantly in the form of gifts, the logic of which is based in cooperative social relationships and which emerge from a fabric of social interaction and reciprocal obligation. To give and receive gifts is overlaid with contextually specific meanings rather than abstract calculation of economic gain. Mauss describes gifting practices as "total" social phenomena expressing all of the institutions of a society within them. They are obligations or informal contracts imposed by collective norms and, as such, are not only exchanges of economically useful goods but also ritualised acts of politeness. Finally, he says, "these total services and counter-services are committed to in a somewhat voluntary form by presents and gifts, although in the final analysis they are strictly compulsory, on pain of private or public warfare" (2002, 6–7). Marshall Sahlins (2004) also depicts gifting in "primitive societies" describing how social relations exert governance over the flow of goods, constraining or enabling certain exchanges. Moreover, he says the relationship between material flows and sociality is reciprocal. Specific relations suggest particular transactions and specific transactions suggest particular relationships to the parties. "If friends make gifts, gifts make friends" (2004, 186).

Because of their inalienability from social contexts, gift exchanges are associated with the transfer of use-values and have served as counterpoints to commodified market exchanges associated with industrial capital; the nature of the product signals the production context of the labour and vice versa. As Appadurai summarises: "Gifts and the spirit of reciprocity, sociability, and spontaneity in which they are typically exchanged, usually are starkly opposed to the profit-oriented, self-centred, and calculated spirit that fires the circulation of commodities. Further, where gifts link things to persons and embed the flow of things in the flow of social relations, commodities are held to represent the drive – largely free of moral or cultural constraints – of goods for one another, a drive mediated by money and not by sociality" (1986, 12).

John Frow contends, however, that there is "nothing inherent in objects that designates them as gifts; objects can almost always follow varying trajectories. Gifts are precisely not objects at all, but transactions and social relations" (1997, 124). Commodities, he later says, are anything that can be governed by the social relationships of the commodity form (1997, 132). He summarises the typical opposition established between the two forms of exchange.

Table 4.1 Distinction between commodity and gift exchanges (Frow 1997, 124)

Commodity exchange	Gift exchange
Alienable objects	Inalienable objects
Reciprocal independence	Reciprocal dependence
Quantitative relationship between objects	Qualitative relationship between subjects

The distinction between gifts and commodities is between particular ordering of social relations in which one model "supposes and enacts a continuity between persons and things and thus the formation of reciprocal obligations by means of the transfer of objects; the other supposes and enacts a discontinuity between persons and things" (1997, 131). What this table emphasises of importance for us then is the inalienability – the persistence of unique use-value – attributed to the gift, as well as its existence only in a context of reciprocal interpersonal connection. Echoed here is the inalienability of affective intensities as described by Massumi and affect's relationality in the terms used by Ahmed. Affect, as a product of domestic work and digitally mediated social exchanges, "supposes and enacts a continuity between persons and things," building the network of interactions between users and platforms that constitute what we now call social media. Affective intensities, as an inalienable product of socially embedded, reciprocal exchange, are clearly aligned with the moral economies of gifting rather than the dominant political economy of today (Prodnik 2012).

Gifts and Commodities in the Digital Economy

The importance of affect to the digital economy can thus be linked to the importance of gifting practices in the history of the Internet. Because at the time the content of its platforms were predominantly provided for free, in 1998 Richard Barbrook (see also Barbrook 2003; Ghosh 1998;

Raymond 1998a; 1998b) described the Internet as a "high-tech gift economy." He argued, though, that exchanges on the Internet were not only gifts because they did not rely on monetary transactions, but also because each input contributed to the cultural commons or general intellect of the Internet. The circulation of gifts was a defining norm of late 1990s Internet culture. For Barbrook, this meant the Internet was a manifestation of anarcho-communism and an anticipation of radical alternatives to capitalist modes of production.

A variety of online communities have been studied for their relationship to gifting practices and moral economies (for example, Bays and Mowbray 1999; Bergquist and Ljungberg 2001; Cammaerts 2011; Dourish and Satchell 2011; Hjorth 2007; Lampel and Bhalla 2007; Pearson 2007; Veale 2003; Zeitlyn 2003). These studies emphasise that it is not that gift giving is outside of economics, it is that its value is realised in forms of capital that are not fiscal. The term "moral economy" refers to an economic system based in endogenous values specific to that cultural context, policed by community norms and social sanctions, rather than drawing on the abstraction of monetary value and contractual relations. These are the kinds of value systems identified in the many studies of consumer practice described in the previous chapter, where the value of users' activity is not centrally concerned with economic gain but in the cultural or social capital it generates. Jenkins (2006), for instance, describes the "self-correcting adhocracy" of Wikipedia as such a system. He argues that for its open-source production of knowledge to work, and in order to maintain respect for diversity and inclusivity, it requires the construction of community norms. He suggests that the "process works because more and more people are taking seriously their obligations as participants to the community as a whole ... What emerges might be called a moral economy of information; that is, a sense of mutual obligations and shared expectations about what constitutes good citizenship within a knowledge community" (2006, 255).

In more Marxist terms, moral economies can be associated with the "self-valorisation" attributed to multitude, and to affect, by Hardt and Negri (see Chapter 1). By drawing on value systems that are outside of capitalist logics, moral economies can be understood as akin to the "self-defining, self-determining process which goes beyond the mere resistance to capitalist valorization to a positive project of self-constitution" (Cleaver 1992, n.p.). They are thus associated with the relative autonomy of workers and multitude. The emergence of socially embedded economies such as those in digital media are integral to capitalist resistance for they refuse to reduce value to exchange-value and, in doing so, reject the alienating logics of capital.

The connection that is made between the production and circulation of use-values in gift/moral economies is part of the reason that it has been difficult to reconcile affect to the capitalist dynamics of digital media. Fuchs (2008; 2009) recognises that gifting practices are at the core of digital media economies. He argues that because the free flow of ideas between users has been associated with the medium since its inception, *native* Internet production can readily be associated with gift exchanges. In *Internet and Society* (2008), he describes an alternative production model to competitive and exploitative capitalist processes. This cooperative model works from the concept of an informational commons "to which all people should have access and from which all should benefit" (2008, 161). It "stresses open knowledge, open access, and co-operative production forms" (2008, 161) such as those associated with open-source communities such as Linux development or Wikipedia and in the free software movement. He links this production model to gifts but also to Marx's idea of a free culture, a realm "characterized by well-rounded individuality, pluralistic activities, abundance, the abolition of hard work and wage labor due to technological productivity, the disappearance of the performance principle and exchange, the free production and distributions of goods ... and free time for idle and higher activity" (2008, 163). Freedom is here conceptualised as the absence of "scarcity and domination and as a community of associated individuals that provides wealth, self-ownership, self-realization of human faculties, and self-determination for all" (2008, 163).

The Internet, he goes on to say, can be closely connected to freedom, partly because the information good is such that it benefits from cooperative production and it is not depleted through use, but rather continues to grow in such conditions. However, in the reality of contemporary global capitalism, information is treated as a commodity and cooperative production has been dominated by competitive, monopolistic production, particularly evident in the false scarcity created by copyright regimes. Fuchs (2008, 178–9) draws a table of key digital media production models and their prevailing relationship to either gift or commodity exchange, indicating the predominance of competitive, market economics. In this table, we also see the domination of use-values by exchange-values in the digital media economy. Thus, while Fuchs argues that cooperation and competition are dialectically productive of the Internet economy – that both gift and commodity exchange are implicated – he nevertheless concludes that market-exchange and the production of commodities is the main mode of production. "Although the principle of the gift points towards a postcapitalist society, gifts today are *subsumed* under capitalism and used for generating profit in the Internet economy" (2008, 185; emphasis added).

What typically underpins discussions of gifting in the digital economy is a profound antagonism between gift and commodity exchange. Barbrook, for instance, notes that although "money-commodity and gift relations are not just in conflict with each other, but also co-exist in symbiosis ... each method of working does threaten to supplant each other ... The potlatch and the commodity remain irreconcilable" (1998, n.p.). Even when acknowledging the complex dialectic between capitalism and gift economics on the Internet, Fuchs (2008; 2009) nevertheless suggests that the two modes of production function as negating binaries. While insisting that competitive and cooperative production relationships are not distinct in the digital media economy, a point developed more effectively through the concept of "sublation" in *Digital Labour and Karl Marx*, in earlier works Fuchs often slips into assuming the absolute subsumption of the gift and its use-value into the debased exchange-value of the commodity form.

Thus, even while *all* commodities have both use-value and exchange-value in the work of Marx (Appadurai 1986, 8; Comor 2010), it is often insisted that use-values are superseded when encountered in the context of commodified exchanges. This position is exemplified by Lewis Hyde (1979, 21) who says: "When gifts are sold, they change their nature as much as water changes when it freezes, and no rationalist telling of the constant elemental structure can replace the feeling that is lost." Like affect and domestic work as theorised by radical feminist theorists, gift giving is typically described as incompatible with *any form* of economic valorisation. Similarly, in much Marxist orthodoxy, the overlaying of economic imperatives into affective relations is also assumed to generate alienating effects. Notably using the example of domestic work, Negri (1999, 79) argues that in capitalism value is assumed *only* by stripping it from the affective relations that underpin that work and thus from the values attributed to it by its subjects. As Viviana Zelizer (2005) puts it, it is often assumed that gifts (use-values) and commodities (exchange-values) exist in necessarily "hostile worlds." It is this binary logic that animates the debates described in the previous chapter in which both those who argue that a social relation of alienation prevails in digital media and those who argue that consumers operate in alternative economies rely on a clear distinction between the fiscal economy and the moral, symbolic and affective economies of digital media users.

Ceasing Hostilities

As the example of *Facebook Stories* suggests though, this hostile world's binary seems untenable in the reality of digitally mediated sociality. But nor has it historically been the case that gifts and commodities do not intersect. It is difficult to associate the commodity form only with industrial and post-industrial capitalism and not with precursor, more "primitive," economic contexts such as gift economies (Read 2003). As Arjun Appadurai (1986, 12) notes, there can be a "calculative dimension" to bartering and gift giving that reflects the abstractions and "economic interests" of capitalist commodity exchange. Furthermore, in contemporary consumer capitalism, there is no clear distinction between alienable and inalienable possessions; both gift and market exchanges are present in all contemporary capitalist societies. Frow says: "Almost all things may move between these contexts, and are defined and valued accordingly. If it is possible for governments to impose a gift tax, for example, it is because almost all gifts can, in the appropriate cultural context, be measured as commodities; conversely, most commodities are capable of being gifted, and indeed the majority of gifts in modern societies with capitalist social relations *are* (purchased but not given as) commodities" (1997, 131). The birthday card I give my sister is one interchangeable commodity amongst many others on the rack in the store, but expresses in the personal inscription and in the act of its exchange, a series of ineffable and inalienable affects and relations of interdependence. It is a commodity experienced as a gift both in the giving and the receiving. Frow's argument draws attention to the simultaneous co-existence of both inalienable affective and abstracted commodified qualities within the same object or, sometimes, the same process of exchange.

This hybridity is also central to Viviana Zelizer's (2005; 2011) studies of the range of complex, multiple and ongoing social negotiations that work to define the boundaries between acceptable and non-acceptable commodification of intimacy. She documents the complex differentiation of monetary transfers in a range of social contexts, based in the definitions being attributed to particular social relationships. She identifies the rituals, symbolic practices and different media of exchange (cash vs. in-kind services vs. commensurate objects) used by people to mark distinct ties with people. Examples of the intertwining of abstract commodities with intimate relations abound, ranging from pocket money for children to the intimate access granted to paid care workers to legal systems' definitions of intimate relationships brought to bear in divorce proceedings or inheritance disputes. Moreover, Zelizer recognises the importance of abstract exchange, including monetary, within intimate relationships. A notable example is in the expatriation of money by female migrant workers to family in their home country (see also Anderson 2003). On one hand, because of its medium of exchange – currency – this could be read as a commodified transaction. On the other hand though, it is experienced as a gift within the context of the political/moral economy, including gender politics, of each worker's family. It is an exchange of money that carries with it the affective intensities of familial relationships which is the context that allows the transfer of currency to assume validity as an expression of care.

Craft, Community and Commercialisation

At first glance, handicrafts seem a peculiar topic for thinking about the ways in which commodity and gift exchanges are negotiated in digital media. The very materiality of such practices seems exterior to the slick binaries of 0s and 1s that make up the digital. But craft-based communities have become increasingly significant on the web. This is not only due to a resurgence of artisanal production in commodities as diverse as beer, cheese and furniture, the growing recognition of craft within "creative industries" discourse (Banks 2010; Luckman 2015; Velkova 2014) or in the revival of domestic handicrafts as a form of leisure (Orton-Johnson 2014; Minahan and Wolfram Cox 2007).

(Continued)

This renaissance has been accompanied by the emergence of new sites for such activity, which includes a "growing presence of 'crafters' on the web, with blogs, podcasts, social networking sites and folksonomies like Flickr and You-Tube connecting a global community … and providing them with a wealth and resources and support" (Orton-Johnson 2014, 305).

These sites range from Etsy, the marketplace for handmade goods, to forums facilitating the offline meetings of Stitch'n'Bitch knitting groups, to YouTube instructional videos to personal and group craft blogs and all shades in between. The kinds of activities undertaken in these spaces are diverse and include learning new skills, following celebrity knitters, selling and exchanging patterns or yarn, documenting projects and social interactions. Because of their "juxtaposition of the technological and the material, the personal and the social" (Orton-Johnson 2014, 306), such sites have been variously understood as expressions of feminist and critical practice (Bratich and Brush 2011; Minahan and Wolfram Cox 2007; Pentney 2008;), grassroots creativity (Hudson 2010; Humphreys 2008a) and as being part of a broader movement transforming product design based on collective intelligence outside of intellectual property regimes (Banks 2010; Bonnani and Parkes 2010; Carpenter 2010).

An important site for "crafters" is the portal Ravelry which, in 2012, registered over 2 million knitters, spinners and crotcheters across the world, 35 million forum posts and 3.5 million craft projects (Orton-Johnson 2014). The site provides its users with a personal page or notebook to record projects and to inventory their resources. These functions sit among many other tools to support individual craftworking and social interaction between Ravelry users. Users can "favourite" other users' activities and use the forums and other messaging systems to communicate and interact with others. The site also offers the ability to search for patterns, needles and yarn, but more importantly to trade or purchase those items in a marketplace open to commercial retailers as well as fellow "Ravelers." There is also a shop for Ravelry themed goods. Like so many other commercial digital media sites, Ravelry is funded by advertising from yarn or fibre-arts related companies rather than subscription.

What even this very brief description points to is the variety of economies at play within Ravelry. Drawing on the concept of "social network markets" identified by Jason Potts and Stuart Cunningham et al. (2008; Potts and Hartley et al. 2008), the nature of these economies has been documented by Sal Humphreys (2008b; 2009). She describes how users can be involved in explicit, monetary commercial transactions by buying merchandise from retailers, or selling their yarn or patterns to other users. These exchanges also work as marketing in the form of implicit user-generated recommendations or as taste data, generating another fiscal economy associated with the audience-commodity. Users may also trade or barter unwanted goods with other users on forums, paying either in cash or in kind. This "destashing" affordance, Humphreys says, is not available to commercial retailers, and users are only allowed to avail of it in order to get rid of unwanted yarn.

There is also a significant set of non-commercial, gift economies associated with "the spirit of Ravelry." Knitters are perceived as "habitual gifters" and this continues in the context of Ravelry (Humphreys 2009, 10). Humphreys also describes how gifting and volunteerism work within the site's reputational economy as user-generated metrics about the popularity of patterns, yarns and project pages subsequently manifest in the ranking of search results for both commercial and non-commercial purposes. Meanings emerging from within the social network thus significantly influence the tenor and tone of the site, and by extension the potential for commercialisation. The most popular, and therefore most visible, sites are often those being used in community events such as "sock wars" or are otherwise shaped by group norms.

What Humphreys describes accords with Zelizer's (2005; 2011) description of the constant negotiations of commodity exchanges in intimate personal relationships. Humphreys documents the tensions between the differing goals, practices and social functions of these economies and how the validity of certain exchanges are not fixed, but are negotiated implicitly in practice and overtly in rules and discussions. In one instance, she describes debates between users over copyright and fair use definitions relating to the use, transformation and redistribution of other users' patterns (2008b) as well as discussion over definitions of when "destashing" becomes commercial activity (2009). Demonstrated in these explicit expressions of otherwise tacit social logics is the tension between, and the negotiation of, a set of distinctions between legitimate and illegitimate user exchanges; the "working out" of a hybrid economy in the practices and discourses of the site. Just as in the intimate, domestic situations described by Zelizer, the particular context of the relationship between Ravelry and its users requires a specific set of symbolic practices and rituals around the disavowal of crass commercialisation. Only when these rituals are appropriately observed can a monetary exchange be legitimated.

What the example of Ravelry shows very clearly is that in user-driven digital media, economic models do not exist in isolation. It also indicates the complex ways in which the social and moral economies of digital media sites intersect with the fiscal. Ravelry cannot be described solely as driven by market or gift exchanges, nor as either a fiscal or moral economy. What Humphreys documents instead are the complex flows between these different kinds of economic models and their associated labouring practices. Moreover, her analysis suggests that it is the ongoing negotiations about what constitutes valid exchanges in different contexts of the site that are constitutive of, and simultaneously constituted by, the culture of the site. The dynamics of these debates and how they change throughout any site and over time are important to capture if we are to define the nature of digitally mediated affective exchanges.

What Zelizer's studies emphasise are the constant personal, cultural, political, economic and ideological struggles over the demarcation of the boundaries between gift and commodity exchanges, between affect and alienation and between use-value and exchange-value (see also Banks and Potts 2010; Skeggs 2010; Velkova 2014; Velkova and Jackobsson 2015). Similar negotiations specific to local context happen within each online community that intersects with commercial interests. This includes, for instance, Facebook users whose interaction with the economics of the site remain at a distance but who negotiate for themselves and in their local networks what constitutes fair intervention by the site, organising protests, boycotts or activating the exit strategy when the perceived balance between commercial imperatives and the tacit values of the social context becomes unacceptable (Bates 2008; Ionescu 2009).

Outside of these moments of crisis though, there is a constant movement between the two sets of interests and a dynamic policing of contingent borders, albeit one that is often experienced seamlessly in everyday use (Light 2014). What is important about Zelizer's analysis is that it points out that the type of production we see in digital media "is generated precisely through a dynamic and co-evolving relationship between the commercial and the non-commercial, rather than a static face-off between these domains in which one side 'wins'" (Banks and Potts 2010, 255).

The Social Life of Things

Arjun Appadurai (1986) and Igor Kopytoff's (1986) related arguments about the movement through inalienable and alienable states in the progression of "the social life of things" offer valuable insight into this flux. Appadurai (1986: Skågeby 2013) argues that because the meanings of objects, including their commodity status, are endowed by human interactions and socio-material practices, emphasis must be given theoretically and methodologically to the concrete and historically specific moments of their circulation. To understand objects and the qualities of the labour they describe, "we have to follow the things themselves, for their meanings are inscribed in their forms, their uses, their trajectories. It is only through the analysis of these trajectories that we can interpret the human transactions and calculations that enliven things" (Appadurai 1986, 5). This involves exploring those moments where commodity logic dominates – the "commodity phase" – and those others shaped more by inalienable sociality and reciprocal obligation. Appadurai and Kopytoff also argue that is important not to view these trajectories from use-value to exchange-value as uni-directional and static. Appadurai argues that we should be cognisant that "things can move in *and* out of the commodity state, that such movements can be slow or fast, reversible or terminal, normative or deviant" (1986, 13; emphasis in original). There may also be more or less coherence in how each actor involved in an exchange understands the nature of the interaction, based in the social or cultural context of each subject and the particularities of the exchange.

What they propose is mapping the different "regimes of value" attributed to the products of labour and how these change over time as labour processes and actors cycle in and out of states of commodification (Velkova and Jackobsson 2015). Many orthodox Marxist arguments, however, document only the progressive extension of commodity logic throughout society.

This is certainly implicit in the critiques of the social factory documented in Chapter 2. However, Frow (1997, 134–5) questions this logic by exploring processes of de-commodification using the example of slave trade abolition as an example. He also notes the uneven success of commodification and its staged progression, insisting that we remember that "every extension of the commodity form has been met with resistance and often with reversals; the struggles over enclosure, over the length of the working day, over the privatization of common resources of many kinds are central to the global development of capitalism" (1997, 135).

Moreover, as Eva Ilouz's (1997) study of the commodification of romantic love argues, the entry of markets into apparently un-commodified areas can have complex and unexpected political consequences. Rather than finding only a lowering of quality and intimacy as consumer goods have come to mediate interpersonal relationships, her study finds that many actors, but particularly women, find agency and power in contemporary relationship norms. Rather than the stifling, paternalistically organised pressures of Victorian dating, contemporary couples encounter greater freedom of choice and movement; they are effectively less alienated because of the commercialisation of the practice. To understand "the role of goods in the romantic bond," one must therefore understand the cultural contradictions of patriarchal capitalism. One must "wrestle with the question of whether direct constraints exerted by some individuals (families most notably) over other individuals (women most notably) are in some sense "preferable" to the fuzzier constraints exerted by the invisible yet all-powerful market forces embodied in consumer goods" (Ilouz 1997, 146). Commodities and gifts have complex life histories and politics that constitute their biography and their relative status in relation to commodification, alienation and abstraction.

What becomes important then, for understanding a hybrid product such as the affectively rich gifts exchanged in the context of advertising-sponsored, commercial digital media, is to engage with the particularities of contexts, actors and economic functions across their cultural/economic life cycle. We can return here to Ahmed's (2004a; 2004b) description of the perpetual circulation of affect, and its punctuation by moments and/or spaces of fixity where it "sticks" to an organic or inorganic body. Such a formal, and temporary, fixing can be seen in the movement from gift to commodity where it is the degree of affective intensity being registered that defines the status of the exchange. Any exchange at any time may thus involve elements associated with gifts, commodities or both, and this status may change as an object or practice circulates, accumulating and losing affective resonance. What is required is the mapping of these transformations in the qualities attributed to the products of labour – the social relations they exemplify over time and space – and thus the nature of the labour involved in that production.

This is particularly so in the case of economies embedded in interpersonal connections and affective intensities such as domestic work, but also that of digital media. In arguing for a multiphasic integration of consumer labour into capital, and highlighting the need to map the dominant relation at given times and the moments of transformation, this framework moves away from traditional understandings of labour, but moves us closer to the image of the Digital Housewife whose labour straddles what Bolin argues are the "rather detached fields of production and consumption" (2012, 809). It is then Marxist feminism, specifically the early work of Leopoldina Fortunati, to which we can turn for a critical model capable of generating such a map of the quotidian uses of affectively rich digital media.

Modelling the Economics of Domestic Work

In *The Arcane of Reproduction*, Fortunati (1995) first emphasises the productive qualities of reproductive domestic labour, going on to describe the historic transformation of that work from activity that solely produces use-values to one that produces value for capital. She says, "it has gone from being *the work of the reproduction of individuals* – posited as a natural condition of human existence and of the exchange between the individual and nature – to *housework and prostitution work, the two principal specifically social forms of the work of the reproduction of labor-power*. It is this passage from the pre-capitalist to the capitalist form of work that reveals the effectively dual character of work" (1995, 105; emphasis in original). This dual character lies in the continued production of use-values even in a capitalist context where exchange-values dominate.

However, her point is that while there has been a shift in the dominant form of exchange, this is not a complete subsumption of one type of labour into the other. Although disguised within the production process, this dual character is true of all work, she suggests. It is, however, integral to domestic labour. She describes the family as having a "double life": "It has an apparent life, as the 'natural' center for the reproduction of individuals as use-value, and a real life, as the center for the production of labor-power as a commodity – the center where the female houseworker produces a huge quantity of surplus-value" (1995, 125–126). The education, health regimes and biological reproduction of the family are about producing "*the pool of labor on which capital draws*" (1995, 126; emphasis in original). Thus, even though the family and the domestic sphere appear as a place of organic "love" it is, in fact, a place of commoditisation and alienation (1995, 126). For Fortunati, the privileged structure of the family is "a secret workshop" in which a worker's labour-power is the key product.

Central to the production of labour-power in Fortunati's reckoning is consumption. The capacity for production of any worker – her/his use-value as labour-power – is produced through consuming the products of domestic work. She describes how, in capitalist societies, workers labour to gain the means of subsistence, which are typically purchased as commodities. In consuming these goods, the worker and thus his/her ability to continue to provide the use-value of their labour-power is reproduced. But, and this is Fortunati's key point, the labour-power of the worker, who she typifies as male, is also produced by consuming the labour-power of the "house-worker," who she typifies as female. The male worker rarely consumes the means of subsistence directly because these are typically translated and transformed through physically, temporally and emotionally demanding domestic work such as shopping, cooking and cleaning. Thus, just as the use-value of a worker's labour-power is consumed during the production process to generate commodities, so too is the energy of the housewife consumed in the generation of the labouring body and subject. The family is therefore the site of the production and consumption of use-values that produce the capacity for work, which can later be transformed into labour-time, the commodity-form of labour-power.

The most important aspect of Fortunati's argument for understanding consumer labour is that that the incorporation of work from the reproductive sphere into capital is not direct, but involves "two distinct phases separated from each other by the moment of consumption" (1995, 72). She argues that the labour-power produced in domestic work has two inter-related characteristics. Firstly, it is the *capacity* to work, and therefore is not an alienable object. Consequently, its second characteristic is that it "does not exist outside of the individual who contains it" (1995, 72). These qualities mean that the "female houseworker cannot directly reproduce the male worker's labor-power" (1995, 73) because it exists only within the body and subjectivity of that worker. To generate that capacity, the worker must individually consume the use-values needed for his own reproduction. There is therefore a two-stage process in the production of labour-power. "Between the female houseworker (who manifests her own labor-power) and the product of her work – the labor-powers of the male worker, of future workers, and her own labor-power – there remains the individual consumption of each of these individuals" (1995, 73). It is only in the case of her own labour-power that a domestic worker can directly produce the final form of labour-power, although this still requires consumption of the products of her own labour. The process of reproduction therefore has two phases: "firstly, the transformation of the means of production of housework into use-values which are directly consumable by the male worker; and secondly, the transformation of the latter into labor-power" (1995, 74). I would also add that there is third phase in which labour-power is transformed into the commodity of labour-time.

A related quality of reproductive work is that it produces both material and non-material goods. The latter of these are the inalienable goods such as esteem and care described in the activities of digital media consumers that satisfy the social, spiritual and psychological needs of an individual and which are "as important to his/her reproduction as a grilled steak or an ironed shirt" (1995, 74). These goods have no measurable exchange-value in capitalist terms and are encountered primarily as use-values. Such products can idealistically be seen as outside of market logics and as objects of reciprocal exchange that mutually satisfy needs. However, in the model Fortunati describes, and despite the potential of such goods to be "the least controllable by capital" (1995, 75), they nevertheless contribute to the generation of surplus-value in the same way as the more material products of domestic work. They all are consumed in the process of producing a worker and once so instantiated become commodifiable. In effect, the production of these products is one phase of a longer value chain associated with the generation of the labouring subject and body. Thus, rather than being detached from the commodity production process, intimate and inalienable use-values such as affection, sex and love are fundamentally implicated in the capitalist circuits of value creation. Fortunati insists, then, that the work of producing workers is not "merely" the production of (pre-capitalist) use-values but a distinct phase in the transfers of value inherent to the capitalist process.

Indirect Incorporation in the Digital Economy

Although this is not underscored in her work, which tends to emphasise the alienating aspects of these processes, Fortunati's model is important because the indirect relationship to capital it describes allows us to understand the production of use-values and the experience of them as use-values while still allowing for their role in the circuits of capital. That they are not directly commodified means that, at various phases of the value creation process, the products and work of housewives retain their inalienability and thus can be interpreted in terms of their distinction from the destructive, exploitative logics of capital. In this form though, they are nevertheless involved in a process of surplus-value production and implicated in the alienation and exploitative logics of capital.

This multiphased process of value generation can be traced in the banality of "liking" on the social networking site Facebook. This ubiquitous feature of the system asks users to respond to the status updates or posts of others by selecting the "like" button. But as Tamara Peyton (2014) argues, this action has a complex ontology, reflecting the long history of labour and its products. She describes the "like" button as "a chimera, meaning multiple things to many people, and acting within the sociotechnical lifeworld in a variety of ways based on the socio-political position of the button publisher, the invoking user, and the neoliberal economic practices of information consumption in which it is embedded" (2014, 116). The "like" button, she says, is a blackboxing of the "complex flows of networked code, financial logic, consumerist aspirations and informational media."

The economic arguments described in Chapter 3 would suggest that as a user selects the "like" button their input is objectified in the back-end databases of Facebook and rendered into the audience-commodity. "Liking" has particular salience for Facebook because, as already noted, the company aggregates not only the information of an individual user or a particular

IP address but also data from across that user's friend network to calculate the commodity it sells to advertisers and the advertising s/he subsequently receives. In the data capture systems of the site, each click of the button, along with all taste indicators contained in status updates, are alienated from the user's individual lived context and rendered into complex formulae for the ascription of advertising formats. When viewed through this prism and at this moment of the life cycle, user activity is helping to generate surplus and so is part of an exploitative and alienating relationship.

In Fortunati's logic, in hitting the "like" button, the consumer uses up their own instantiated affective, psychic and physical energies. The data this generates correspond with labour-time, the abstract representation of labour-power that circulates in capitalist accounting (Elson 1979). But the labour-power – the capacity and desire to "like" something in the first place – must first be produced and reproduced through a prior consumption of use-values. In this example, these use-values are the non-material products of social interaction, esteem or affective response that each user experiences when engaged with others through the sites. Even though Peyton (2014) suggests "liking" does not always reflect what we understand as the experience of liking something – it may in fact register ironic pleasure, anger, duty and so on – it nevertheless begins as a reflection of some kind of affective state. Before it becomes user (and useable) data, the "like" is first a manifestation of a set of social affinities, affective interactions or personal desires that satisfy some non-material need. We "like" things first and foremost because we like them, or because they affect us in certain ways, and it is our production and consumption of this use-value that produces the instantiated capacity and desire to generate user data. The affective intensities invoked by our "liking" in turn generates more and more affective products for consumption by others to sustain their interactions. Like domestic work, "liking" a Facebook page is simultaneously the raw material and auxiliary material of the digital media production process.

For users though, Facebook is experienced primarily as an exchange of use-values. The site can only convert the labour-power of user experience into the commodified form of user data (labour-time) *after* its experience as inalienable use-value by the user. And because it remains use-value, the affective intensity associated with exchanges on Facebook does not lose its capacity to build and sustain rich social formations even as it almost simultaneously enters the commodity circuit. Contrary to the logics of the alienation thesis, "liking" a friend's status update continues to manifest an inalienable and affectively powerful social relationship, or even asserts a political statement. Thus, while the generation of user data on Facebook is deeply implicated in the capitalist valorisation process, it is not an inherently exploitative or wholly commodified process across its whole life cycle. A multiphasic relationship with capital accumulation such as that proposed by Fortunati leaves open the capacity for a single exchange to retain its non-alienated value to users while also, in a different step of the exchange process, to generate exchange-value and become saturated with alienating and exploitative logics.

The model Fortunati proposes enables the rich description of consumer pleasures and agency, and asserts that these are able to remain meaningful and potentially disruptive of capitalist logics, allowing for their (potential) role in capital to be identified. Like domestic work, which can be almost simultaneously burdensome and delightful; exploited and richly rewarding; a scene for degradation and site for self-actualisation, consumer labour can be both alienated and disenfranchising and individually and socially meaningful. Feminist perspectives on domestic work, such as Fortunati's, not only challenge the hierarchy between production and reproduction that animates the concept of the social factory, they also complicate the binary between alienation and agency that has dogged studies of digital media consumers. Fortunati's model suggests that it is not necessarily true that in capitalist market contexts the reciprocal dependence of use-values is eradicated so that "anything socially useful that lacks exchange-value becomes worthless, dispensable, and irrelevant" (Prodnik 2012, 298). These goods or experiences are still encountered and consumed as use-values.

A multiphasic model of incorporation into capital like Fortunati's thus enables mapping the longer biographies or "social lives" of labour practices and their commodities as advocated by Appadurai and Kopytoff. It demands attention to the specificity of value creation across the various phases of production associated with digital media use, and a specific focus on the political consequences of the varying degrees of exploitation and alienation during each of these phases. This model also calls upon us to map the transformations back and forth between use-value and exchange-value throughout the circuits of capital exchange and in doing so map the dynamic relationship between exploited and self-actualising labour. It is this emphasis on the particular, but mutable, status of the products and inputs of domestic and consumer labour that is important for understanding affect's economic role. Such a model offers the hybridity that moves us away from unfruitful squabbling over which logic is *the* logic that defines the economic or social significance of this practice. It is only by embracing uncertainty that we can properly understand the labour of the Digital Housewife.

Marx Is Not the Only Fruit

There is one final point to be made about this model. The persistence of use-values within capital that it allows opens the way for understanding the circulation and valorisation of such activity in circuits other than capital and for incorporating that understanding into a critical economic, materialist, analysis. Clarifying some confused phrasing in Marx, Fortunati (1995, 80) insists that commodities like labour-power have value distinct from use-value and particularly exchange-value, which is merely the capitalist measure of value. The refusal here to reduce value to *only* fiscal surplus is particularly useful for understanding the production of non-material goods that have a cultural as well as an economic function, such as those generated by the Digital Housewife.

By continuing to recognise the importance of use-values within capitalism, this model makes it possible to explore various labour practices as examples of social reproduction, with an emphasis on their role in reproducing social norms. Understanding value creation in this arena must necessarily entail understanding the creation of subjects embodied in and through cultural practices. It is to explore the ways in which the socialisation of labourers, whether in the context of the domestic sphere or in their online activities, perpetuates cultural logics, or the superstructure, of capitalism. The emphasis on social reproduction opened up through this model encourages the incorporation of a broader range of critical perspectives into Marxist-driven analysis of this kind of activity.

As I have argued elsewhere (Jarrett 2015), a multiphasic model of labour allows for the meaningful observation of pleasure, agency and empowerment in digital media work. At the same time, it also offers critical appraisal of how those use-values (may) emerge from, or are implicated in, the inequitable distribution of resources and power in contemporary global capitalism. The political critique of such work can be widened beyond Marx and the alienation thesis to include theorists like Williams, Bourdieu, hooks, Althusser, Butler, Said, Foucault, or Deleuze and Guattari (to name but a few) and their ways of conceptualising the nature of cultural production and production of economic subjects. For instance, it allows us to look more closely at the agency experienced by digital media consumers in terms of how that may emerge from a particular class, gender, racial, sexual or other status and to query whether the practices we are exploring recreate those subject positions and the exclusions of capitalist economies alongside their economic function. This is a crucial understanding if we are to fully reckon the value of consumer labour to capitalism.

The approach advocated here thus can incorporate the insights of Cultural Studies and cultural Marxism into analysis of the political economy of digital media, ending the false binary between these fields (Peck 2006). The figure of the Digital Housewife allows for a return to the tradition of the formative texts from which the discipline of Cultural Studies emerged, in which questions of culture were taken seriously "as a dimension without which historical transformations, past and present, simply could not adequately be thought" (Hall 1980, 58). This tradition refuses to conceptualise base and superstructure as separate spheres but focuses instead on the "radical interaction" between economics and the organisation of lived experience (Skeggs 2014). In effect, this approach looks for how labour activities, but particularly consumer activities, can be both value-generating by contributing to surplus, but also *of value* by reproducing the capitalist social factory. The multiphasic model for the incorporation of culturally meaningful labour into capital that the Digital Housewife leads us to, and the persistence of use-values that this figure reminds us of, mirrors this logic and provides a means for conceptualising the place of such interactions within capitalist circuits.

To explore how consumer labour produces and reproduces these subject positions alongside economic value is thus to generate a more holistic understanding of value and of value-creation that avoids fruitless squabbles over the primacy of any one theoretical paradigm. It bridges what Natalie Fenton (2007) refers to as "the mythical divide" between political economy approaches and Cultural Studies. Perhaps more importantly though, by expanding what we interpret as valuable in the capitalist mode of production, this approach also complicates and extends our view of the social importance of consumer labour and digital media. The next chapter takes up this opportunity, bringing together the various threads of this study to explore a particular example of consumer labour and its various relationships to capitalism.

References

Ahmed, Sara. 2004a. "Affective Economies." *Social Text* 22 (2): 117–139.
———. 2004b. *The Cultural Politics of Emotion.* New York: Routledge.
Alexa. n.d. "The Top 500 Sites on the Web." Accessed May 27, 2015. http://www.alexa.com/topsites.
Anderson, Bridget. 2003. "Just Another Job? The Commodification of Domestic Labour." In *Global Woman: Nannies, Maids and Sex Workers in the New Economy*, edited by Barbara Ehrenreich and Arlie Russell Hochschild, 104–114. London: Granta Books.
Appadurai, Arjun. 1986. "Introduction: Commodities and the Politics of Value." In *The Social Life of Things: Commodities in Cultural Perspective*, edited by Arjun Appadurai, 3–63. Cambridge: Cambridge University Press.
Arvidsson, Adam and Elanor Colleoni. 2012. "Value in Informational Capitalism and on the Internet." *The Information Society* 28 (3): 135–150.
Ash, James. 2012. "Attention, Videogames and the Retentional Economies of Affective Amplification." *Theory, Culture & Society* 29 (6): 3–26.
Banks, John and Jason Potts. 2010. "Co-creating Games: A Co-evolutionary Analysis." *New Media & Society* 12 (2): 253–270.
Banks, Mark. 2010. "Craft Labour and Creative Industries." *International Journal of Cultural Policy* 16 (3): 305–321.
Barbrook, Richard. 1998. "The High-tech Gift Economy." *First Monday* 3 (12). doi:http://dx.doi.org/10.5210/fm.v3i12.631.
———. 2003. "Giving is Receiving." *Digital Creativity* 14 (2): 91–94.
Bates, Claire. 2008. "Facebook Fury: One Million Users Protest at Re-design of Social Networking Site." *The Daily Mail*, September 11. http://www.dailymail.co.uk/sciencetech/article-1053525/Facebook-fury-One-million-users-protest-design-social-networking-site.html.
Bays, Hilary and Miranda Mowbray. 1999. "Cookies, Gift-giving and the Internet." *First Monday* 4 (11). doi:http://dx.doi.org/10.5210/fm.v4i11.700.
Benksi, Tova and Eran Fisher, eds. 2014. *Internet and Emotions.* Oxon: Routledge.
Bergquist, Magnus and Jan Ljungberg. 2001. "The Power of Gifts: Organizing Social Relationships in Open-source Communities." *Information Systems Journal* 11: 305–320.

Bolin, Göran. 2012. "The Labour of Media Use: The Two Active Audiences." *Information, Communication & Society* 15 (6): 796–814.

Bolton, Sharon C. 2009. "The Lady Vanishes: Women's Work and Affective Labour." *International Journal of Work Organisation and Emotion* 3 (1): 72–80.

Bonnani, Leonardo and Amanda Parkes. 2010. "Virtual Guilds: Collective Intelligence and the Future of Craft." *The Journal of Modern Craft* 3 (2): 179–1990.

Bratich, Jack Z. and Heidi M. Brush. 2011. "Fabricating Activism: Craft-work, Popular Culture, Gender." *Utopian Studies* 22 (2): 233–260.

Bruns, Axel. 2008. "Life Beyond the Public Sphere: Towards a Networked Model for Political Deliberation." *Information Polity* 13 (1–2): 65–78.

Bruns, Axel, Jean Burgess, Tim Highfield, Lars Kirchoff and Thomas Nicolai. 2011. "Mapping the Australian Networked Public Sphere." *Social Science Computer Review* 29 (3): 277–287.

Cammaerts, Bart. 2011. "Disruptive Sharing in a Digital Age: Rejecting Neoliberalism?" *Continuum* 25 (1): 47–62.

Carpenter, Ele. 2010. "Activist Tendencies in Craft." *Concept Store #3: Art, Activism and Recuperation*. http://research.gold.ac.uk/3109/.

Cleaver, Harry. 1992. "The Inversion of Class Perspective in Marxian Theory: From Valorization to Self-valorization." In *Open Marxism Volume 2*, edited by Werner Bonefeld, Richard Gunn and Kosmas Psychopedis. Available from libcom. org. https://libcom.org/library/inversion-class-perspective-marxian-theory-valorization-self-valorization.

Clough, Patricia Ticineto with Jean Halley, eds. 2007. *The Affective Turn: Theorizing the Social*. Durham and London: Duke University Press.

Comor, Edward. 2010. "Digital Prosumption and Alienation." *ephemera* 10 (3/4): 439–454.

Coté, Mark and Jennifer Pybus. 2007. "Learning to Immaterial Labour 2.0: MySpace and Social Networks." *ephemera* 7 (1): 88–106.

Davidson, Martin. 1992. *The Consumerist Manifesto: Advertising in Postmodern Times*. London: Routledge.

Dourish, Paul and Christine Satchell. 2011. "The Moral Economy of Social Media." In *From Social Butterfly to Engaged Citizen: Urban Informatics, Social Media, Ubiquitous Computing and Mobile Technology to Support Citizen Engagement*, edited by Marcus Foth, Laura Forlano, Christine Satchell and Martin Gibbs, 21–37. Cambridge, Massachusetts: MIT Press.

Elson, Diane. 1979. "The Value Theory of Labor." In *Value: The Representation of Labour in Capitalism*, edited by Diane Elson, 115–180. London: CSE Books.

Facebook Stories. n.d. https://www.facebook.com/FacebookStoriesEnglish?fref=ts.

Federici, Silvia. 2011. "On Affective Labor." In *Cognitive Capitalism, Education and Digital Labor*, edited by Michael A. Peters and Ergin Bulut, 57–73. New York: Peter Lang.

Fenton, Natalie. 2007. "Bridging the Mythical Divide: Political Economy and Cultural Studies Approaches to the Analysis of the Media." In *Media Studies: Key Issues and Debates*, edited by Eoin Devereux, 7–31. London: Sage.

Fortunati, Leopoldina. 1995. *The Arcane of Reproduction: Housework, Prostitution, Labour and Capital*. Translated by Hilary Creek. New York: Autonomedia.

Frow, John. 1997. *Time and Commodity Culture: Essays in Cultural Theory and Postmodernity*. Oxford: Clarendon Press.

Fuchs, Christian. 2008. *Internet and Society: Social Theory in the Information Age*. London: Routledge.

———. 2009. "Information and Communication Technologies and Society: A Contribution to the Critique of the Political Economy of the Internet." *European Journal of Communication* 24 (1): 69–87.

Ghosh, Rishab Aiyer. 1998. "Cooking Pot Markets: An Economic Model for the Trade in Free Goods and Services on the Internet." *First Monday* 3 (3). http://www.firstmonday.org/htbin/cgiwrap/bin/ojs/index.php/fm/article/view/580/501.

Gill, Rosalind and Andy Pratt. 2008. "In the Social Factory? Immaterial Labour, Precariousness and Cultural Work." *Theory, Culture & Society* 25 (7–8): 1–30.

Gillespie, Tarleton. 2014. "Facebook's Algorithms – Why Our Assumptions Are Wrong, and Our Concerns Are Right." *Culture Digitally*, July 4. http://culturedigitally.org/2014/07/facebooks-algorithm-why-our-assumptions-are-wrong-and-our-concerns-are-right/.

Gray, Mary. 2014. "When Science, Customer Service, and Human Research Subjects Collide. Now What?" *Mary L. Gray*, July 8. http://marylgray.org/?p=288.

Gregg, Melissa and Gregory J. Seigworth, eds. 2010. *The Affect Theory Reader.* Durham: Duke University Press.

Grimmelmann, James. 2014. "The Facebook Emotional Manipulation Study: Sources." *The Laboratorium*, June 30. http://laboratorium.net/archive/2014/06/30/the_facebook_emotional_manipulation_study_source.

Grohol, John M. 2014. "Emotional Contagion on Facebook? More Like Bad Research Methods." *World of Psychology*, June 29. http://psychcentral.com/blog/archives/2014/06/23/emotional-contagion-on-facebook-more-like-bad-research-methods/.

Hakim, Simon. 2002. "Making the Emotional Connection." *Professional Marketing* February: 11.

Hall, Stuart. 1980. "Cultural Studies: Two Paradigms." *Media, Culture and Society* 2 (1): 57–72. http://xroads.virginia.edu/~drbr/hall.html.

Hardt, Michael and Antonio Negri. 2000. *Empire.* Cambridge, Massachusetts: Harvard University Press.

Hesmondhalgh, David and Sarah Baker. 2008. "Creative Work and Emotional Labour in the Television Industry." *Theory, Culture & Society* 25 (7–8): 97–118.

Hill, Kashmir. 2014. "Facebook Added 'Research' to User Agreement 4 Months After Emotion Manipulation Study." *Forbes*, June 30. http://www.forbes.com/sites/kashmirhill/2014/06/30/facebook-only-got-permission-to-do-research-on-users-after-emotion-manipulation-study/.

Hillis, Ken, Susanna Paasonen and Michael Petit, eds. 2015. *Networked Affect.* Cambridge, Massachusetts: MIT Press.

Hjorth, Larissa. 2007. "*Home and Away*: A Case Study of the Cyworld Mini-hompy by Korean Students Living in Australia." *Asian Studies* 31 (4): 397–407.

Hudson, Tracy P. 2010. "Spin Artists, and How the Internet Fuels the Art Yarn Movement." Paper presented at *Textiles and Settlement: From Plains Space to Cyber Space* Textile Society of America 12th Biennial Symposium, Lincoln, Nebraska, October 6–9. http://digitalcommons.unl.edu/tsaconf/22/.

Humphreys, Sal. 2008a. "Grassroots Creativity and Community in New Media Environments: Yarn Harlot and the 4000 Knitting Olympians." *Continuum: Journal of Media and Cultural Studies* 22 (3): 419–433.

———. 2008b. "The Challenges of Intellectual Property for Users of Social Networking Sites: A Case Study of Ravelry." Paper presented at *MindTrek '08*, Tampere, Finland, October 7–9.

———. 2009. "The Economies within an Online Social Network Market: A Case Study of Ravelry." Paper presented at *Communication, Creativity and Global Citizenship, ANZCA conference*, Brisbane, Queensland, July 8–10.

Hyde, Lewis. 1979. *The Gift: Imagination and the Erotic Life of Property*. New York: Vintage Books.

Ilouz, Eva. 1997. *Consuming the Romantic Utopia: Love and the Cultural Contradictions of Capitalism*. London: University of California Press.

Ionescu, Daniel. 2009. "Facebook Redesign Revolt Grows to 1.7m." *PCWorld*, March 23. http://www.pcworld.com/article/161752/facebook_users_against_redesign.html.

Jarrett, Kylie. 2015. "Devaluing Binaries: Marxist Feminism and the Value of Consumer Labour." In *Reconsidering Value and Labour in the Digital Age*, edited by Eran Fisher and Christian Fuchs, 207–223. Basingstoke: Hampshire: Palgrave Macmillan.

Jenkins, Henry. 2006. *Convergence Culture: Where Old and New Media Collide*. New York: New York University Press.

Karatzogianni, Athina and Adi Kuntsman, eds. 2012. *Digital Cultures and the Politics of Emotion: Feelings, Affect and Technological Change*. Basingstoke: Hampshire: Palgrave Macmillan.

King-O'Riain, Rebecca Chiyoko. 2014. "Transconnective Space, Emotions and Skype: The Transnational Emotional Practices of Mixed International Couples in the Republic of Ireland." In *Internet and Emotions*, edited by Tova Benksi and Eran Fisher, 131–143. Oxon: Routledge.

Kopytoff, Igor. 1986. "The Cultural Biography of Things: Commoditization as Process." In *The Social Life of Things: Commodities in Cultural Perspective*, edited by Arjun Appadurai, 64–91. Cambridge: Cambridge University Press.

Kramer, Adam. 2014. Facebook post, June 29. https://www.facebook.com/akramer/posts/10152987150867796.

Kramer, Adam D. I., Jamie E. Guillory and Jeffrey T. Hancock. 2014. "Experimental Evidence of Massive-scale Emotional Contagion Through Networks." *Proceedings of the National Academy of Sciences of the United States of America* 111 (24). http://www.pnas.org/content/111/24/8788.full.

Lampel, Joseph and Ajay Bhalla. 2007. "The Role of Status-seeking in Online Communities: Giving the Gift of Experience." *Journal of Computer-Mediated Communication* 12: 434–455.

Lazzarato, Maurizio. 1996. "Immaterial Labor." In *Radical Thought in Italy: A Potential Politics*, edited by Paolo Virno and Michael Hardt, 132–146. Minneapolis: University of Minnesota Press.

Leder Mackley, Kerstin and Angelina Karpovich. 2012. "Touching Tales: Emotion in Digital Object Memories." In *Digital Cultures and the Politics of Emotion: Feelings, Affect and Technological Change*, edited by Athina Karatzogianni and Adi Kuntsman, 127–143. Basingstoke, Hampshire: Palgrave Macmillan.

Light, Ben. 2014. *Disconnecting with Social Networking Sites*. Basingstoke, Hampshire: Palgrave Macmillan.

Liljestrom, Marianne and Susanna Paasonen, eds. 2010. *Working with Affect in Feminist Readings: Disturbing Differences*. Oxon: Routledge.

Lindstrom, Martin. 2002. "Web Branding: Take it Personally." *Clickz* March 19. http://www.clickz.com/clickz/column/1708675/web-branding-take-it-personally.

Luckman, Susan. 2015. *Craft and the Creative Economy*. Basingstoke and New York: Palgrave Macmillan.

Lury, Celia. 2004. *Brands: The Logos of the Cultural Economy*. Oxon: Routledge.

Massumi, Brian. 2002. *Parables for the Virtual: Movement, Affect, Sensation.* Durham and London: Duke University Press.

Matthews, Dylan. 2014. "Facebook Tried to Manipulate Users' Emotions. But We Have No Idea If It Succeeded." *Vox*, June 30. http://www.vox.com/2014/6/30/5856938/the-facebook-study-wasnt-just-creepy-it-was-bad-research.

Mauss, Marcel. 2002. *The Gift: The Form and Reason for Exchange in Archaic Societies.* London: Routledge. Originally published in 1954.

McAllister, Matthew P. 1996. *The Commercialization of American Culture: New Advertising, Control and Democracy.* Thousand Oaks, CA: Sage.

McNeil, Gregory S. 2014. "Controversy Over Facebook Emotional Manipulation Study Grows as Timeline Becomes More Clear." *Forbes*, June 30. http://www.forbes.com/sites/gregorymcneal/2014/06/30/controversy-over-facebook-emotional-manipulation-study-grows-as-timeline-becomes-more-clear/.

Meyer, Michelle N. 2014. "Everything You Need to Know About Facebook's Controversial Emotion Experiment." *Wired*, June 30. http://www.wired.com/2014/06/everything-you-need-to-know-about-facebooks-manipulative-experiment/.

Miller, Vincent. 2008. "New Media, Networking and Phatic Culture." *Convergence* 14 (4): 387–400.

Minahan, Stella and Julie Wolfram Cox. 2007. "Stitch'n'Bitch: Cyberfeminism, a Third Place and the New Materiality." *Journal of Material Culture* 12 (1): 5–21.

Mowlabocus, Sharif. 2010. "Porn 2.0: Technology, Social Practice, and the New Online Porn Industry." In *Porn.com: Making Sense of Online Pornography*, edited by Feona Attwood, 69–87. New York: Peter Lang.

Negri, Antonio. 1999. "Value and Affect." *Boundary 2* 26 (2): 77–88.

Orton-Johnson, Kate. 2014. "Knit, Purl, and Upload: New Technologies, Digital Mediations and the Experience of Leisure." *Leisure Studies* 33 (3): 305–321.

Paasonen, Susanna. 2011. *Carnal Resonance: Affect and Online Pornography.* Cambridge, Massachusetts: MIT Press.

Paasonen, Susanna. 2015. "A Midsummer's Bonfire: Affective Intensities in Online Debate." In *Networked Affect*, edited by Ken Hillis, Susanna Paasonen and Michael Petit, 27–42. Cambridge, Massachusetts: MIT Press.

Papacharissi, Zizi. 2010. *A Private Sphere: Democracy in a Digital Age.* Cambridge, UK: Polity Press.

———. 2015. *Affective Publics: Sentiment, Technology and Politics.* New York: Oxford University Press.

Papacharissi, Zizi and Maria de Fatima Oliveira. 2012. "Affective News and Networked Publics: The Rhythms of News Storytelling on #Egypt." *Journal of Communication* 62 (2): 266–282.

Pearson, Erika. 2007. "Digital Gifts: Participation and Gift Exchange in LiveJournal Communities." *First Monday* 12 (5). doi:http://dx.doi.org/10.5210/fm.v12i5.1835.

Peck, Janice. 2006. "Why We Shouldn't Be Bored with the Political Economy vs. Cultural Studies Debate." *Cultural Critique* 64: 92–126.

Pentney, Beth Ann. 2008. "Feminism, Activism and Knitting: Are the Fibre Arts a Viable Model for Feminist Political Action?" *thirdspace: a journal of feminist theory & culture* 8 (1). http://journals.sfu.ca/thirdspace/index.php/journal/article/viewArticle/pentney.

Peyton, Tamara. 2014. "Emotion to Action? Deconstructing the Ontological Politics of the 'Like' Button." In *Internet and Emotions*, edited by Tova Benksi and Eran Fisher, 113–128. Oxon: Routledge.

Potts, Jason, Stuart Cunningham, John Hartley and Paul Ormerod. 2008. "Social Network Markets: A New Definition of the Creative Industries." *Journal of Cultural Economy* 32 (3): 167–185.

Potts, Jason, John Hartley, John Banks, Jean Burgess, Rachel Cobcroft, Stuart Cunningham and Lucy Montgomery. 2008. "Consumer Co-creation and Situated Creativity." *Industry and Innovation* 15 (5): 459–74.

Prodnik, Jernej. 2012. "A Note on the Ongoing Processes of Commodification: From the Audience Commodity to the Social Factory." *Triple C* 10 (2): 274–301.

Raun, Tobias. 2012. "DIY Therapy: Exploring Affective Self-Representations in Trans Video Blogs on YouTube." In *Digital Cultures and the Politics of Emotion: Feelings, Affect and Technological Change*, edited by Athina Karatzogianni and Adi Kuntsman, 165–180. Basingstoke, Hampshire: Palgrave Macmillan.

Raymond, Eric S. 1998a. "The Cathedral and the Bazaar." *First Monday* 3 (3) doi:http://dx.doi.org/10.5210/fm.v3i2.578.

———. 1998b. "Homesteading the Noosphere." *First Monday* 3 (10) doi:http://dx.doi.org/10.5210/fm.v3i10.621.

Read, Jason. 2003. *The Micro-politics of Capital: Marx and the Prehistory of the Present*. Albany: State University of New York Press.

Sahlins, Marshall. 2004. *Stone Age Economics*. Oxon: Routledge. Originally published 1974.

Sirisena, Mihirini. 2012. "Virtually Yours: Reflecting on the Place of Mobile Phones in Romantic Relationships." In *Digital Cultures and the Politics of Emotion: Feelings, Affect and Technological Change,* edited by Athina Karatzogianni and Adi Kuntsman, 181–193. Basingstoke, Hampshire: Palgrave Macmillan.

Skågeby, Jörgen. 2013. "The Performative Gift: A Feminist Materialist Conceptual Model." *communication +1* 2 (7). http://scholarworks.umass.edu/cpo/vol2/iss1/7/.

Skeggs, Beverley. 2010. "The Value of Relationships: Affective Scenes and Emotional Performances." *Feminist Legal Studies* 18 (1): 29–51.

———. 2014. "Value Beyond Value? Is Anything Beyond the Logic of Capital?" *British Journal of Sociology* 65 (1): 1–20.

Slayden, David. 2010. "Debbie Does Dallas Again and Again: Pornography, Technology, and Market Innovation." In *Porn.com: Making Sense of Online Pornography*, edited by Feona Attwood, 54–68. New York: Peter Lang.

Sugiyama, Satomi. 2009. "Decorated Mobile Phones and Emotional Attachment for Japanese Youths." In *Electronic Emotion: The Mediation of Emotion via Information and Communication Technologies*, edited by Jane Vincent and Leopoldina Fortunati, 85–100. Bern: Peter Lang.

Sullivan, Gail. 2014. "Cornell Ethics Board Did Not Pre-approve Facebook Mood Manipulation Study." *The Washington Post*, July 1. http://www.washingtonpost.com/news/morning-mix/wp/2014/07/01/facebooks-emotional-manipulation-study-was-even-worse-than-you-thought/.

Tufekci, Zeynep. 2008. "Grooming, Gossip, Facebook and MySpace." *Information, Communication & Society* 11 (4): 544–564.

van Doorn, Niels. 2011. "Digital Spaces, Material Traces: How Matter Comes to Matter in Online Performances of Gender, Sexuality and Embodiment." *Media Culture & Society* 33 (4): 531–547.

Veale, Kylie J. 2003. "Internet Gift Economies: Voluntary Payment Schemes as Tangible Reciprocity." *First Monday* 8 (12). doi:http://dx.doi.org/10.5210/fm.v8i12.1101.

Velkova, Julia. 2014. "Workflows, Labour and Value in Open Animation Production: An Ethnographic Study of a Distributed Animation Training Creation." Paper presented at Dynamics of Virtual Work conference, Hatfield, UK, September 3–5.

Velkova, Julia and Peter Jakobsson. 2015. "The Production of Difference and Commensurability between Regimes of Value in Open Source Cultural Production." Paper presented at International Communication Association conference, San Juan, Puerto Rico, May 21–25.

Vincent, Jane. 2009. "Emotion, My Mobile, My Identity." In *Electronic Emotion: The Mediation of Emotion via Information and Communication Technologies*, edited by Jane Vincent and Leopoldina Fortunati, 187–202. Bern: Peter Lang.

Vincent, Jane and Leopoldina Fortunati, eds. 2009. *Electronic Emotion: The Mediation of Emotion via Information and Communication Technologies*. Bern: Peter Lang.

Waldman, Katy. 2014. "Facebook's Unethical Experiment." *Slate*, June 28. http://www.slate.com/articles/health_and_science/science/2014/06/facebook_unethical_experiment_it_made_news_feeds_happier_or_sadder_to_manipulate.html.

Warner, Michael. 2002. "Publics and Counterpublics." *Public Culture* 14 (1): 49–90.

Ze-ev, Ben. 2004. *Love Online: Emotions on the Internet*. Cambridge: Cambridge University Press.

Zeitlyn, David. 2003. "Gift Economies in the Development of Open Source Software: Anthropological Reflections." *Research Policy* 32 (7): 1,287–1,291.

Zelizer, Viviana A. 2005. *The Purchase of Intimacy*. New Jersey: Princeton University Press.

———. 2011. *Economic Lives: How Culture Shapes the Economy*. New Jersey: Princeton University Press.

5 I Can Haz False Consciousness?
Social Reproduction and Affective
Consumer Labour

The goal of this book has been to validate a model of consumer labour and its relationship to value creation that draws on insights provided by Marxist feminist interrogations of domestic work. Through critical appraisal of ideas within dominant Autonomist Marxist frameworks and by identifying the complexity that feminist approaches bring to debates about exploitation and alienation, I have advocated a hybrid approach in order to understand the affectively rich consumption and production contexts of digital media. This is an approach that rejects the binaries between productive and unproductive activity, production and reproduction and between gifts and commodities. In doing so, the argument of this book has placed the creation of use-values, such as affect, at the centre of capitalism not only when they are transformed into commodities with exchange-value, but also for their role in reproducing social norms. Fortunati's (1995) model of the multiphasic incorporation of domestic labour into capitalism described in *Arcane of Reproduction* has been offered as a useful model for understanding this dynamic, as well as allowing for the continued importance of immaterial labour's reproductive role.

This is not a simple analytical model. But the approach advocated throughout this book allows for a more thorough understanding of the dynamics of consumer labouring practices and how/if these are shot through with patriarchal capitalism's repressive logics. By refusing the separation of production and reproduction in both lived experience and analysis, the model outlined in this book usefully complicates how we understand the significance of our lives being mediated through commercial digital media sites. The approach validates explorations of pleasure and desire as a form of agency, which is crucial to understanding the kinds of social and cultural consumer practices associated with the web, but it also allows us to see how these may be implicated in capital with or without their conversion into exchange-value. It challenges us to look more closely at the products of this labour, in particular the subjectivities that are produced and reproduced in these interactions, for how they intersect with economics and other social power relations.

Advocating this approach is where we left the previous chapter. This chapter, then, works to summarise the argument of this book and demonstrate the relevance of what the Marxist feminist politics of the Digital Housewife tell us is important about consumer labour. It will draw inspiration from the work of Fortunati (1995), Appadurai (1986) and Kopytoff (1986) into the process of commodification and decommodification to explore how we might generate a biography of the products of the affectively rich consumer labour in this example. It will also add to this an emphasis on subjectivity and subjection drawn from radical feminist and Cultural Studies paradigms.

Consequently, in a break with the form of this book, rather than bracketing out significant examples from the theoretical exploration, this chapter will focus throughout on one specific instance: a Facebook conversation between my friend, Sheamus, and me. This exchange, known amongst my friends as "The Ballad of Kylie and Sheamus," generated the "Engels Cat" meme "I can haz false consciousness" that provides the title of this chapter. This example is a banal exchange of the kind many would have every day but, when examined as an instance of the multiphasic work of the Digital Housewife, such banality can encapsulate the tensions and complexities of digital media consumers' labour. This chapter will explore the multifaceted ways in which this exchange and the affects it relies on, and generates, are used to produce fiscal value. It also examines the moments prior to this phase of the commodification process, looking at the inalienable use-values that are also produced. It then complicates this biography of value-generation by exploring how the affective intensities of the Ballad of Kylie and Sheamus serve as a disciplining mechanism, not value-generating in the economic sense but of value to capital nonetheless.

By applying the model outlined in this book to this exchange, this chapter takes up the challenge made by Bev Skeggs (2014; Arruzza 2013) when she decries the long history of analytically separating out economic and non-economic forms of value. As she says, "they must be understood together and rather than assuming we know what either is we should interrogate their relationship and production" (2014, 4). The analysis in this chapter is not intended to be exhaustive though. It is designed to cover enough instances of the socioeconomic relations associated with this exchange to demonstrate the diversity and complexity that come from applying this model. The insights generated by the metaphor of the Digital Housewife will also demonstrate that there are more than the processes of alienation that make digital media consumers valuable to capitalism.

The Ballad of Kylie and Sheamus

This exchange began when Sheamus – who has given permission for me to discuss this exchange here – shared a cat meme describing religion as "the catnip of the purrrrrrletariat." Sitting at my desk on campus, I was amused by "Lenin Cat." I replied "Aren't LOLcats the opiate of the masses?" followed

Figure 5.1 Screenshot of Facebook post, 24 March 2013.

quickly by a hyperbolic underscoring of my statement: "I'm serious about that." Sheamus "liked" my comments and the conversation continued:

Sheamus: I can haz false consciousness. (You're right though. The sharing of memes in general, lolcats, condensing Wonka etc, are all forms of displacement. Says the meme sharer.)

Kylie: ermagerd, you must make a meme of "I can haz false consciousness". NOW!

At this point, there was a brief hiatus as Sheamus searched the web for appropriate images.

Sheamus: I need to find a cat that looks like Engels first.

Kylie: Surely there's a tumblr devoted to that?

Sheamus: Seems not. All I can find is that a bloke called Donald Engels wrote a book about cats.

This was then followed by another pause where I toggled to Google Image to search for the term "cats with beards." After trawling through various images of hipsters holding cats – there are more of these than one might expect – I came across an appropriate bearded cat image and sent it to Sheamus through the Facebook private messaging facility. Ten minutes later, he shared the meme he had created through the meme generator site, Quickmeme.com.

Figure 5.2 Screenshot of Facebook post, 24 March 2013.

I liked the image, as did another mutual friend, and I added "Purrfect" as a comment. A little more banter followed – with Sheamus expressing horror at my appalling pun – and the exchange came to an end twenty-five minutes after it began.

Undoubtedly, this is a very banal example of the kinds of exchanges that are constantly taking place on Facebook all over the world. For me, it filled some dead time in my workday with humour and interpersonal connection, but was one of many such moments, as well as only one of the many activities I undertook. It was rich with affective intensities but was not an exceptional event. For all its banality though, or perhaps because of this banality, this Facebook exchange usefully maps a range of dynamics associated with the economics of digital media, both fiscal and cultural. The affective work done by Sheamus and me in this interaction cycles through various economic dynamics, demonstrating the multiphasic relationship to capital brought into view by the prism of domestic work. To map this biography, this exchange will be disassembled and re-assembled in various configurations to demonstrate these dynamics and to explore the range of ways in which consumer labour contributes to capitalism.

Commodification

The most obvious economic relationship to point out is the exploitation of user data that occurs in this instance. Facebook, as has already been referenced, makes most of its income from advertising and so is reliant on generation of the audience-commodity. Consequently, every aspect of this exchange, from Sheamus' initial sharing of the image, the liking of particular posts and the content of each comment is expropriated and transformed into taste-identifying data points that have value in the advertising marketplace. Even the ostensibly private message containing the image of the bearded cat that I sent to Sheamus was expropriated and exploited in this fashion. Throughout the exchange, we were also exposed to advertising in sidebars, although the exchange occurred before the incorporation of overt advertising into newsfeeds. These ads were generated by Facebook's algorithms that parsed our user data to send (ostensibly) relevant advertising. Facebook is, however, notoriously bad at translating its data into appropriate advertising. The persistent appearance of weight loss ads for female-identifying users, despite no indicators that this is relevant to them, is one irritating example of this. As badly targeted as these ads may be, they nevertheless indicate how user inputs are transformed into advertising and, thus, into revenue for the company. Because our data had been sold, or would be in the future, Sheamus and I were generating surplus-value for Facebook, regardless of how much attention we paid to these ads.

It may seem meaningless for Facebook to know that Sheamus and I are familiar with the work of Marxist theorists and indeed such knowledge may seem contrary to the goals of marketing companies. But the information these posts contain are aggregated and, over time, work to develop a picture of us at our respective IP addresses, also adding to the data about the interests of people within our friends lists and in our broad demographic areas. This former information is more relevant for the small advertisers that Facebook caters for, while the latter, even when not used directly, can be sold to larger advertisers for wider market research purposes.

Rob Heyman and Jo Pierson's (2013) analysis of Facebook's basic advertising targeting practices identifies how the company aggregates what the authors call "personal identifying information" into various categories from which advertisers can select when choosing where to place their ads. They typify these categories as having three overlapping qualities: information based on taste, presumably drawn from "liking" and keyword data; that based on technical and subscription data such as the kind of operating system, age, educational attainment, or geography; and finally, that based on inferences from various data sources such as family, relationship or employment status. Furthermore, that Sheamus and I are "friends" and in regular contact through the site is a further data point that allows the company to assume we share similar tastes, make inferences about relevance based on that assumption and target advertising accordingly. The existence of an affective connection between Sheamus and me is of value (Arvidsson and Colleoni 2012).

However, it is not only for Facebook that this exchange generated value. In using both Google and Quickmeme.com, Sheamus and I contributed user data to two other sites. Google, as has already been discussed (see *Google-nomics* in Chapter 3), also relies on the audience-commodity to generate its enormous profits. Quickmeme is also a commercial provider relying on the aggregation of audiences. Launched in 2010, Quickmeme offers a simple process of image captioning and distribution that lies at the heart of meme culture. By 2012, Quickmeme was a significant Internet property, registering 70 million unique visitors and half a billion page views (Alonso 2013). While the home page at the time of writing this chapter had little to no information, Quickmeme's advertising-driven economic model was visible in the sponsored links (predominantly generic clickbait) and video advertising displayed on its home page. The flow of audiences to the site is clearly crucial, as evidenced in the founder's alleged attempts to manipulate traffic from Internet portal Reddit (Alonso 2013). Sheamus' use of the Quickmeme page and my viewing of it as I clicked through the small image embedded in the Facebook comment thus form part of the valorised product of our exchange.

It is important to recognise that even when using any one particular site, we may also be generating data that are incorporated into the advertising machinery of another commercial entity. Through its Connect protocol, Facebook can draw on third-party information, relying on the relationality between its own database and customer-relationship management systems on other commercial sites (Constine 2012; Heyman and Pierson 2013). Google is particularly skilled at using information from cookies drawn from across the web, sometimes startling me with advertising directly referencing recent online exploration or transactions I have conducted completely outside of the search engine's formal jurisdiction. In the Ballad of Kylie and Sheamus, the linking of databases was made explicit. To use Quickmeme to generate or upload an image, the user is required to login through their Facebook or Twitter account, a process that grants the site access to that user's public profile (which includes demographic details such as name, age range, gender and geographic location), friends list and email address. Facebook Connect presumably also allows Facebook access to our meme consumption.

Viewed through the logic of Marxism, bolstered by Marxist feminism's expansion of the kinds of work that can/must be defined as contributing to surplus, the Ballad of Kylie and Sheamus can be read as a formally exploited exchange. Critics of the audience-commodity thesis such as Lee (2014), Bolin (2011) and Meehan (1984) would suggest that because it is the labour of paid Facebook employees that produces the audience data that actually generate revenue, the work Sheamus and I do cannot be considered productive. However, as argued in Chapter 3, this position relies on a limited model of value-creation. While Facebook, Inc. bears the costs of producing and maintaining the site, including the technical infrastructure to process the content, collect and manipulate user data, to manage advertising clients and their payments (transforming raw user inputs into a commodity consumable by advertisers) and all the other functions of a publicly listed company, they do not bear all the costs of producing their user data. The raw materials with which they work are created by the unpaid labour of users, with marginal costs to the provider. To make an analogy with industrial contexts, Facebook can be viewed as an assembly line in which certain paid workers produce a website which serves as the materials transformed by another set of workers – the unpaid consumers involved in "liking" and generating status updates – into raw data, which then move along the value chain to another set of paid workers who transform those data into saleable commodities.

Like the relationship of domestic work to capital, it is by drawing on this unwaged work that capitalist producers like Facebook generate greater surplus. In this banal and short online exchange, Sheamus and I are working for Facebook, Google, Quickmeme, our respective Internet service providers and myriad other sites for whom our data serve as infinitely replicable and recombinable raw materials.

The Alienation of Copyright

There is another economic relationship that occurs in the extended biography of The Ballad of Kylie and Sheamus that is important to note. When Sheamus shared the Engels Cat meme, it appeared in my Facebook newsfeed as an embedded link to the Quickmeme page (see Figure 5.2 above). I shared this post on my own feed, but it continued to appear as a link to the Quickmeme website. Rather than being accessible as a disembedded, stand-alone file that could be viewed from Facebook, as is possible with YouTube videos for instance, to view this image required following the link to the Quickmeme page and being exposed to the advertising and data capture systems there (see Figure 5.3). While it is possible to identify the link for the meme and to paste that to Facebook or to drag the image from the web as a .jpeg file and upload that to avoid linking through to Quickmeme, these are not the default options for this image, not least because in order to use the meme generator the user is required to login via Facebook or Twitter. Nor are these alternative distribution mechanisms the simplest of operations, requiring wider engagement with image properties and alternative menus. By default, the Engels Cat meme is tied inextricably to Quickmeme and to generating surplus for the site.

Figure 5.3 Screenshot of Engels Cat meme on Quickmeme.com site
   (http://www.quickmeme.com/meme/3ti6jy/).

This set of affordances is obviously a means by which user traffic is shepherded towards the site and so feeds directly into Quickmeme's economic logic. But it also speaks to the political critique of user labour described in Chapter 3 in that it clearly demonstrates the alienation associated with consumer labour. Control over where and how this image is distributed is curtailed for those whose labour has generated the product. Despite being its creator, Engels Cat did not belong to Sheamus. This is emblematised in the Quickmeme copyright logo just discernible in the bottom right-hand corner of the image. At the time, the Terms of Use Agreement of the site declared:

> By submitting User Content through the Services, you hereby do and shall grant us a world-wide, non-exclusive, royalty-free, fully paid, sublicensable and transferable license to use, edit, modify, reproduce, distribute, prepare derivative works of, display, perform, and other-wise fully exploit the User Content in connection with the Site, the Services and our (and our successors' and assigns') businesses, includ-ing without limitation for promoting and redistributing part of all of the Site or the Services (and derivative works thereof) in any media formats and through any media channels.
>
> (Quickmeme 2013)

The conditions also require that the creator grant non-exclusive licence for all users of the site to access their image, to generate derivative works from it and to distribute or perform the content as desired.

This legal claim is then bolstered by the technological affordances of the site to further limit the capacity for the image creator to distribute the image outside of the Quickmeme domain. These design features attempt to create the conditions of artificial scarcity that is the economic function of copyright. Sheamus labour in producing the image – conceiving the phras-ing and using the online tools to generate the meme – and my labour in searching for and sharing the bearded cat image is thus appropriated and "made strange" as it enters Quickmeme's copyright regime. The legal condi-tions and technological affordances of the site have effectively constrained Sheamus' agency over the product of his own labour, limiting his control over its future uses. In this aspect of the labour process, exchange-value is the dominant logic. This is the essence of alienation.

For this example, the consequences of this alienation are negligible. But when we consider the vast architecture of data collection that constitutes digital media – even this small and banal exchange intersects with at least three different databases – the consequences become more significant. The surveillance capacities of digital media and the relationality of databases mean that it is possible to gather finely grained pictures of a user's tastes and online activities, or at least those linked to a particular IP address. As I have explored more thoroughly elsewhere (Jarrett 2014), Google has a pretty thorough picture of my tastes and interests based on my search his-tory, the data gathered under my profiles distributed across Gmail, YouTube and Google Scholar and from the cookies embedded in browsers on my various devices. This is the version of "Kylie Jarrett" that Google mobilises in its personalisation algorithms, in Autosuggest, in the advertising options it displays for me and in the lists of search results it provides as answers to my searches. This digital proxy may not necessarily be a direct equivalent of the biological "Me," but it nevertheless functions as me within Google's domains. This "algorithmic identity" (Cheney-Lippold 2011) grows and adapts with each instance of data that are entered either actively or passively and attributed to the IP addresses and profiles that constitute the entity Google recognises as Kylie Jarrett.

In 1995, Mark Poster warned us against becoming dominated by such digital doppelgangers. Long before the ascendancy of search and the emergence of the social media network sites into which we pour various kinds of personal information, Poster raised concerns about the "database subjects" being built from credit card use, marketing surveys, insurance information, electoral registers and government institutional systems. He argued that the portraits of consumers built up in the relational databases of these institutions "become additional social identities as each individual is constituted for the computer, depending on the database in question, as a social agent. Without referring the database back to its owner and his or her interests or forward to the individual in question as a model of its adequacy or accuracy, we comprehend the database as a discursive production which inscribes positionalities of subjects according to its rules of formation" (Poster 1995, 87–88).

Like Poster's database subjectivities, the person Google and Facebook believe me to be lacks subtlety and is reductive and incomplete, and the subjectivity ascribed to me is shaped by the limitations of its data capture systems. However, that the subject is not really me becomes irrelevant. I am functionally and practically the subject cached in digital media's databases for any who draw on these resources. Ascribed (fallacious) qualities that are then inscribed (Poster 1995) into my digital existence, my online experience becomes that which is constituted by the database's expectations.

The Ballad of Kylie and Sheamus is saturated by mechanisms that capture, translate, relate, interpret and assemble user data into semi-autonomous database subjects. It is a mechanism for generating digital identities for both of us. These ascribed and inscribed identities go on to serve as the subjects for whom personalisation systems are built, for whom suggestions are made in Autocomplete and which can be sold to other marketing firms or digital media providers without our knowledge or specific consent. More importantly, it is the traces of this subject that state surveillance organisations will pick over to identify our roles in the economy and the polity. With this agency, the database subject assumes a capacity to act upon us and to potentially act against us. Given that Sheamus and I are politically active, the alienation of our data could have significant repercussions in the future. Thus, while it may not be important to Facebook's advertisers that we are interested in Marxist thinking, it may be of interest to other, as yet unknown, actors who access this construct. This alienation of our online personae – our limited ability to control their make-up and the ways in which they are used – is the most serious consequence of the alienation of consumer labour.

The labour involved in generating Engels Cat and in the Ballad of Kylie and Sheamus is alienated because neither Sheamus nor I have any control over the final products – the image itself and our user data. Short of activating limited privacy options, the use of adblocking software (which still does not stop Facebook collecting our user data), or not using the site at all, we cannot control how, where or in what ways these data are immediately used. We also cannot control what functions they may have as they enter into massive, aggregating marketing databases with untold future uses. This is the alienating capitalist logic enshrined in the Facebook's EULA. What we do on Facebook, as much as what we do in our employer's workplace, belongs to the capitalist who provides the raw materials for that productive activity and sells its products in the marketplace. For all its affective complexity, my interactions with Sheamus that are mediated by Facebook can be interpreted as a debased exchange, perpetuating the economic and social logics of capitalism.

Affective Resonance

If we apply Fortunati's model of domestic work's incorporation into capital to this analysis though, the question of alienation becomes more complicated. User labour has at least two distinct products. On one hand, there are the keystrokes and mouse clicks, the products of which are the raw user data that ultimately become the commodity sold to advertisers, the content of Engels Cat and this exchange. On the other hand, there is the affective and cognitive intensities that both result from the substantive qualities of these exchanges and which are also what drives the actions captured by the system's databases. Like the fruits of domestic work, the product of this activity – anger, pleasure, ennui, laughter, repulsion, self-affirmation – are encountered and experienced primarily as use-values.

The products of each phase of consumer labour, while interlinked, are not coterminous. Consider the difference between my liking a post, but not manifesting a physical response, and "liking" it by selecting the appropriate button on the site. Facebook cannot capitalise on the first instance of liking for, as I have argued in relation to Google's description as a "database of intention" (Jarrett 2014), it can only capture the material manifestation of our affective intensities. Facebook captures my clicks, not my affect, not least because these may not correspond. What animates behaviour is not necessarily co-extensive with its manifestation, for both of these arenas are shaped by complex psychological, social, cultural and technological factors. The underlying drives of online exchange – the more or less rational, more or less purposive, more or less knowable cognitions, experiences or embodied desires that shape them – cannot be read directly off a user's externalised activity. Google and Facebook, therefore, can read and capture the extensive output of my online activity, but this is merely the mapping of my behaviour rather than real insight into its underlying affect.

If, as Massumi (2002) has argued, affect is the autonomous energy that motivates and non-rationally shapes our practices and intentions, it is a state of potential that cannot be captured or confined within a body, perception or cognition. It can only be captured in the form of emotion that draws on pre-existing regimes of knowledge about our affective states. Our work for Facebook has a similar duality. It can be affective and unknowable and then codified in the form of "likes" or status updates, but it is only these latter forms that can be isolated and exploited. Facebook, therefore, does not exploit our affect per se, for it can only capture a limited manifestation of our embodied affective logics. No matter how sophisticated its technologies may be, our affective intensities are simply not available to its algorithms and data capture systems.

In the case of Facebook, the affective intensity must precede its incorporation into capital. In this instance, it was only *because* I consumed the affective intensity generated by Sheamus' original post that I produced the taste-identifying information and user data (the "like") that were exploited in the generation of Facebook's surplus. In media driven by affects and/ or forms of cultural capital, it is the registration of an affective intensity that generates the desire and capacity to interact and contribute data. As in Fortunati's description of domestic work where it is the consumption of the use-values of food, care and affect provided by the domestic worker that produces the labour-power which is then exploited by the capitalist in the workplace, the registration of affect by a user precedes the manifestation of the capacity, desire and intention to contribute user data. Even if these activities are produced almost simultaneously, they are analytically separate. It is the consumption of the use-values of affect by an individual that generates the labour-power that is then captured by the capitalist in the form of user data (the equivalent of labour-time).

Use-values, as I will go on to discuss in more detail shortly, are thus implicated throughout this model of accumulation, corresponding with, but not being co-extensive with, those commodities with exchange-value in this market. User affect is not user data. It is this duality that allows Facebook use to remain pleasurable and desirable, even for users like Sheamus and me who, by virtue of being media researchers, are more than typically aware of the exploitation at its core. The persistence of these use-values within commodified exchanges is what allows my Facebook friends to be my real friends, to return to the theme of an earlier chapter.

Indeed this is the case in my friendship with Sheamus. At the time of the interaction documented here, I had only met Sheamus once and he could, quite literally, have passed me on the street and I would not have recognised him. However, since we had friended each other on Facebook, he had become an important part of my everyday social experience and, consequently, my self-actualisation. Because he was in the final stages of completing his doctorate, Sheamus was a heavy Facebook user with an insightful ironic wit and Left politics akin to my own. His posts would consistently make me laugh out loud, literally. Even though I arguably did not know Sheamus in a meaningful way, if he had stopped posting to Facebook or defriended me, I would have suffered an acute sense of loss. Since the time of the exchange documented here, Sheamus and I have become good friends offline as well, and are involved in political activism together, often using Facebook to coordinate these activities. But in both periods, our relationship has been one that is rich in inalienable use-values, despite its "debased" beginnings in a context of capitalist exploitation. This is not to diminish the exploitative dynamic at the core of social media, nor to minimise the alienation that inheres to the identities we build up through these exchanges, but to underscore the persistence of use-values in that context. Like the housewife whose labour maintains a happy, healthy home of intrinsic social value within capitalist contexts, the affection between Sheamus and me is ineffable, inalienable and very real.

Disciplining the Digital Housewife

The lens provided by the concept of the Digital Housewife, however, also highlights an important and typically overlooked aspect of the work associated with this exchange; it is the work of social reproduction. As I also argue in Chapter 2, domestic work's role is to reproduce bodies and subjectivities appropriate for consumption by the labour process. As Federici (2012, 33) summarises: "Far from being a precapitalist structure, the family, as we know it in the 'West,' is a creation of capital for capital, as an institution that is supposed to guarantee the quantity and quality of labor power and its control." Not only is this function policed by the disciplining work of a variety of mechanisms ranging from parenting advice books, social etiquette guides to domestic violence, it is also disciplining in and of itself as it provides the normative conditions for the development of appropriate labouring bodies and subjectivities. Most importantly though, it does not serve this role because its products are directly commodified. What domestic work demonstrates is that the production of use-values serves a role in capitalism, even when those products are not directly transformed into commodity form.

This is evident in the Ballad of Kylie and Sheamus. It was entirely because of the affective intensities of this exchange – the inalienable use-values it generated – that it was possible for it to become saturated by capitalist logics. For instance, our pleasure in this interaction lead us both to use the Quickmeme site where we became further incorporated into alienating economies in the form of its copyright regime, in our viewing of its advertising displays and its alienation of our data. If I had not laughed at his original post, nor been driven to comment on his post by my affection for Sheamus, or my desire for reciprocal social affirmation, there would have been no data nor any reason to link with Quickmeme. This is perhaps an obvious point to make, but it is nevertheless an important argument because it challenges the logic that first privileges fiscal capital circuits over other circuits of exchange and which also assumes an autonomous economic actor for whom social contexts are separate and distinct from economic activity. It challenges the naturalisation of a binary divide between masculinised and feminised contexts that underpins much traditional Marxist thought.

We can develop this argument more thoroughly by returning to the consideration of gifting practices described in the previous chapter. Gift giving in Mauss estimation is a "total social phenomenon." Like domestic work, gifting is not "naturally" occurring but is governed by systems of rules that are translations of the social order of society. Each gift demands reciprocity, the form of which is shaped by, and is shaping of, the power relations associated with that object and the relational status of exchange participants. The rules of reciprocity governing a gift create social interdependencies and become "a web upon which social structure is organized" (Bergquist and Ljunberg 2001, 308). To receive a gift is to be bound to the politics of reciprocity encoded into that gift and through which it takes meaning. Not reciprocating gifts or using what Zelizer (2005) would describe as an inappropriate medium for the context (cash instead of in-kind goods, for instance) is to risk censure or various kinds of social exclusion. Reciprocal obligations such as these reflect and thereby perpetuate existing power dynamics, leading Marx to suggest that gift economies are inherently conservative (Marx 1973; Read 2003, 45).

Because of this involvement in producing and reproducing social relations, gifts are normatively disciplining. I mean here the Foucauldian concept of disciplining, which is not to be confused with negative, violent coercion or repressive outcomes. All social practices, including the pleasurable, encode and perform a particular mode of being associated with some ideological formation. They reward and punish, in more or less subtle ways, any individual's alignment with that ideology's behavioural norms. In this context, even to be socialised into a subjectivity expressing positively valued behaviours such as care for others, is an effect of disciplining techniques and technologies embedded throughout the wide social fabric. Discipline is a product of mechanisms of social reproduction like domestic work.

Because they are based primarily on social exclusion, gift practices discipline at the level of inalienable use-values. In this instance, Sheamus and I were rewarded for our use of Facebook with sensorily or affectively intense experiences – we laughed, we experienced interpersonal connection, we took pleasure in ideas. To have not contributed to the thread would have reduced the social interactions in our lives and the affective intensities that ensued from continuing that dialogue. In my case, the day would have been much less pleasurable without this exchange. To have not contributed would have "punished" me by increasing my sense of social alienation. Consequently, it was affect that disciplined us to labour for Facebook. A gift exchange like that represented here can therefore be associated with the reproduction of the social order *through use-values*; it is the inalienability of the gift that provides it with the resonance to effect social ordering. When that order is fundamentally shaped by capitalism, it is possible then for a gift to reproduce capitalist logics prior to, or even without, any transformation into exchange-value. This is not because it directly generates fiscal value, but because it generates subjective orientations that are *of value* to the maintenance and perpetuation of capitalist social relations.

Reproducing the Phatic Subject

What is re/produced through the consumption of inalienable use-values in social media is a subject disciplined to engage in practices that perpetuate the site's popularity and also its particular economic/cultural logic. For both of us, the successful intensification of social relations engendered in the production of Sheamus' status update, and the ensuing affirmations of "likes" and commentary, created rewards for engaging with others through a mediated microblogging site. It added value to our commitment of time and energy in Facebook by adding more and more inalienable sensation to the experience, encouraging us to continue mediating our friendship through its platforms. Thus, we were not only overtly disciplined into capitalist logics by the fixity of the code that limited our ability to subtract the fruits of our labour from the site, or by the EULA that articulated that agreement. We were also subtly disciplined by our own pleasures in this interaction. It was our mutual desire to make each other laugh that lead us from Facebook to Google and then Quickmeme, expanding our incorporation into capitalist systems. Giovanna Franca Dalla Costa (2008) describes how the love contract between a husband and wife is the only legitimate means through which capital can extort the "labours of love" that constitute domestic work. Similarly, it is only through the affective social bonds between Sheamus and me that Facebook could legitimately claim and exploit our labour.

This affective investment and the need for its constant renewal is the source of brand value – a key reciprocal obligation associated with exchange-value and central to the economics of digital media companies like Facebook which typically generate revenue only as they enter financial markets (Arvidsson and Colleoni 2012). To feel something – anything – via a digital media platform is to become a source of fiscal value (user data), but moreover to become the endlessly phatic subject who continues to express his or herself through, and because of, these mediated platforms. It is therefore to become a resource of capital. The intensification and extensification of affective exchange made possible in digital media thus bind our subjectivity to a communicative rich capitalism that demands affective responses from us and through which it reproduces the hegemony of particular sites. On Facebook, even negative responses can support further engagement with others and the site. In this way, the intensity of our affective responses becoming indexed to the legitimacy we attribute to the site and social networking sites (SNS) more generally as valid mediators of our interpersonal relations.

The Ballad of Kylie and Sheamus demonstrates the continued performance of the kinds of disciplined subjects willing, indeed often eager, to engage affectively through digital platforms. The constant becoming of digital media users as they create and recreate their online identity reflects a particular ideological position where even the most intimate of relations are open to, albeit never entirely captured by, the structures of exploitation associated with capital. Coté and Pybus say: "Through the user's built up network of social relations comes a sense of connectivity and belonging amidst the multiple on-line communities. And it is this sense of connection and participation in something that is larger then [sic] one's self, which provides the impetus for exploring new techniques and practices of communicative and affective productions" (2007, 96). Consequently, these affective relations serve as "the binding dynamic force which both animates those subjectivities and provides coherence to the networked relations" (Coté and Pybus 2007, 90).

When articulated within the broad range of similar interpellations across the social fabric, the cultural logics normalised through the affective intensities of commercial digital networks become powerful agents of social organisation. Thus Facebook, and SNS more generally, come to exert agency – to have power to shape our engagement with the world – *because of* the value generated in the intensity of the affective exchanges they facilitate. In the form of their use-value, the gifts exchanged between users contribute to the symbolic dominance of Facebook but more importantly to the naturalisation of the commercial mediation of our inalienable relationships. We reproduce ourselves as consumer labourers in these digital gift exchanges.

But this is not all that is re/produced here. The constant making and remaking of affective intensities also produces appropriate subjects for contemporary capitalism and neoliberal governance structures. In their study of MySpace, the most successful social media network precursor to Facebook, Coté and Pybus (2007) argue that it is in social networking sites that young people "learn to immaterial labour." Riffing from Paul Willis' famous study of the social reproduction of working class labour-power through the acculturation of working-class boys, they suggest that it is in social media that today's young people learn the communicative capacities appropriate for contemporary capitalism. I have similarly argued (Jarrett 2008) that interactivity in media disciplines users into the active, responsibilised and flexible subjectivity associated with neoliberal governance. In offering the illusion of autonomous control over communicative choices, and by encouraging the constant articulation and re-articulation of subjectivity, digital media is a powerful disciplining machinery. As I contend, it is a technological system that "enables the reproduction of neoliberal regimes of power by producing subjects fit for the continuation of that system of power and its particular regimes of control. The interactive Web 2.0 consumer is, therefore, not only the *subject of* advanced liberal government as previously argued, but is also *subject to* that particular form of governance" (2008, n.p.; emphasis in original). This is not a fixed and static subjection, but one that, like the subjectivities it describes, is dynamic and flexible – a recurring *disciplining*, not a single, fixed instance of discipline – and experienced as a legitimate source of pleasure. Digital media is thus a site where "users enthusiastically respond to the call, 'become subjects'" (Coté and Pybus 2007, 89) and to reproduce their own labour-power.

Despite the claims of Engels Cat, it would be problematic to call this an example of "false consciousness." What is described is the production of subjectivity that is more emergent, socially embedded and necessary to human and social flourishing than is implied by that term. It is certainly a subjectivity that lacks "authenticity," but no more than any other socially produced identity. Indeed, the disciplined subject of Facebook closely resembles the social subjects often attributed to pre-capitalist contexts in that they are intensely bound to the construction and maintenance of intimacy and connection with others. And while it is true that the endlessly phatic subject of social media may mask its own exploited status, and in doing so whitewash the problems of capitalism, this figure is not only an exploited labourer. This identity, and the work done to produce it, is shot through with the radical potential that inheres to all use-value production and consumption. It manifests the radical potential of the general intellect and multitude.

Federici (2012, 99) argues that the work of social reproduction is "simultaneously a production and valorization of desired human qualities and capacities, and an accommodation to the externally imposed standards of the labor market." These processes may be impossible to differentiate in practice, but there is still an inherent duality and tension to reproductive labour and its products that "suggests a world of conflicts, resistances, contradictions that have political significance" (2012, 99). This is the autonomous energy that can be the source of alternative politics and provide the impetus for further struggle. This is also inherent to the Ballad of Kylie and Sheamus and all other digitally mediated social exchanges. For Federici, reproductive work – the production and maintenance of bodies and subjectivities – is "ground zero" for political resistance and struggle. For all her/his value-generating capacity, in the many senses used here, the Digital Housewife nevertheless "haz" a potentially powerful consciousness.

Radical Thoughts

There are many more moments that could be analysed in the long biography of both the labour and products of this exchange. We could, for instance, have explored, how the Ballad of Kylie and Sheamus continues to do work in the moral economy of our friendship and within our wider social network. We could also have explored the labour involved in the production of the Lenin Cat meme that began our exchange and the economic and social processes by which it came to Sheamus' possession, or paid some further consideration to the copyright regimes that shape it and the original images that it uses. The particular cat image I extracted from a now unknown source on the web could be similarly interrogated. It would also be valuable to know more about the particular ways that Facebook, Quickmeme and Google have used our data and the particular fiscal value that can be articulated to them. It would also be interesting to explore the social and economic relationships enacted by this image as it circulates not as a link to Quickmeme, but as a quasi-autonomous .jpeg image, albeit one branded with the Quickmeme logo. There is a lot more that even the very simple exchange that is the Ballad of Kylie and Sheamus could tell us about the complex movements in and out of states of commodification of any form of labour and of any product generated by such work. What even this limited analysis has done though, is demonstrate the value of adopting a holistic approach to this form of value-creation, exploring both fiscal and social value in a complementary fashion. It has also demonstrated that processes of alienation and subjection are not simply aligned with the market but are intertwined with our sociality in ways that challenge certain Marxist orthodoxies.

To discuss the Ballad of Kylie and Sheamus through the lens provided by Marxist feminist frameworks is thus a radical act. No longer can we categorically state that this is an alienating or empowering exchange. Moreover we cannot find an adequate critical position by comparing the labour involved in it to mythical wholeness that exists "outside the market." This uncertainty about the political significance of this exploitation of labour is important for how we understand and critically appraise the work of consumers in digital media. There is a much greater complexity in how this activity works within capitalism than is usually attributed.

Marxist feminist arguments also suggest that the easy solution to capitalism provided by the kinds of "cooperative social relations" proposed by Fuchs (2008) is not viable. The critique described across the many pages of this book cannot simply celebrate this answer. Rather, it holds them to account by recognising how other forms of inequity manifest in these relations. We cannot simply remove the monetised economic contexts of capital and assume the end of exploitation. The long history of unpaid, feminised domestic work and the subjugation of women (and various others subaltern groups) documented in Chapter 2 puts the lie to that. If we lack the appropriate autonomy, we may no longer be working for capital in these contexts, but nevertheless be alienated from the fruits of our labour and coerced by more or less subtle mechanisms of social control. Not only then does the Digital Housewife represent a means by which to more fully understand the labour of consumers and its role in capitalism. The radical critique it presupposes has significant implications for the eternal question of critical theory: "What is to be done?" It is, then, to the broader implications of this figure for understanding other kinds of labour and for political activism to which I will turn in order to conclude this book.

References

Alonso, Fernando III. 2013. "The Reddit Sleuths Who Brought Down an Empire." *The Daily Dot*, July 1. http://www.dailydot.com/business/reddit-quickmeme-banned-miltz-brothers/.S.

Appadurai, Arjun. 1986. "Introduction: Commodities and the Politics of Value." In *The Social Life of Things: Commodities in Cultural Perspective*, edited by Arjun Appadurai, 3–63. Cambridge: Cambridge University Press.

Arruzza, Cinzia. 2013. *Dangerous Liaisons: The Marriages and Divorces of Marxism and Feminism*. Wales: Merlin Press.

Arvidsson, Adam and Elanor Colleoni. 2012. "Value in Informational Capitalism and on the Internet." *The Information Society* 28 (3): 135–150.

Bergquist, Magnus and Jan Ljungberg. 2001. "The Power of Gifts: Organizing Social Relationships in Open-source Communities." *Information Systems Journal* 11: 305–320.

Bolin, Göran. 2011. *Value and the Media: Cultural Production and Consumption in Digital Markets*. Farnham, Surrey: Ashgate.

Cheney-Lippold, John. 2011. "A New Algorithmic Identity: Soft Biopolitics and the Modulation of Control." *Theory, Culture and Society* 28 (6): 164–181.

Constine, Josh. 2012. "Facebook Lets Businesses Plug in CRM Email Addresses to Target Customers with Hyper-relevant Ads." *TechCrunch*, September 20. http://techcrunch.com/2012/09/20/facebook-crm-ads/.

Coté, Mark and Jennifer Pybus. 2007. "Learning to Immaterial Labour 2.0: MySpace and Social Networks." *ephemera* 7 (1): 88–106.

Dalla Costa, Giovanna Franca. 2008. *The Work of Love: Unpaid Housework, Poverty and Sexual Violence at the Dawn of the 21st Century*. Translated by Enda Brophy. New York: Autonomedia.

Federici, Silvia. 2012. *Revolution at Point Zero: Housework, Reproduction and Feminist Struggle*. Oakland, California: PM Press.

Fuchs, Christian. 2008. *Internet and Society: Social Theory in the Information Age*. London: Routledge.

Fortunati, Leopoldina. 1995. *The Arcane of Reproduction: Housework, Prostitution, Labour and Capital*. Translated by Hilary Creek. New York: Autonomedia.

Heyman, Rob and Jo Pierson. 2013. "Blending Mass Self-communication with Advertising in Facebook and LinkedIn: Challenges for Social Media and User Empowerment." *International Journal of Media & Cultural Politics* 9 (3): 229–245.

Jarrett, Kylie. 2008. "Interactivity is Evil! A Critical Investigation of Web 2.0." *First Monday* 13 (3). doi:http://dx.doi.org/10.5210/fm.v13i3.2140.

———. 2014. "A Database of Intention?" In *Society of the Query Reader: Reflections on Web Search*, edited by René König and Miriam Rasch, 16–29. Amsterdam: Institution of Network Cultures.

Kopytoff, Igor. 1986. "The Cultural Biography of Things: Commoditization as Process." In *The Social Life of Things: Commodities in Cultural Perspective*, edited by Arjun Appadurai, 64–91. Cambridge: Cambridge University Press.

Lee, Micky. 2014. "From Googol to Guge: The Political Economy of a Search Engine." In *The Audience Commodity in the Digital Age: Revisiting a Critical Theory of Commercial Media*, edited by Lee McGuigan and Vincent Manzerolle, 175–191. New York: Peter Lang.

Marx, Karl. 1973. *Grundrisse: Foundations of the Critique of Political Economy.* Translated by Martin Nicolaus. London: Penguin. Originally published 1939.

Massumi, Brian. 2002. *Parables for the Virtual: Movement, Affect, Sensation.* Durham and London: Duke University Press.

Meehan, Eileen R. 1984. "Ratings and the Institutional Approach: A Third Answer to the Commodity Question." *Critical Studies in Mass Communication* 1 (2): 216–25.

Poster, Mark. 1995. *The Second Media Age.* Cambridge, UK: Polity Press.

Quickmeme. 2013. "Licence Grant." Accessed 23 April 2013. http://buzz.quick-meme.com/2013/04/23/quickmeme-terms-of-use.

Read, Jason. 2003. *The Micro-politics of Capital: Marx and the Prehistory of the Present.* Albany: State University of New York Press.

Skeggs, Beverley. 2014. "Value Beyond Value? Is Anything Beyond the Logic of Capital?" *British Journal of Sociology* 65 (1): 1–20.

Zelizer, Viviana A. 2005. *The Purchase of Intimacy.* New Jersey: Princeton University Press.

Conclusion
Beyond Consumer Labour

The Digital Housewife as s/he has been articulated throughout this book does not supply us with a simple narrative of subjection nor one of celebration, but forces us into a more considered reflection on capitalist structures' capture, use and reliance upon the culturally significant activities undertaken by digital media consumers. I have first documented a set of dominant ideas about consumer labour and their basis in the work of Autonomist Marxism and, in particular, in the work of Hardt and Negri. I then reiterated their argument that contemporary capital is driven by the cognitive, communicative and affective energies of workers and consumers alike and then placed the digital media user's activity in that context. The book began, then, by aligning itself with the Autonomist Marxist argument that describes the incorporation of the whole of life into capitalism's social factory and, in accordance with that, associated digital media consumers' activities with exploited labour.

The argument in this book then went on to apply a Marxist feminist critique of domestic work to this position, demonstrating that there is a longer history to immaterial labour's exploitation and the existence of a social factory than usually ascribed. This set the scene for using more feminist frameworks, including a few radical ideas about domestic work to understand this labour more thoroughly. These frameworks suggest that there is a rich hybridity to both domestic work and consumer labour that allow them to be both socially meaningful and exploited. They also suggest that there is not a singular, uni-directional and exhaustive incorporation of such work into capitalist circuits. I argued that work and its products have long life cycles that potentially involve moving in and out of commodity relations. Subsequently, I identified Fortunati's model of the two-phase incorporation of domestic work as a useful framework for interrogating consumer labour to document such processes of commodification and decommodification. I then applied this model to the example of a banal Facebook exchange, demonstrating the complexity of how socially and affectively meaningful labour is incorporated into, and how it exceeds, capital. The goal of this book has been to argue for this more holistic approach to understanding labour and capitalism.

It is difficult, though, to contain this analysis to its putative subject: consumer labour in digital media. The final contention of this book is that

Marxist feminism is a useful tool for understanding various kinds of paid labour, but particularly those associated with the creative, high-technology or cultural industries. The critique enabled by Marxist feminist analysis of domestic work also has implications for how we must analyse capital and subsequently, the forms of struggle in which we need to engage. Outlining some of these further applications of Marxist feminist frameworks is the work of this short concluding chapter. It will place the Digital Housewife in a wider narrative, revealing the greater salience of this figure and the theoretical frameworks through which s/he is animated.

Creative Work

The multiphasic model of incorporation into capital of the kind proposed here is particularly valuable for understanding creative work such as that within the paid digital media economy, particularly when it draws on the insights about processes of commodification and decommodification described by Kopytoff (1986) and Appadurai (1986). This is an approach being used by Julia Velkova and Peter Jakobsson (2015; Velkova 2014) who are producing research exploring the shifting valorisation regimes at play in the work of independent animation film producers, noting the complex ways in which moral and fiscal economies intersect in the logics of these workers. Their approach, and the one advocated in this book, also accord with that of Potts et al. (2008), who propose exploring digital media production as a series of overlapping and emergent social network markets, each with a different valorisation system. While I would argue that Potts et al.'s economic model is slightly limited in that it does not inherently manifest the criticality associated with a Marxist paradigm, it nevertheless offers a useful tool for examining the long biographies of labour and the shifting dynamics of commodification within that work. Similarly, the "circuits of labour" model proposed by Jack Linchuan Qiu et al. (2014) to explore the work associated with the iPhone from manufacturing to everyday use also offers a multiphased approach to understanding work and value generation in digital media contexts. Marxist feminist models of domestic labour though, with their necessary engagement with a longer value chain than more orthodox Marxist approaches, seem ready-made for exploring the dynamics of such labour, but with an integrated critical explanatory force.

However, it is the intersection of culture and economics, and the importance paid to the ways subjection emerges from that nexus within Marxist feminist critiques of domestic work, that I suggest is its greatest tool for understanding the relations of paid production. Marxist and radical feminist positions, particularly when allied together, recognise that the patriarchal, subjective dimensions of capitalism shape work, especially the primary division of labour that identifies domestic work as unproductive, "natural" (for women) and outside regimes of compensation. A broader application of this concept suggests that any paid labour context will include various subjective structures that materially support, or potentially undermine, both the capital relation and other relations of dominance (Adkins and Lury 1999). For instance, women and men do not encounter the same work in the same way because of the pre-existing subjugation of women in patriarchy (Pateman 1988). The prevalence of sexual harassment and the continuing existence of "glass ceilings" attest to this fact. These subjective and subjugating structures are important to identify if we are to truly understand work.

Moreover, these structures are deeply embedded in personal and social identities and so are not experienced as alienating impositions. The Marxist feminist framework that allows us to see that domestic work plays a role in reproducing capitalism through the construction and consumption of use-values also allows us to understand that subjugating processes are often encountered in the form of pleasurable, inalienable relations. This occurs in the marriage contract or, for digital media work, in the ostensible autonomy of the labouring subject of the creative industries. Attention to the ways in which the material relations of capitalism are produced and reproduced in the subjective qualities of workers, both in and outside the factory walls, is therefore an important tool for understanding contemporary capitalism.

As Lazzarato (2014, 52) sees it, contemporary capitalism demonstrates the successful integration of the desire for the type of "self-steering Self" described by Nikolas Rose (1999) and similarly Berardi (2009) and Virno (1996). This dynamic is clearly evident in the paid work of the creative/cultural industries in which digital media production resides. In this labour context, the distribution of cultural capital, or "cool," serves as a powerful motivator for working and also as the myth that conceals or "renders unsayable" the inequities and insecurities of the industry (Gill 2002; Liu 2004; Ross 2003). "Cool" here can be allied with freedom and agency. For Angela McRobbie (2003), artists are pioneers of the contemporary economy because the creative autonomy they are ostensibly offered – the promise of non-alienated labour – can be mobilised as a tool to encourage the continued exploitation, precarious labour conditions and under-compensation of the creative sector. Even outside this particular industry, the directive to find work that "you love," or indeed to find love in your work, has become an important disciplining technology of capitalism (Duffy 2015; Gibson 2003; Gill 2007; Gill and Pratt 2008; Neff et al. 2005; Thrift 2005; Tokumitsu 2014).

This is Ergin Bulut's (2015) argument (discussed in *Work and Play in the Games Industry* in Chapter 3) about the exploited and precarious labour of game-testing where "fun" and passion become the motivation for work that is notoriously precarious. Fred Turner (2009, 88) similarly documents how, at Google, the framing of engineering as a form of "artistic creativity"' has allowed the firm's workers to "reimagine themselves collectively as autonomous creators and restore to their labor, if only for a while, the sense of social value that is so often falsely claimed for it by corporate marketers." This couples with the expansive employee perks such as high salaries and benefits, on-site childcare, catering, laundry facilities and a variety of leisure facilities such as gyms and foosball tables that has Google consistently top-ping the Fortune "best company to work for" lists and which are integral to its "cool" image (Stabile 2008). However, these conditions also form the "cultural infrastructure" that supports the unsustainable work practices associated with the high-tech industry.

The desire for creative self-expression coupled with an entrepreneurial subjectivity is the cornerstone of the creative industries (Gill 2002; Leadbeter and Oakley 1999). The mobilisation of these "artistic subjectivities" also has wider economic repercussions, as evidenced in the continued salience of the concept of "bohemia" and the romantic image of the artist in urban gentrification such as that associated with the Silicon Valley social factory. These kinds of geographic, economic and social processes are described by Kristin Forkert (2013) as "culture-driven." To understand labour in these sectors, and its capacity for generating value across a wide range of economic fields, the subjective dimensions of work, and their relationship to social and personal use-values, cannot be ignored.

Economy, Culture, Self, Labour

The interconnection between economy, culture, self and labour that the Digital Housewife articulates is also important as a critical tool. As a matter of urgency, the digital media sector must be interrogated for the ways in which the dynamics of subjectivity impact on labouring practices. When men out-number women 4 to 1 in the large technology companies (Lien 2015) and more than half of employees in most major technology companies iden-tify as "white" (Forrest 2014) there is a clear problem with the relations of power in the sector. This inequity is not only to do with hiring practices but also with the privileging of particular subjectivities in these workplaces. Rosalind Gill (2011, 35–37) describes the mobilisation of a static idea about the relationship between gender and technical abilities in the discourses of the new media workers she studied. Elsewhere, she describes gendered exclusions generated by contract work emerging from an "old boys net-work" (Gill 2002; O'Brien 2014; 2015).

A *Harvard Business Review* study in 2008 (Hewlett et al. 2008), updated in 2014 (Hewlett 2014), found that over 50 per cent of women leave these industries due to social contexts at work and a "hostile" male culture. "Gender bias is the common denominator, manifesting in cultures hostile to women: the 'lab-coat culture' in science that glorifies extreme hours spent toiling over experiments and penalizes people who need the flexibility to, say, pick up their kids from day care; engineering's 'hard-hat culture' whose pervasive *maleness* makes women do a 'whistle-check' on their work clothes to avoid a barrage of catcalls; and tech's 'geek workplace culture' that women in our study often compared to a super-competitive fraternity of arrogant nerds" (Hewlett 2014, n.p.). As Judy Wajcman (2010, 146) summarises, because of the "engrained cultures of masculinity" within these industries, "women are being asked to exchange major aspects of their gender identity for a masculine version, whilst there is no similar 'degendering' process prescribed for men."

Even in industries where women are present in greater numbers than the high-technology or digital media sectors, inequality is rife as traditional gender politics (re)-assert themselves. Christina Scharff (2012; Gill 2002), for instance, describes the repudiation of feminism by young women in the workplace based in assumptions about the cultural valence of this political alignment and a consequent move towards (typically unsuccessful) individualised responses to labour inequities rather than collective struggle against systemic problems. Adkins and Lury (1999; Adkins 1995; 2001; 2002; Veijola and Jokinen 2008) also provide a valuable analysis of how feminine gender performances such as affect and embodied communicative ability become part of value creation in the contemporary workplace, but because these are assumed "natural" behaviours of women, male colleagues are more often acknowledged for this performance. In creative workplaces driven by immaterial labour, the rewards, and indeed the very possibility, of performing the appropriate flexible, feminised, entrepreneurial subject are not available to all in equal measure. Ironically perhaps, gender mobility in the workplace is itself highly gendered (Adkins 2002) and, as Dan Irving's (2015) study of the labour experiences of twenty-three US and Canadian trans women reveals, generative of material and economic deprivation for those for whom such mobility is actively and/or passively rejected.

Despite the varying conclusions and focus of all of these studies, what is consistent is that cultural and social processes of subject making are integral to relations of production and cannot be considered separately. This is not a matter of teaching women to "lean in" and claim masculine corporate power as Facebook CEO Sheryl Sandberg (Sandberg and Scovell 2013) advocates, but understanding and intervening in the subjective structuring of labour in patriarchal capitalism. Gender, race and other identity politics work as both cause and effect of material exploitation and labour inequalities. If we are to critique contemporary capitalism, particularly with a view to effecting industry or wider sociopolitical change around work, we must meaningfully engage with these arenas of subjectivity and their materialisation and reproduction in labour.

For instance, it would be useful to understand more about what "cool" means to people in the creative industries, how it comes to be constituted as an object of desire and how its articulation in labour practices draws on and/or reproduces social categories of exclusion such as gender and race. Not only must we ask how "cool" is mobilised in facilitating the exploitation of workers, but also interrogate the economic, social and personal consequences for various workers and their families of the privileges granted to the masculinised figure of the independent, autonomous creative actor. We must draw on Marxist feminism's insights and assume the existence of power relations impacting on how work is structured that intersect with class, but cannot be reduced to only that.

McRobbie (2010) underscores this point, provocatively suggesting that class may be in its twilight as a critical tool for understanding labour. Class politics, she says, are forged in a particular antagonistic struggle between capital and labour, predicated on the particular and distinctive relation to work associated with industrialisation. In a context where work has become less distinct from life, and where, as I have argued here, we recognise that life has always been part of work, we become much less engaged solely as "workers." Consequently, class is not necessarily the key frame through which we engage with, understand or experience our exploitation. McRobbie argues that by drawing almost solely on class as their central antagonism, Hardt and Negri are unable to see "the centrality of gender and sexuality in a post-Fordist era, with the result that there is a failure to consider the meaning of what is often referred to as the feminisation of work" (2010, 62). She asks: "Who exactly are the exemplary class (non)-subjects called into being by the labour process? Is it not the case that the gender or ethnicity of such subjects provides a more significant dimension in the forms and the locations of struggle?" (2010, 62). I would not, perhaps, be as dismissive of class as a continuing cultural organisational principle, but McRobbie's point that what has often been disregarded as mere "identity politics" are, in fact, integral to the configuration of contemporary capitalism is profoundly important. To return to a quote from Judith Butler (1997) used earlier, identity politics are not "merely cultural."

Activism and Critique

What the framework of domestic work also does is de-naturalise the subject of critical theory and political economy. In doing so, it insists that we reconsider the assumption that re-shaping or overturning capitalist class relations will necessarily end the exploitation, alienation and other pernicious effects of social inequality associated with capitalism. It cannot be assumed that there is a universal experience of commons-based production. Therefore, even when capitalist relations have been supplanted, there may remain other social structures that perpetuate similar inequalities. This is evident when we consider how women are obligated by sexual and marriage contracts to be given as gifts in various patriarchal systems including capitalism, a practice Claude Lévi-Strauss (1969, 481; Pateman 1988) defines as "the supreme rule of the gift." Rather than merely willing a return to a mythical autonomous, unified, self-possessed subject who exists prior to capitalism (or ideology generally) (Weeks 2007, 234; Eisenstein 1979), it is important to identify the dominant arrangements of power/knowledge in order to rearrange them so truly alternative subject positions that articulate resistant politics can be generated. The reproductive role of domestic work and its construction within and through inequitable power relations that is revealed by the Digital Housewife also tells us that the immediate solution to capitalism's inequalities is not *inherent* to the sphere primarily concerned with the production of use-values. While it can and must emerge in that context, as Federici suggests, it is not an intrinsic quality of that domain.

This framing raises issues for the concept of multitude as it is articulated by Hardt and Negri (see Chapter 1) which is often posed as the model of contemporary activist politics. While Hardt and Negri certainly provide a complicated and sometimes contradictory description of this concept, there is a tendency to assume that there is something inherently progressive in the energies that emerge from "the commons." This often draws on assumptions that the "social space of communication" (2005, 222) from which multitude emerges is somehow organic and not riven by deeply entrenched power imbalances and divisions that support and reproduce capitalism as well as other inequalities. For instance, in *Commonwealth*, they call on Marx from the *Economic and Philosophical Manuscripts* to claim that, when freed from private property relations, labour engages all of our human relations such as smell, taste, sight, loving, thinking, contemplating. They go on to say: "When labor and production are conceived in this expanded form, crossing all domains of life, bodies can never be eclipsed and subordinated to any transcendent measure or power" (2009, 38). They propose that the answer to the problems of capitalism therefore lies in the commons for, in this context, "valorization and accumulation necessarily take on a social rather than an individual character" (2009, 283).

However, if gifting – the model typically used to exemplify commons-based exchanges – can be, and arguably typically is, conservative in its social effects, the commons can only take on established social dynamics (such as its patriarchal and racist structures). Therefore, we cannot simply assume that in the near future radical political action emerging from multitude will articulate positive outcomes for all, or even manifest anti-capitalist sentiment. McRobbie points out that the emphasis on the "putative creativity of the multitude" in Hardt and Negri's work has often lead to a "naïve celebration of the vitality and apparent proto-communism of contemporary economic forms, while ignoring the aggressive neo-liberal underpinning of immaterial labour and the forms of biopower which shape up amenable kinds of subjectivities, giving rise to a new kind of society of control" (2010, 69).

This dynamic can be seen in Mathieu O'Neil's (2009) study of open-source production in Wikipedia. Often feted as the leading example of alternative commons-based production, O'Neil's study reveals that Wikipedia manifests hierarchical systems and power struggles that delimit the agency of women and other subaltern actors. Wikipedia may in fact *be* the commons, but access to that commons is not open to all on the same terms. Like other kinds of spaces, it is organised by hierarchies of access and agency that define its economy. While for Hardt and Negri such inequitable relations may merely be inauthentic expressions of the commons, their failure to be suitably cautious about the nature of power residing in social relations and to address the political relevance of existing divisions within the working class (Federici 2006; Pateman 1988), undermines a simple equation between multitude and progressive political change.

Furthermore, recognition of the value to capitalism of our inalienable affect collapses the traditional Marxist alienation critique because it breaks the necessary correlation of non-market activity and freedom. It challenges the assumption that our labour that is not directly commodified is automatically outside of market logics and therefore inherently self-actualising. This is the same logic through which domestic work has been defined as "natural" and consequently devalued. It is also this logic that cast the private sphere, women's labour and women's bodies as the "reward" or compensation for the iniquities of capital (Adkins 2008; Federici 2004; Folbre 1991). This idea also underpins the division of labour between public and private domains that was essential to establishing the capitalist mode of accumulation (Dalla Costa and James 1975; Federici 2004). To reproduce that logic in the political critique of capitalism seems not only misogynist, but also counter-productive. As Federici argues in a 2006 talk at Bluestockings Radical Bookstore in New York, the "gender-blindness" of much contemporary capitalist critique renders it an inadequate tool for political struggle. She says: "It assumes that the reorganization of production is doing away with the power relations and hierarchies that exist within the working class on the basis of race, gender and age, and therefore it is not concerned with addressing these power relations; it does not have the theoretical and political tools to think about how to tackle them" (2006, n.p.).

Activists on the Left need to look more closely at the subjectivating dynamics of all social systems in order to identify future subject positions that will reflect a more equitable distribution of power and to deploy this alongside critique of the ways in which we are "enslaved" by capitalist machinery (Lazzarato 2014). The feminist slogan from the 1970s that the personal is political remains not only apposite but also useful for the work that needs to be done. We must be attuned to, critical of and intervene in the micropolitics of everyday life. The focus needs to be on re-articulating the hegemonic value system and economic order but also on how to produce and reproduce subjects that can be mobilised in establishing and maintaining these politics. Political change cannot be wished into being but requires active participation and action. For a political avant garde, that requires mechanisms to expand alignment with their political goals. As Lazzarato (2014, 38–39) says, revolutionary political action "must operate against both subjection and enslavement, refusing the former's injunction to inhabit certain places and roles in the social distribution of labor while constructing, problematizing, and reconfiguring the machinic assemblage, in other words, a world and its possibilities."

How this happens in a context already saturated with capitalist subjective dynamics is an important challenge but one that is rarely effectively addressed. In *Commonwealth* (2009; Hardt 2011), Hardt and Negri raise concern about the political direction that may emerge from multitude in their discussion of love as the "field of battle" against capitalism. They suggest that, because love can be diverted to "production of corrupt forms of the common" (2009, 169), it is important that it be shaped in the right directions; it is not about *being* multitude but *making* multitude. "The deployment of love has to be learned and new habits have to be formed through the collective organization of our desires, a process of sentimental and political education. Habits and practices consolidated in new social institutions will constitute our now transformed human nature" (2009, 196). What is missing from their analysis is any detail about mechanisms for producing this new subjectivity. There is more required than merely intervening in the activity of ideological state apparatus to "change the message" to ensure successful reproduction of radical concepts. Rather, it is about effecting and sustaining change in power relations at both social and interpersonal levels. Certainly some of these changes may emerge from altered production relations, but others require a holistic politics working at the level of subjectivity and identity.

This is where feminist critiques are again of intrinsic value. The making of non-capitalist subjects, as lived experience and as an analytical site, has historically been attributed to the domain of domestic work, interpersonal, sociocultural relations and individual psychology – effectively outside of "the economic." Consequently, it has been a subject of critical interrogation primarily by feminists (of all stripes) as well as queer, post-colonial and other cultural theorists. Insights from these theoretical contexts, therefore, can demonstrate how the necessary re-organisation of subjectivity can proceed. For instance, the refusal of housework movement, as Federici (2006; Weeks 2007; 2011) argues, teaches us to reject work that only reproduces us as labour-power, which leaves work that reproduces us as social beings intact.

Feminist approaches also teach us that political movements that function without consideration for the reproduction of their members are destined to fail. We must also ensure our politics focused on justice and equity permeate all facets of our lives, recognising and building alliances against other destructive socially produced divisions such as age, sex, sexuality, ability or race. Federici says: "We have to ensure that we do not only confront capital at the time of the demonstration, but that we confront it collectively at every moment of our lives" (2006, n.p.). It may be a little churlish to critique the obviously schematic analysis of Hardt and Negri because it fails to attend to these details and I certainly am not able to provide particular models of the subject and the processes of its (re)-production in this book. But the omission of research that investigates these domains and provides models for action – feminist theories and Cultural Studies – in their idea of multitude seems self-defeating. Combining the critical insights provided by Marxist economics with these other domains seems to be a valuable route for understanding current social dynamics, but also for answering the question of what must be done.

Back to the Digital Housewife

This conclusion seems to have wandered far from questions of consumer labour and the specificity of digital media; far from the Digital Housewife. But this has been a deliberate and legitimate move. Being emblematic of the social factory, consumer labour in digital media captures in its remit the premise that all of life is saturated by mechanisms that support capitalism, either in the production of economically valuable data or of individual subjectivities. At the same time it also offers insight into how these practices offer resistance and value beyond capitalist capture. To critique the labouring consumer is thus to critique a model of the contemporary capitalist system. This renders the Digital Housewife a valuable tool for engaging broadly with contemporary capitalism as a mode of production but also as a site of struggle.

Consequently, in documenting a framework for thinking about the role played by digital media's consumers, my goal was never merely to provide a better economic or critical model for understanding this realm (although this was important and central). It was also to document and highlight the value of Marxist feminist critiques for critical thought, identifying the rich insights they can provide into everyday life under capitalism. The elision of this analytical lens from Internet research but also from the particular suite of Marxist ideas increasingly being brought to bear upon contemporary capitalism is counter-productive. We will never understand capitalism as an economic and/or social system unless we appreciate all the forms of oppression it entails. The argument traced in this book that the Digital Housewife brings valuable insight thus has consequences reaching beyond the ways in which we conceptualise consumer labour. It penetrates directly into more important arenas of exploitation that require urgent action.

I want to close this book by returning to the anecdote that opens Chapter 2 in which I described the wholesale rejection of my claim that capitalism has always needed immaterial labour. My chagrin at the time, and my ongoing irritation at the absence of engagement with domestic work in studies of labour in digital media and in Autonomist Marxism, was thus not mere petulance. It was a profound frustration that such a useful and important framework had been left lying fallow. Not only does a Marxist feminist framework usefully describe the incorporation into capital of consumer labour, it has vital importance for how we conceive of political engagement. It is my hope that in the preceding pages I have done justice to the arguments of the many theorists, mostly women, whose work has been so profoundly important to how I conceptualise my own politics. I also hope that others take value from the many insights I have gained about my own agency while researching the Digital Housewife. For Silvia Federici (2012), domestic work and arenas of social reproduction are "ground zero" for revolution. In claiming our capacity to resist our subjection, and by building better subjective structures within our personal and professional contexts, we can also rewrite our subjection to capitalist patriarchy and from there begin to dismantle its infrastructure. This is the key lesson I have learned from the Digital Housewife.

References

Adkins, Lisa. 1995. *Gendered Work: Sexuality, Family and the Labour Market.* Buckingham: Open University Press.

———. 2001. "Cultural Feminization: 'Money, Sex and Power' for Women." *Signs* 26 (3): 669–695.

———. 2002. *Revisions: Gender and Sexuality in Late Modernity.* Buckingham: Open University Press.

———. 2008. "From Retroactivation to Futurity: The End of the Sexual Contract?" *NORA – Nordic Journal of Feminist and Gender Research* 16 (3): 182–201.

Adkins, Lisa and Celia Lury. 1999. "The Labour of Identity: Performing Identities, Performing Economies." *Economy and Society* 28 (4): 598–614.

Appadurai, Arjun. 1986. "Introduction: Commodities and the Politics of Value." In *The Social Life of Things: Commodities in Cultural Perspective*, edited by Arjun Appadurai, 3–63. Cambridge: Cambridge University Press.

Berardi, Franco "Bifo". 2009. *The Soul at Work: From Alienation to Autonomy.* Translated by Francesca Cadel and Giuseppina Mecchia. LA: Semiotext(e).

Bulut, Ergin. 2015. "Playboring in the Tester Pit: The Convergence of Precarity and the Degradation of Fun in Videogame Testing." *Television and New Media* 16 (3): 240–258.

Butler, Judith. 1997. "Merely Cultural." *Social Text* 15 (3–4): 265–277.

Dalla Costa, Mariarosa and Selma James. 1975. *The Power of Women and the Subversion of the Community.* 3rd edition. London: Falling Wall Press.

Duffy, Brooke Erin. 2015. "The Romance of Work: Gender and Aspirational Labour in the Digital Cultural Industries." *International Journal of Cultural Studies* Online First. doi:10.1177/1367877915572186.

Eisenstein, Zillah R. 1979. "Developing a Theory of Capitalist Patriarchy and Socialist Feminism." In *Capitalist Patriarchy and the Case for Socialist Feminism*, edited by Zillah R. Eisenstein, 5–40. New York: Monthly Review Press.

Federici, Silvia. 2004. *Caliban and the Witch: Women, the Body and Primitive Accumulation.* New York: Autonomedia.

———. 2006. "Precarious Labour: A Feminist Viewpoint." Lecture at Bluestockings Radical Bookstore, New York, October 28. *In the Middle of the Whirlwind.* https://inthemiddleofthewhirlwind.wordpress.com/precarious-labor-a-feminist-viewpoint/.

———. 2012. *Revolution at Point Zero: Housework, Reproduction and Feminist Struggle.* Oakland, California: PM Press.

Folbre, Nancy. 1991. "The Unproductive Housewife: Her Evolution in Nineteenth Century Thought." *Signs* 16 (3): 463–484.

Forkert, Kirsten. 2013. "The Persistence of Bohemia." *City: Analysis of Urban Trends, Culture, Theory, Policy, Action* 17 (2): 149–163.

Forrest, Conner. 2014. "Diversity Stats: 10 Tech Companies That Have Come Clean." *Tech Republic*, August 28. http://www.techrepublic.com/article/diversity-stats-10-tech-companies-that-have-come-clean/.

Gibson, Chris. 2003. "Cultures at Work: Why 'Culture' Matters in Research on the 'Cultural' Industries." *Social & Cultural Geography* 4 (20): 201–215.

Gill, Rosalind. 2002. "Cool, Creative and Egalitarian? Exploring Gender in Project-based New Media Work in Europe." *Information, Communication and Society* 5 (1): 70–89.

————. 2007. *Technobohemians of the New Cybertariat? New Media Work in Amsterdam a Decade After the Web*. Amsterdam: Institute of Network Cultures. http://networkcultures.org/blog/publication/no-01-technobohemians-or-the-new-cybertariat-rosalind-gill/.

————. 2011. "'Life as a Pitch': Managing Self in New Media Work." In *Managing Media Work*, edited by Mark Deuze, 249–262. London: Sage.

Gill, Rosalind and Andy Pratt. 2008. "In the Social Factory? Immaterial Labour, Precariousness and Cultural Work." *Theory, Culture & Society* 25 (7–8): 1–30.

Hardt, Michael. 2011. "For Love or Money." *Cultural Anthropology* 26 (4): 676–682.

Hardt, Michael and Antonio Negri. 2005. *Multitude*. London: Penguin.

————. 2009. *Commonwealth*. Cambridge, Massachusetts: Harvard University Press.

Hewlett, Sylvia Ann. 2014. "What's Holding Women Back in Science and Technology Industries." *Harvard Business Review*, March 13. https://hbr.org/2014/03/whats-holding-women-back-in-science-and-technology-industries.

Hewlett, Sylvia Ann, Carolyn Buck Luce and Lisa J. Servon. 2008. "Stopping the Exodus of Women in Science." *Harvard Business Review*, June. https://hbr.org/2008/06/stopping-the-exodus-of-women-in-science.

Irving, Dan. 2015. "Performance Anxieties." *Australian Feminist Studies* 30 (83): 50–64.

Kopytoff, Igor. 1986. "The Cultural Biography of Things: Commoditization as Process." In *The Social Life of Things: Commodities in Cultural Perspective*, edited by Arjun Appadurai, 64–91. Cambridge: Cambridge University Press.

Lazzarato, Maurizio. 2014. *Signs and Machines: Capitalism and the Production of Subjectivity*. Los Angeles: Semiotext(e).

Leadbeter, Charles and Kate Oakley. 1999. *The Independents: Britain's New Cultural Entrepreneurs*. London: Demos.

Lévi-Strauss, Claude. 1969. *The Elementary Structures of Kinship*. Translated by James Harle Bell, John Richard von Sturmer and Rodney Needham. Boston: Beacon Press. Originally published 1949.

Lien, Tracey. 2015. "Why are Women Leaving the Tech Industry in Droves?" *LA Times*, February 22. http://www.latimes.com/business/la-fi-women-tech-20150222-story.html#page=1.

Liu, Alan. 2004. *The Laws of Cool: Knowledge Work and the Culture of Information*. Chicago: University of Chicago Press.

McRobbie, Angela. 2003. "'Everyone is Creative.' Artists as Pioneers of the New Economy?" Be Creative project. http://www.k3000.ch/becreative/texts/text_5.html.

————. 2010. "Reflections on Feminism, Immaterial Labour and the Post-Fordist Regime." *New Formations* 70: 60–76.

Neff, Gina, Elizabeth Wissinger and Sharon Zukin. 2005. "Entrepreneurial Labour Among Cultural Producers: 'Cool' Jobs in 'Hot' Industries." *Social Semiotics* 15 (3): 307–334.

O'Brien, Anne. 2014. "'Men *Own* Television': Why Women Leave Media Work." *Media, Culture & Society* 36 (8): 1,207–1,218.

————. 2015. "Producing Television and Reproducing Gender." *Television & New Media* 16 (3): 259–274.

O'Neil, Mathieu. 2009. *Cyber-chiefs: Autonomy and Authority in Online Tribes*. London: Pluto Press.

Pateman, Carole. 1988. *The Sexual Contract*. Cambridge, UK: Polity Press.

Potts, Jason, Stuart Cunningham, John Hartley and Paul Ormerod. 2008. "Social Network Markets: A New Definition of the Creative Industries." *Journal of Cultural Economy* 32 (3): 167–185.

Qiu, Jack Linchuan, Melissa Gregg and Kate Crawford. 2014. "Circuits of Labor: A Labor Theory of the iPhone Era." *TripleC* 12 (2). http://www.triple-c.at/index.php/tripleC/article/view/540/607.

Rose, Nikolas. 1999. *Powers of Freedom: Reframing Political Thought*. Cambridge: Cambridge University Press.

Ross, Andrew. 2003. *No-Collar: The Humane Workplace and its Hidden Costs*. Philadelphia: Temple University Press.

Sandberg, Sheryl and Nell Scovell. 2013. *Lean In: Women, Work and the Will to Lead*. London: WH Allen.

Scharff, Christina. 2012. *Repudiating Feminism: Young Women in a Neoliberal World*. Surrey: Ashgate.

Stabile, Susan J. 2008. "Google Benefits or Google's Benefit?" *Journal of Business and Technology* 3 (1): 97–107.

Thrift, Nigel. 2005. *Knowing Capitalism*. London: Sage.

Tokumitsu, Miya. 2014. "In the Name of Love." *Jacobin* 13. https://www.jacobinmag.com/2014/01/in-the-name-of-love/.

Turner, Fred. 2009. "Burning Man at Google: A Cultural Infrastructure for New Media Production." *New Media and Society* 11 (1–2): 73–94.

Veijola, Soile and Eeva Jokinen. 2008. "Towards a Hostessing Society? Mobile Arrangements of Gender and Labour." *NORA – Nordic Journal of Feminist and Gender Research* 16 (3): 166–181.

Velkova, Julia. 2014. "Workflows, Labour and Value in Open Animation Production: An Ethnographic Study of a Distributed Animation Training Creation." Paper presented at Dynamics of Virtual Work conference, Hatfield, UK, September 3–5.

Velkova, Julia and Peter Jakobsson. 2015. "The Production of Difference and Commensurability between Regimes of Value in Open Source Cultural Production." Paper presented at International Communication Association conference, San Juan, Puerto Rico, May 21–25.

Virno, Paolo. 1996. "The Ambivalence of Disenchantment." In *Radical Thought in Italy: A Potential Politics,* edited by Paolo Virno and Michael Hardt, 12–33. London: Routledge.

Wajcman, Judy. 2010. "Feminist Theories of Technology." *Cambridge Journal of Economics* 34: 143–152.

Weeks, Kathi. 2007. "Life Within and Against Work: Affective Labor, Feminist Critique, and Post-Fordist Politics." *ephemera* 7 (1): 233–249.

———. 2011. *The Problem with Work: Feminism, Marxism, Antiwork Politics, and Postwork Imaginaries*. Durham: Duke University Press.

Index

For Product Safety Concerns and Information please contact our
EU representative GPSR@taylorandfrancis.com Taylor & Francis
Verlag GmbH, Kaufingerstraße 24, 80331 München, Germany